Space, Time, and Crime

Kim Michelle Lersch

University of South Florida

Carolina Academic Press

Durham, North Carolina

ISBN 0-89089-470-1
LCCN 2004100446

CAROLINA ACADEMIC PRESS
700 Kent Street
Durham, North Carolina 27701
Telephone (919) 489-7486
Fax (919)493-5668
www.cap-press.com

Printed in the United States of America

Space, Time,
and
Crime

Contents

Acknowledgments

As is the case with most projects, this one would have died a slow, painful death were it not for the guidance, encouragement, and prodding of a number of individuals. First and foremost, I must thank Paul Cromwell and Quint Thurman for their sage advice at the very early stages of this book. Without their enthusiasm and interest, this book never would have gotten past the outline stage. Thanks for picking me up, dusting me off, and sending me back into the ring after I had run into a few obstacles along the way.

I'd also like to thank my colleagues at the University of South Florida for their support, especially during the doldrums. Tom Mieczkowski and Wilson Palacios could always be counted on for a shoulder to whine on and a swift boot in the pants. Lenny Territo, a respected colleague whose expertise will be sorely missed when he retires, was always available to answer questions and provide advice along the way. Richard Dembo always made time for a kind word of encouragement. To all, thanks.

Carolina Academic Press has been absolutely wonderful to work with. I'd like to offer special thanks to Tim Colton for his technical expertise and patient responses, and to Keith Sipe and Paul Knepper for their interest and encouragement. Also, as you will see, there are a number of article reprints that appear throughout the text. The inclusion of these pieces has greatly contributed to the overall quality of the project. I'd like to thank Elijah Anderson, Tom Mieczkowski, David Belluomini, Conrad Clay, Bob Hopkins, John Chaffin, Christopher Bruce, Rachel Boba, and Mary Velasco for their contributions.

Last but certainly not least, I'd like to thank my best friend and husband, John 'Buzz' Lersch, for his patience, support, and gentle prodding throughout all phases of this project. You've always been behind me, encouraging me to achieve higher levels of success. Without your support and belief in my abilities, I would still be making pizzas on 4th Street.

Introduction

In the fall of 2002, residents of the Washington D.C. metropolitan area were absolutely terrified by a pair of serial snipers who had roamed the region, shooting 14 innocent people as they conducted the every-day business of their lives: shopping, pumping gas, dropping by the post office, running errands, or just going to school. There was no rhyme or reason to the selection of the victims. Men and women, old and young, and members of various racial and ethnic groups were slain at the hands of the well-trained shooter and his young stepson. In the days prior to their arrest, the gunmen had even issued a warning to parents that their children may be the next victims. No one was immune from this indiscriminate violence.

The most terrifying aspect of these incidents was the sheer randomness of their timing and place of occurrence. There was no pattern in the shootings. Some of the victims were shot in the early morning hours, others at various times throughout the late morning and afternoon, while still others were gunned down in the late evening. A Florida tourist was wounded outside of a Ponderosa restaurant; a terror analyst for the Federal Bureau of Investigation was killed in a Home Depot parking lot. It seemed that no one was safe at any time or at any place in the region. Schools were closed and outdoor events such as high school football games were cancelled as the area was paralyzed by fear.

While the case of the Beltway snipers garnered international attention, it should be noted that this type of violence targeted against random victims is the exception, not the rule. In fact, one could argue that the lack of a pattern in the location, time, and victim selection is what made this horrible tragedy especially newsworthy. If these same madmen had been targeting drug dealers or prostitutes in poor urban neighborhoods, more than likely this book would have had a different introduction since few of us would have been able to recall any details from the media reports of the incident (if there had been any national coverage at all).

Our journey through space, time, and crime begins with a basic statement of fact: Crime is not evenly distributed across locations, times, victims, or targets. In every city in America, there are "safe" areas where serious crimes are a relatively rare event. There are also not-so-safe areas where crimes — especially violent, predatory street crimes — are an everyday occurrence. Certain times of the day are safer than others, although this varies with the type of crime. While one is much less likely to become a victim of a violent assault during the daytime hours, one's home is at greater risk for an attack by a burglar during the same time frame. While some will (fortunately) live their entire lives free from serious incidents of crime, others, especially those who happen to be young, single, members of a minority group, and/or urban residents have a much higher likelihood of becoming a victim of crime. Far from being a random event that occurs without rhyme or reason, crime is concentrated in certain areas and at certain times.

The purpose of this book is to explore issues related to the spatial and temporal clustering of crimes. The book is divided into four sections. The first section, which includes Chapters 2 and 3, explores the issues of "why." Why are some neighborhoods overrun with crime, while others enjoy safety, peace, and harmony among the local residents? In the second section, Chapters 4 and 5 explore the issue of "what." Once a high crime location or time is identified, what can we do about it? How do the theories get translated into policy? The third section, which is comprised of Chapters 6 and 7 , explores the issues of "how." How do we know where the crimes are located? How do police agencies, security managers, and others identify the areas that need more crime prevention services or special patrol operations? The book ends with a critical examination of the various theories, policies, and strategies that have been presented throughout the text.

Space, Time, and Crime

Chapter 1

The Basics of Space, Time, and Crime

Crime Places and Spaces in History

There has been a great deal of renewed interest in the study of space, time, and crime in the past 20 years. To some, this may seem like a hot "new" area in crime fighting. More and more police agencies are adopting technology that allows them to easily identify "hot spots" or clusters of criminal activity. Television programs regularly portray the use of crime mapping technology, displaying brightly colored maps of policing beats and zones. The highly publicized COMPSTAT system, made popular by the New York City Police Department, is based on a philosophy of geographic accountability in which a team of officers and supervisors are responsible for crime occurrences in specified areas. In the wake of the Beltway Sniper case, software programs designed to develop a geographic profile of the shooters received international media attention. While there is a great deal of excitement in the study of the geography of crime, it should be noted that interest in the examination of crime and space dates back to the early 1800s.

Adriano Balbi and Andre-Michel Guerry are usually credited as being the first creators of maps of crime (Weisburd & McEwen, 1998). The first national crime statistics were released in France in 1827, and Balbi and Guerry were intrigued. The pair combined the crime data with other demographic figures from the recent census, mapping areas based on the level of poverty, education, and crime. Their findings were of interest: the wealthy areas of France reported high levels of property crimes, while the

3

areas with the lowest levels of education had the lowest rates of violent crimes (Vold, Bernard & Snipes, 2002).

Another early pioneer in the area of crime and space was Adolphe Quetelet, a Belgian mathematician and astronomer. Quetelet was also interested in the newly released crime statistics from France and, with the use of his mathematical talents, was able to perform rather sophisticated statistical analyses with the data.

Working in the 1830s, Quetelet examined both the characteristics of those accused of criminal activity as well as the locations in which the crimes had occurred. He was able to determine that some individuals were more likely to commit crime than others, especially those who were young, poor, male, and unemployed. However, Quetelet also found that areas with high concentrations of poverty and unemployment actually had fewer reported crimes. Quetelet concluded that instead of victimizing other poor and unemployed persons close to home, crimes were more likely to be committed by poor and unemployed individuals against wealthy and educated persons. For Quetelet, inequality was an important factor in tempting individuals to commit crimes. The poor were drawn into areas of relative affluence in order to commit their crimes (Vold, Bernard & Snipes, 2002).

While the work of Quetelet was influential, interest in the geography of crime decreased in the late 1800s for a variety of reasons. First, without the use of calculators or statistical programs, it was difficult to create maps and conduct meaningful spatial comparisons between the crime data and the census data. Data availability was also an issue, especially in the United States. While France had a great deal of relatively modern, national-level data readily available for analysis, in other counties (such as the United States) crime data and census data were not collected on such a wide-scale basis (Weisburd & McEwen, 1998).

In the United States, the study of crime and place sat dormant until the birth of the Chicago School of Criminology. In the early 1900s, a group of innovative sociologists found themselves working and writing in a rapidly changing urban environment. While the contributions of the Chicago School are explored at length in Chapter 2, one of the rather puzzling issues that intrigued researchers was why crimes were concentrated in certain areas of the city. Why did certain areas of the city seem to be troubled not only by crime but also by other social problems? Why were other areas relatively safe and healthy spaces—neighborhoods where one would not hesitate to walk around at night, raise a family, or conduct the everyday business of life? One hundred years later, the same issues are being explored.

What Is "Space?"

Throughout this text, a number of different terms are used to refer to "space," such as location, place, address, neighborhood, census tracts, policing zones or crime reporting districts, or an entire city. While at times these terms may appear to be interchangeable, it is important to note that there are some subtle differences in the meanings of these words.

Most of the words describing an area or location listed above may be grouped into two general terms: place and space (Block & Block, 1995). **Places** might include a house, business, classroom, individual address, street corner, or other individual location. A place is a much smaller area than a space—it is an individual point in a space. A **space** may include such areas as neighborhoods, census tracts, or other larger territories.

The actual boundaries for spaces can be formed in a number of ways. For example, a police agency normally divides its area of responsibility into a number of small geographic areas. The specific term given to these smaller areas varies with the individual agencies, although names such as reporting districts, recording districts, or crime tracts seem to be the most common. These boundaries form the spaces as far as the police agency is concerned. These smaller crime tracts are then grouped into even larger spaces, sometimes called zones or districts. A municipal police department may have 50 different crime tracts that are grouped into three different districts.

Cities may also create space boundaries by posting signs at specific street boundaries such as "Welcome to the Kenwood Neighborhood Area" or "You are now entering the Seminole Heights Neighborhood." In one city where I lived for a number of years, there was a great push by the local municipal government to build a sense of community among its residents. The city invested thousands of dollars in signs to alert people that they were passing from one community space into another. These officially recorded boundaries for community spaces had been established long before homes were built and neighborhoods were formed. These "official" boundaries often did not coincide with the informal boundaries that had historically developed among the local residents, as their own ways of dividing spaces often do not respect police or city boundaries. As illustrated later in this text, this can be somewhat problematic, especially when well-intentioned outsiders — like police agencies, social service agencies, and others — try to "force" official community boundaries in areas where local residents have defined their own spaces quite differently.

Space definition can also be made on a more personal, internal level. While driving or walking to work or school, certain areas along the way may be identified based on visual cues important to some individuals and not others. Spaces, then, may be defined based on a personal cognitive or internal mental map of a city, county, or region. An entertainment district, a cluster of apartments, or an area of single-family homes may all be defined as spaces.

Another interesting characteristic of spaces is that they tend to take on lives of their own. The spaces become more than just the sum of all of the individual places located within them. A stroll down Bourbon Street in New Orleans may present this sort of phenomenon. The individual bars, clubs, and restaurants become a blur as you are drawn into the overall feel of the larger space — the sights, smells, and sounds of the space are an experience beyond the individual places.

Of course, the distinction between places and spaces can get a bit blurred. For example, is a high school a place or a space? The answer depends on the person making the distinction between place and space. A school resource officer assigned to a high school would probably view the school as a space filled with many individual places — classrooms, hallways, auto shop area, cafeteria, etc. A resident of the local neighborhood might view the school as just another individual place located within the larger neighborhood space. This sort of same confusion may arise when talking about large public housing projects — is it a space or a place?

What Is Time?
The Language of Temporal Analysis

Time is an important consideration in the study of crime. As seen in Table 1, just as there are dangerous high-risk places and spaces, there are also blocks of time in which victimization for certain types of crimes is more likely than in others. An individual is much more likely to become a victim of a homicide or aggravated assault during the evening hours on a weekend, especially Saturday nights (Miethe & McCorkle, 2001). As discussed in Chapter 3, many of these high-risk times can be traced to how we live our daily lives. Weekends are found to be especially dangerous times because people tend to venture out and involve themselves in social events that occur in public areas. They come into greater contact with problematic situations and problematic people. Throw in a good healthy dose of drugs and/or alcohol (remember the old advertisement slogan "Weekends were made for Michelob?") and you've got a good recipe for crime.

In addition to time of day and day of the week, there are other important considerations with respect to time. These include the week of the month, quarterly and yearly fluctuations, and seasonal trends. Some analysts even consider crime changes during full moon phases (Vallani & Nahoun, 2001). The study of time in relation to the occurrence of crimes is often called **temporal analysis**.

High Risk Places and Times

Type of Crime	High Risk Places	High Risk Times	High Risk Days/Periods
Homicide	Victim's home	Evening Hours (6 p.m.–6 a.m.)	Weekends
Aggravated Assault	Within 1 mile of victim's home	Evening Hours (6 p.m.–Midnight)	Weekends
Sexual Assault	Within 1 mile of victim's home	Evening Hours (6 p.m.–Midnight)	Weekends, especially in summer months
Personal Robberies	Within 1 mile of victim's home	Daytime Hours (6 a.m.–6 p.m.)	Late summer, Fall, and Winter (esp. January)
Residential Burglaries	Victim's home	Daytime (especially 10:00–11:00 a.m.; 1:00–3:00 p.m.)	Weekdays
Motor Vehicle Theft	Near victim's home	Late Evening Hours (Midnight–6 a.m.)	Summer months

Adapted from Miethe & McCorkle (2001)

Moments in Time

Understanding the concept of time can be a bit more elusive than the concept of space. This becomes especially problematic when one considers both time and space together. As discussed by Harries (1999:11), there are a number of concepts to consider in the temporal and geographic analysis of crime. First, there is the issue of **moments**. A moment provides the time that a crime occurred in space — when and where the crime occurred. While pinpointing the exact time and location of a crime seems like a basic issue, it can be a bit complex for certain types of crimes.

With respect to identifying the moment of a crime occurrence, there are two important concepts that must be introduced: **exact time crimes** and **time span crimes** (Gottlieb, Arenberg, & Singh, 1998). An exact time crime is a crime in which the victim can identify the time that the crime occurred with relative accuracy. Violent personal crimes, such as robbery, rape, and assault, are more likely to be exact time crimes. Consider the following example: You are walking out of class today and encountered by a young man who demands your money. You hand over your wallet and immediately run into the nearest building to notify the campus police of the incident. Even if you were unable to check a clock on the wall, you could give the responding officer a good estimate of the exact time that the robbery took place. For example, "Gee, my class ends at 1:00, but we got out a few minutes early...the crime occurred about 1:15 or so." Additionally, the campus police would have a record of your initial call for service, which would provide further information on the exact time of the crime. Crimes against persons are more likely to be exact time crimes.

Consider another scenario. You leave your apartment for school at 9:00 a.m. You attend your classes, and then go directly to work from the campus. You log in a few hours at work, and then you decide to drop by your friend's house to watch a game on television. After the game, you return to your apartment. When you arrive back at your apartment at 1:00 a.m., you find that your home has been burglarized. The police arrive and ask "What time did this happen?" The only information that you can give is the time span — you left your home at 9:00 a.m. and returned at 1:00 a.m. The crime occurred somewhere between these two known time values — you know when you left and when you returned home. Property crimes, in particular burglary and auto theft, are more likely to be time span crimes.

Researchers and police agencies have a number of ways of dealing with time span crimes. For purposes of temporal analysis, a "best guess" single time is often much more useful than a large time span. Temporal analysts employ a number of techniques to assign a single "best guess" value to better identify the moment of a crime occurrence.

One of the more basic techniques is called **midpoint analysis.** In midpoint analysis the time value that is in the middle of the known range of times is reported as the "best guess." In the previous example, since you left your home at 9:00 a.m. and returned at 1:00 a.m. (a span of 16 hours) the midpoint for this range would be 5:00 p.m. The value of 5:00 p.m. would then be reported as a **split time** value to estimate the moment of the crime occurrence (for a more detailed discussion of the various estimation techniques for dealing with time span crimes, please see Gottlieb et al. 1998).

Duration

According to Harries (1999:11), **duration** is defined as how long an event or process continued in a specific space. Duration may refer to a specific criminal incident, such as how long it took to resolve a hostage situation. It may take on broader meanings: How long did the number of reported crimes remain above a specific level in a certain area? For how many days, weeks, months did a jurisdiction experience a high level of residential burglaries? How long was a "hot spot," or a specific place with a high level of criminal activity, active or "hot"? Duration may also refer to the length of time that a specific perpetrator was active. For example, what was the duration of the Beltway Snipers' activity?

Distance As Time

I live in a rural area about 30 miles away from the University. When students or colleagues on the campus ask me where I live, most do not recognize the name of the town. Their next question is usually "Wow, how far is that?" I usually respond "About 45 minutes away." Distance can be expressed as a time value, and the inquirer gets a good idea of how far away I live from the campus. For some people, a time value can even be more informative than a mile value when expressing distance.

Things get even more interesting with respect to space, time and crime when one considers issues related to travel time. For example, consider the case of a detective investigating reports of an individual who is exposing himself to women during the hours of noon to 1:00 p.m. The activities are limited to the downtown business district on weekdays only. The detective might begin to develop a theory that this perpetrator works downtown and is exposing himself during his lunch break. The locations of the reported events may be examined to visualize how far the perpetrator could travel in a rather limited period of time from his workplace location. Once a limited geographic area for the possible location of his workplace has been developed the information may be cross checked against registered sex offenders to see if any of these known individuals work at businesses in the target area.

What Is Crime?

Though the discussions of the concepts of place and time thus far may seem surprisingly complex, answering the question "What is crime?" can actually take up an entire book. Part of the complexity is that crime is not absolute. What is considered "criminal" in one state may be acceptable behavior in another. What is considered a "normal" activity one year may violate a newly passed law the next. Laws that define what is and is not a crime are relative to both time and space.

A Note on Crime and Deviance

As a sociologist (as most criminologists are), it is easy for me to slip into sociological vocabulary when discussing issues related to crime. On the graduate level, sociologists do not study crime, but deviance. **Deviance** is broad sociological term used to describe behavior that violates generally accepted expectations. These generally accepted expectations or rules for behavior are called **norms**. Criminals violate laws, while someone described as **deviant** violates a norm.

Similar to laws, norms are also not absolute and vary with time and space. The expectations for behavior in the classroom are much different than the norms governing behavior while attending a party on a Saturday night. If you walk into a local tavern, pull out your notebook and pen, and prepare to take notes on whatever pearls of wisdom the bartender shares, other people in the bar will look at you a bit strangely. Norms that define expected behavior in one location might be very different from norms in another time and place. Over time, some norms become more formalized into laws. Many norms, however, just stay norms. Though informal, they are powerful rules for controlling behavior.

It is important to consider norms and norm violations along with the discussions of laws and crimes. Oftentimes, norms can exert stronger influence over daily lives than criminal law and its accompanying threat of sanctions. Within the same city, the laws are the same regardless of the neighborhood in which one lives. However, the behaviors that are exhibited by the local residents with respect to themselves, their property, and their neighbors may be very different.

For example, in some neighborhoods there may be fairly rigid, shared expectations for behavior. People keep their yards well-mowed and carefully maintain flowerbeds and other decorative landscaping. Garage doors are rarely left open, and homes are tastefully painted (in pre-approved colors only) and well cared for. Even though there may not be direct criminal sanctions for violating the "thou shalt mow once a week" commandment, few violate this norm. Children play outside under the watchful eyes of parents and other neighbors. If a child gets out of line, a neighbor may step in and correct the situation and/or inform the child's parents. Residents chat with each other over their fences and wave at passers-by.

In other neighborhoods, the norms may be quite different. People park cars on their front lawns, where one would be more likely to find empty beer cans than a decorative marigold or petunia. Grass mowing may be optional (if grass exists at all), and homes may sport broken windows, peeling paint, or gang-related graffiti. Unsupervised children play in the street, and few adults are outside. A group of teenagers often loiters in front of a vacant house, throwing rocks at the windows and playing loud music. Neighbors do not recognize their neighbors, and there is little conversation (if any) among the residents. Residents are generally suspicious and fearful of each other. While the laws governing these two neighborhoods are identical, the day-to-day lives of the residents and the level of social control may be very, very different.

Defining norms can be a bit difficult. For example, when first starting college, a good part of the adjustment period is trying to figure out how you are supposed to act. Of course, you are given a student code of conduct with the formal rules and regulations carefully laid out, but what about the all-important informal norms? How do you address your professor? Is it normal to raise your hand if you have a question, or should you go to office hours, or ask the teaching assistant? Do you have to set up an appointment for office hours, or do you just go? Are you going to be defined as a geek if you sit in the front of the classroom? What should you wear to class? Figuring out what the shared expectations for behavior are in a new setting can be a painful experience, especially since oftentimes it is not known that a norm exists until it is violated.

Defining Crimes

While defining norms can be a bit difficult, defining crimes is very easy. How does one know what is and is not considered a crime? In contemporary societies, one need look no further than the **penal code,** a highly organized, detailed record of all of the written criminal laws in a specified jurisdiction. Each state has its own set of written laws, as do different municipalities. There are also Federal level laws that can be found in the United States Code. The penal codes for all states can be found with a little digging on official state-sponsored websites.

The written criminal law is divided into two types: **procedural** and **substantive.** Substantive criminal law includes detailed definitions of what behaviors constitute a crime as well as what punishments go along with violations of the law. For example, according to the New York State Penal Code S 130.25, the crime of rape in the third degree is defined in the following manner:

Section HA130.25 Rape in the third degree.

A person is guilty of rape in the third degree when:

1. He or she engages in sexual intercourse with another person who is incapable of consent by reason of some factor other than being less than seventeen years old;

2. Being twenty-one years old or more, he or she engages in sexual intercourse with another person less than seventeen years old; or

3. He or she engages in sexual intercourse with another person without such person's consent where such lack of consent is by reason of some factor other than incapacity to consent.

Rape in the third degree is a class E felony.

There are a couple of things to note in the above definition. First, in the State of New York, the legal age of consent for sexual intercourse is seventeen. The legal age of consent may be higher or lower in other states. Second, in New York State the victim of rape may be male or female. In some jurisdictions, the crime of rape has not occurred if the victim is male. Finally, the classification of rape in the third degree as a class E felony means that the punishment for conviction of this crime in New York State is four years. In other states the punishment for a similar act may be more lenient or more punitive.

While the substantive criminal law applies to all members of a society, procedural law regulates the conduct of actors in the criminal justice system as they enforce elements of the substantive criminal law.

Rules governing searches and seizures, rules of evidence, and trial proceedings fall under procedural law. This text does not concern violations of the procedural law. It does concentrate on allegations that someone has violated some element of the substantive criminal law.

Counting Crimes: Official Statistics

Penal Codes are sources for defining crimes. But how does one find how many crimes occur in a specific area? Law enforcement agencies are the most popular source of crime data. Federal, state, county, and local law enforcement agencies compile and report data from various sources regarding the number and types of crimes that have occurred in their jurisdiction. Many technologically advanced agencies make this data readily available to interested citizens on their websites. Data collected by law enforcement agencies are often called "official statistics" and include such things as calls for service, incident reports, and the Federal Bureau of Investigation Uniform Crime Reports. Depending on the source of data used, one can get a very different view of the level of criminal activity in an area.

Calls for Service

Calls for service are a rather crude measure of the level of criminal activity in an area. Police agencies have records of the number of citizen-initiated calls for assistance based on their small geographic units (referred to here as recording districts). Each recording district reports the number of calls received (both 911 emergency and non-emergency calls), the preliminary nature of the call, the time that the call was received, and the location of the complaint. This data is often automatically compiled by computer-assisted dispatch (CAD) software systems. CAD systems allow vast amounts of data to be compiled over time, which can assist in identifying areas with high service demands (Swanson, Territo & Taylor, 1998). Using calls for service data, one can get a basic picture of the crime problem in an area. Does the area seem to generate a higher than average number of calls? Has there been an increase or decrease in the number of calls over the past 5 years? Are the calls for relatively minor offenses, or are they primarily regarding serious felony allegations?

Unfortunately, one of the drawbacks of using calls for service as a primary measure of the level of crime in an area is that citizen reports of criminal activity are often not valid. One agency representative that I worked with found the "gang problem" in his zone rather humorous. The area had a large elderly population especially fearful of teens and pre-teens. Whenever several young people gathered in the street to ride their skateboards, the police were immediately called to investigate allegations of gang activity in the neighborhood. When the police arrived, oftentimes the youths had already left the area or, upon investigation, found to be just harmless bored kids getting in a little exercise. Regardless of the reality of the situation, if one relied solely on the calls for service data in this example one would expect that a gang war was about to break out at any time.

Relying on calls for service data presents a second problem often described as the **dark figure of crime**, or crimes that go unreported to police. The crimes known to police are viewed as only the tip of the iceberg, with vast amounts of criminal activity never officially counted. People choose not to call the police to report a crime for a number of reasons. A citizen may fear reprisal by the offender if their identity as the complainant is somehow revealed. A citizen might assume that someone else has called the police to report the crime. The citizen may also feel that the police are not able to do anything about the crime or that the matter is not important enough to merit the attention of the police. If the relationship between the police and the local residents is strained, citizens are not likely to summon the police into their homes especially for relatively minor criminal incidents. Regardless of the justification, in reality, many legitimate crimes go unreported and hence, do not show up in any official crime reports.

Incident Data

As calls for service may not be the most accurate source of data, some researchers have turned to incident data. Incident data are based on reports written by a responding officer regarding the nature of the call. For example, a patrol officer may be dispatched to a citizen's home based on the complaint of a barking dog. Upon arriving at the address, the officer may find a very different situation. There may be evidence of forced entry into the home and, upon further investigation, the body of the unconscious homeowner may be found. Calls for service and actual incident reports can be very different.

Reliance upon incident data, however, is not without its problems. If there is no call for service, it would logically follow that there would be no incident report. The problem of measuring the dark figure of crime applies here as well. Beyond the underreporting issue, in many calls for service the responding police officer has the power to decide whether or not a crime has actually occurred. Patrol officers have a great deal of unchecked discretion in this area. One patrol officer shared an experience he had in responding to a disturbing the peace call. Upon arrival, the officer found a crying woman with a fresh bruise on her face. Her husband, who was still at home at the time of the officer's arrival, had struck her during an argument. There was clear evidence of battery. She begged the officer not to arrest her husband as was required under the domestic violence laws of this state. According to the woman, her husband would lose his job and push the family into even greater financial and emotional distress. After careful deliberation, the officer classified the incident as "NR" — no report needed. Even though there was clear evidence that a crime had occurred and an arrest was mandated, no official report of the incident was ever made.

Federal Bureau of Investigation Uniform Crime Reports (FBI UCR)

The oldest and most widely recognized source for all crime related data is the FBI Uniform Crime Reports. At least once a year local papers will carry front-page headlines that herald the release of the latest FBI UCR statistics. Did crime go up? Did crime go down? Where is the new murder capital of the U.S.? How do we account for changes in the level of criminal activity? Since these numbers are so widely reported, it is useful to discuss this data source at some length.

The FBI UCR began in 1930 at the request of the International Association of Chiefs of Police (IACP). The IACP, which exists to this day, recognized the importance of having a standardized national database of criminal activity. The goal of the FBI UCR was to collect data from law enforcement agencies across the country on a limited number of crimes. To ensure standardized responses, the FBI provided very clear definitions as to what constituted each crime and under what circumstances the crimes should be reported. While all law enforcement agencies were encouraged to report the crimes that had occurred in their jurisdiction, reporting was and continues to be voluntary.

Today, the FBI groups crimes into two general categories: Part I or Index Crimes and Part II or Non-Index Crimes (see Table 1.1). As a whole, Part I offenses are viewed as more serious offenses and are usually garner much more publicity than the Part II offenses. The FBI provides very clear definitions for Part I offenses which are as follows:

- **Criminal Homicide.** A. Murder and non-negligent manslaughter: the willful (non-negligent) killing of one human being by another. Death caused by negligence, attempts to kill, assaults to kill, suicides, accidental deaths, and justifiable homicides are excluded. Justifiable homicides are limited to: (1) the killing of a felon by a law enforcement officer in the line of duty; and (2) the killing of a felon, during the commission of a felony, by a private citizen.

  B. Manslaughter by negligence: the killing of another person through gross negligence. Traffic fatalities are excluded. While manslaughter by negligence is a Part I crime, it is not included in the Crime Index.

- **Forcible Rape.** The carnal knowledge of a female forcibly and against her will. Included are rapes by force and attempts or assaults to rape. Statutory offenses (no force used—victim under age of consent) are excluded.

- **Robbery.** The taking or attempting to take anything of value from the care, custody, or control of a person or persons by force or threat of force or violence and/or by putting the victim in fear.

- **Aggravated assault.** An unlawful attack by one person upon another for the purpose of inflicting severe or aggravated bodily injury. This type of assault usually is accompanied by the use of a weapon or by means likely to produce death or great bodily harm. Simple assaults are excluded.

- **Burglary.** The unlawful entry of a structure to commit a felony or a theft. Attempted forcible entry is included.

- **Larceny-theft.** The unlawful taking, carrying, leading, or riding away of property from the possession or constructive possession of another. Examples are thefts of bicycles or automobile accessories, shoplifting, pocket picking, or the stealing of any property or article which is not taken by force and violence or by fraud. Attempted larcenies are included. Embezzlement, confidence games, forgery, worthless checks, etc., are excluded.

Table 1.1. FBI UCR Part II Offenses

• Assaults	• Curfew and Loitering Violations	• Disorderly Conduct
• Drug Violations	• Drunkenness	• Driving under the Influence
• Embezzlement	• Forgery and Counterfeiting	• Fraud
• Gambling	• Liquor Law Violations	• Prostitution and Commercialized Vice
• Receiving, Buying, Possessing Stolen Property	• Runaways	• Vagrancy
• Vandalism	• Weapons Related Offenses	• All other Offenses

- **Motor vehicle theft.** The theft or attempted theft of a motor vehicle. A motor vehicle is self-propelled and runs on the surface and not on rails. Specifically excluded from this category are motorboats, construction equipment, airplanes, and farming equipment.
- **Arson.** Any willful or malicious burning or attempt to burn, with or without intent to defraud, a dwelling house, public building, motor vehicle or aircraft, personal property of another, etc.

(Source: Federal Bureau of Investigation, 2001:446).

Based on information provided by local law enforcement agencies, the FBI compiles the data and reports the total number of crimes based on various geographic areas such as cities, states, and national regions. The FBI also calculates the **Crime Index**, which is the total of all the Part I index crimes excluding arson. Two other useful statistics are the **Violent Crime Index**, which is the total number of reported murders, aggravated assaults, forcible rapes, and robberies, and the **Property Crime Index**, which is the total of all reported burglaries, larceny-thefts, and motor vehicle thefts. Arson was not added as a Part I Offense until 1979 and is not included in the calculation of the Crime Index. The various crime indices as well as the individual crime counts for the Part I Offenses for 2001 are reported in Table 1.2 on the next page.

The FBI UCR has a number of problems. First, since it is based on the crimes reported to police, the accuracy of the numbers is affected

Table 1.2. 2001 Part I Index Crimes

Measure	Total
Crime Indices	
Crime Index	11,849,006
Violent Crime Index	1,436,611
Property Crime Index	10,412,395
Individual Part I Crime Counts	
Murder	15,908
Rape	90,491
Robbery	422,921
Aggravated Assault	907,219
Burglary	2,109,767
Larceny	7,076,171
Motor Vehicle Theft	1,226,457
Arson (not included in Crime Index)	68,967

Source: Federal Bureau of Investigation (2001:64)

by underreporting by citizens. The FBI UCR does not include the dark figure of crime. Second, since the state definitions and the FBI definitions of crime are often not consistent, individual agencies may not have the time or the resources to separately calculate separate crime reports for the FBI. Consider the crime of rape. According to the FBI definition, only women can be raped. Some states (like New York) have adopted gender-neutral language in their laws, which means that their internal crime statistics count forcible rapes of both men and women. Some agencies may separate their counts by victim gender and only report the forcible rapes as defined by the FBI to the UCR accounting office. Other agencies may report the same number of forcible rapes for both their internal purposes as well as for the FBI UCR. There is no formal audit of the data provided to the FBI, so in spite of their best efforts, oftentimes the FBI has no control over the statistics it receives.

Third, police agencies may intentionally manipulate their data. As an example, consider college and university police departments. These law enforcement agencies must report their Part I Index crimes to the FBI. These reports are then published in national and international newspapers and magazines (*The Chronicle of Higher Education*, which is more than likely available in your university's library, regularly reports annual crime figures for a large number of colleges and universities). Imagine that a string of rapes has occurred in campus dorms. From a very cold business stance this sort of criminal incident is not good for the University's reputation and may impact potential enrollment. Part I offenses (including forcible rape) are widely reported; Part II offenses (which includes simple assault) are not. Instead of reporting the incident as a forcible rape, the police agency may report the crime as a simple assault. This is often very true with attempted crimes. While the FBI requests counts for attempted violent crimes, once again it does not have control over the statistics it receives.

A fourth problem concerns the **hierarchy rule**. According to the FBI UCR guidelines, only the most serious crime should be reported. This seriously under-reports the occurrence of crimes. Imagine this example: Someone breaks into your house and you come home and surprise the burglar. The burglar demands your wallet, beats you to a pulp with a baseball bat, and then steals your television, stereo, and computer. While numerous Part I crimes have been committed in this example, the FBI only wants the top charge reported, which in this example would be the aggravated assault.

A fifth and final problem concerns what I call "the show must go on" issue. The FBI must have all of the requested data from local law enforcement agencies by a specific date. Sometimes agencies miss the due date. When this happens, "the show must go on," meaning the FBI publishes the data that was received by the due date. Crimes that occurred in areas policed by agencies that were unable to meet the due date would then be excluded from any annual reports. I have witnessed this in the state of Florida, where a highly publicized decrease in the level of crime (as measured by the FBI UCR statistics) was reported by the local media. Politicians congratulated themselves for a job well done, taking credit for the decline as a direct result of their "get tough" policies. Interestingly, a few weeks later an article buried on the back page of the metro section critiqued the accuracy of the UCR data. It seemed that a number of agencies had not reported their crime figures to the FBI. The highly publicized reduction in the number of crimes was due to the missing data and did not reflect an actual decline in the level of criminal activity. If all the agencies had reported their crime figures, an increase in the level of crime would have been reported for the state!

Despite its flaws, the FBI UCR remains one of the most widely cited sources of data on crime. This is especially true with respect to studies of the geography of crime. Most agencies do report their crime figures along to the FBI, so one can compare the number of homicides in Portland, Maine with the number of homicides in Honolulu, Hawaii. City, county, state, and regional totals of Part I Index crimes are readily available for analysis. Additionally, because the FBI has collected data for over 70 years, one can readily monitor changes in the level and type of criminal activity over time. Even though the accuracy of the data may not be the best, it is generally recognized as one of the stronger sources of data. One of my first criminology professors described the FBI UCR data in the following manner: "It *is* bad, but at least it is *consistently* bad."

Counting Crimes: "Unofficial" Data

Because of the inaccuracies surrounding the FBI UCR data and other official data sources, some researchers have turned to other sources for data on the level of crime including surveys and qualitative research techniques. Results from these "unofficial" data sources can provide a much different (and in many cases, much more accurate) picture of the crime problem in an area.

Surveys:
The Good, the Bad, and the Ugly

Surveys of local citizens can provide a great deal of information on the level and type of crimes that are occurring in a neighborhood. At one end of the extreme, surveys can be well funded, highly organized, and scientifically administered projects. At the other end, they can be loosely constructed, poorly administered, and yield questionable results. Regardless of the data source (whether official or unofficial), there are always problems with accuracy.

A substantial portion of courses in research methods is devoted to survey research and includes a number of important elements one must consider when designing and administering a "good survey." The following discussion will present a brief overview of a number of critical points.

In a survey to a group of local residents, one must first decide how one is going to administer the survey: in-person, mail, or phone? The mode of administration may be determined by cost. Phone surveys are cheaper than mail or in-person surveys, especially if only a local neighborhood or community is being contacted. However, the **response rate** of phone surveys is not great. The response rate is defined as the number of people who complete the survey based on the number of people contacted. Since people can easily hang up the phone when contacted for a survey, lower response rates can be expected. In-person surveys tend to have the highest response rate of the three methods, but usually take longer to complete and require a higher number of costly assistants to administer the survey.

Second, who will be surveyed? This sounds like an easy question, but it is not. Even in a door to door survey with each resident, are questions posed to the entire household, the head of the household, or whoever answers the door? What if a teenager answers the door? Will the survey be administered to every resident of a community (called a **population**) or will a subset of the population (called a **sample**) be selected? If a sample of residents is used, there are a number of **sampling techniques** that are used to decide which members of a population will be selected into a sample. One can randomly select households from an accurate list of all possible households in the neighborhood, or set up a booth at a local grocery store and ask customers to fill out the survey as they walk by. The quality of the results of the survey will be determined by how accurately the sample represents the target population.

The actual wording of the survey can significantly impact the results. If a vocabulary that is above your target audience is used, the results will not be worth the paper they are printed on. In a survey I once worked on, sixth graders were asked if they felt that police officers were prejudiced against minority persons. As the survey was administered, the children immediately began to overwhelm us with questions. This age group did not know what the words "prejudice" and "minority person" meant. Because we were in the classroom and were able to recognize their confusion, not much stock was put in their answers. Imagine if the surveys had been sent out by mail and we had no feedback from the students that they simply did not understand the wording. In addition to vocabulary, question order (earlier responses may affect later responses), poorly worded questions, or questions that direct the respondent to a preferred answer ("There's a lot of crime around here, isn't there?") may also influence an answer.

While only a small part of survey construction and administration has been introduced it should be clear that some surveys (and some results) are better than others. Bear in mind that some surveys may be very poorly constructed and administered. For example, it is not uncommon for a police chief to mandate that a survey of local residents be conducted. However, few police department employees have any formal training or education in survey construction. As explained later, many crime analysts who are often given responsibility for completion of such tasks only have a high school education.

National Crime Victimization Survey

While results from surveys conducted at the local level may elicit a bit of skepticism, there is one national survey that is held in high regard: the National Crime Victimization Survey (NCVS). The **National Crime Victimization Survey** is sponsored by the United States Department of Justice. Since its inception in 1973, the NCVS has grown into a widely respected source of data. According to the Bureau of Justice statistics, nearly 50,000 household units are interviewed twice a year. Those individuals living in the selected households age 12 and older are asked about the frequency, characteristics, and consequences of crime victimizations. Only the following crimes are included in the survey: rape, sexual assault, robbery, assault, theft, household burglary, and motor vehicle theft. This limited range of crimes was selected in order to make comparisons with the FBI UCR findings.

The strongest aspect of the NCVS is that it provides an estimate of the dark figure of crime. Data is collected on crimes regardless of whether or not the police are notified. Based on data provided by the NCVS, it is estimated that as much as half of all violent crimes and two thirds of all property crimes that occur go unreported to the police (Rand & Rennison, 2002). Clearly, the NCVS provides a needed complement to the FBI UCR statistics.

Additionally, the NCVS provides much more detailed descriptions of the crime as well as the victim characteristics. For example, in the FBI UCR if a robbery occurred one would only be able to tell that the crime had taken place. With the exception of homicide, the FBI UCR does not include detailed data on crime and victim characteristics. Conversely, the NCVS asks respondents when and where the crime occurred, if a weapon was used, how the offender gained access to their property, if there were any injuries, the actions of the victim (did they resist, escape, etc.), and whether or not the police were notified of the crime. This more detailed information on victim characteristics and offender actions is very useful in developing explanations as to why certain victims and/or targets were selected by offenders. These issues will be discussed in much greater depth in Chapter 3.

As is the case with all data sources, there are limitations on the accuracy of the findings. One problem is called **sampling error**, a consideration in all surveys of samples. When a sample is surveyed, responses from this smaller group of people are used to estimate the responses of the whole group (the population). It would be surprising if the sample values were exactly equal to the population values. The values would be close, but not exact. For example, in a survey investigating the overall grade point average for all of the students enrolled in this course, students would write down their grade point averages and the class average would be calculated. This is the population value. If a sample was randomly selected from the class and the sample average was calculated, the sample value and the population value would be close, but not exactly the same. This difference between the sample value and the population value is known as the sampling error.

In addition to sampling error, there are other issues that may affect the accuracy of NCVS findings. Respondents are asked questions about criminal events that occurred over the past six months. Some victims may not be able to remember all of the crimes that occurred during this time frame, especially if they experience high levels of victimizations. A **series victimization** is defined as six or more similar but separate crimes in which the victim is unable to individually distinguish one crime from another. This can be a problem, as the NCVS interviewer will attempt to get as much detailed information on each incident as possible. In cases where detailed events cannot be recalled, one report is taken for the entire series of crimes. This policy for counting such multiple incidents can underestimate the actual number of crimes that have occurred (Rand & Rennison, 2002).

While the hope is that people readily report their victimizations to the NCVS interviewer, in reality some individuals do not disclose all of their personal experiences. Incidents of domestic violence may go underreported, since victims may not wish to share the details of such personal crimes. The same may be said of the crime of rape. Even though it may be much less intimidating to disclose details to a NCVS interviewer than to a (oftentimes male) police officer or detective, the victim still has to reveal very personal, intimate details of their lives. Some may choose not to relive the details of such victimizations.

Self Report Surveys

Self-report surveys are a common source of data for studies of criminal behavior. In this type of survey, respondents are asked about their personal involvement in a variety of criminal and deviant acts. Only the imagination and interests of the person who constructed the survey instrument limit the actual questions included in these surveys. People may be asked what crimes they have committed, why they committed them, and what happened to them as a result. Similar to the NCVS, self-report surveys allow a better estimate of the dark figure of crime.

Self report surveys do have their own limitations. Because the surveys are individualized to meet the specific needs of each researcher and/or project, it is difficult to compare the results of one survey to the results of another. Further, because few people actually commit serious criminal offenses, oftentimes self-report surveys tend to focus on relatively minor crimes or acts of deviance. In order to conduct statistical analyses of the data, a good number of respondents who indicate that they did commit the crime in question is necessary. It is much easier to find a teenager who has skipped school, stayed out past curfew, or consumed alcoholic beverages than it is to find one who has committed a burglary, robbery, or aggravated assault.

The quality of the samples of respondents used in self-report surveys has also been scrutinized. For example, a researcher is interested in adolescent substance abuse and constructs a self-report survey to find out what kinds of drugs kids are taking, how often they are taking them, and why they feel the need to use drugs. What will be the sample? High school students would only represent teens that are still enrolled in school and are in attendance on that particular day. Dropouts, truants, and others who would be absent would not be included in the sample. What about the local juvenile detention center? This sample would only represent kids who have been picked up by the police on various charges of criminal activities.

It can be very difficult to identify a good representative sample of individuals. As a result, many self-report surveys are administered to **convenience samples** — large, but unrepresentative groups of people that may be quickly found in one location. If you have ever completed an attitude or behavioral survey in one of your larger social science classes, you were a part of a convenience sample. When you read the results of a self-report survey, in the back of your mind you might ask yourself who completed the survey? Are the respondents similar to all teens (adults, offenders — whatever)? Since the goal of many surveys is to generalize the results to the larger population, it is very important that the sample is a good representation of the population.

Qualitative Techniques

The last unofficial data source is qualitative techniques. While there are a variety of qualitative techniques out there, two will be discussed: in-depth interviews and participant observation studies.

For the skilled researcher, **in-depth interviews** may provide a wealth of information. The word "skilled" is stressed since conducting a good interview requires much training and practice. The researcher needs to gain the trust of the respondent, know when to probe and push for more information, and know when to respectfully back off. I personally find qualitative research much more challenging than number crunching statistical analysis.

In-depth interviews may be conducted in a variety of settings—homes, offices, street corners, wherever. Whenever possible, the researcher often records the responses with a tape recorder in order to preserve the exact words of the respondent. Similar to a self-report survey, the questions posed during an in-depth interview are limited only by the imagination of the person conducting the exchange. Some in-depth interviews are highly structured with specific questions and probes (follow-up questions) while others are loosely constructed with few formal requirements.

The benefit of in-depth interviews is that the direction of the data collection may be modified during the course of the interview. The questions can go anywhere and are often driven by the responses of the person being questioned. In a pre-printed forced response survey, the survey instrument remains just as it was constructed. Hence, in-depth interviews are much more flexible than traditional surveys. In-depth interviews allow the respondent to elaborate, question, go off on (informative) tangents, and often provide answers to questions that the interviewer did not foresee being asked.

In-depth interviews may be conducted as part of a larger qualitative research effort called a **participant observation**. In this type of study, researchers climb down from their ivory towers and immerse themselves in the "real" world. It is one thing to study arrest statistics from the FBI UCR or examine results of self-report surveys on substance abuse, and quite another to spend the evening in a crack house, observing and talking with the houseguests. Participant observations can provide data from an insider's perspective. When properly conducted, the quality of this type of data is unparalleled by any of the other official or unofficial data sources we have discussed so far.

There are different types of participant observation studies that are based on the degree of participation and involvement of the researcher in the chosen site. In some studies, researchers essentially operate undercover. A researcher is simply an observer and individuals in the setting are unaware that the researcher is actually there to collect data. In other types of studies, a researcher makes his or her presence known to those in the site. This type of technique was used by Tom Mieczkowski as he studied drug distribution networks in Detroit. The results of this study will be presented later in this text. A third type of participant observation is the case where the researcher is a complete participant—this type of study can be a bit problematic, especially when studying criminal activities!

Unfortunately, qualitative studies do not always get the respect that they deserve. Critics argue that the results are unrepresentative and heavily influenced by the personal perceptions of the researcher. For some, if a study does not feature the use of high-powered statistical tests as a central part of its data analysis, the quality of the study is severely undermined. Thankfully, there are still those who do value the unique perspective that qualitative research can provide.

Summary

A number of terms and concepts were examined that will assist with more in-depth discussions of space, time, and crime presented in later chapters. The basic vocabulary of spatial and temporal analysis has been introduced and the various methods by which criminal justice researchers measure crime and deviance have been explored. Comprehending these basic elements will assist in developing a better understanding of why certain locations seem to be more prone to crime than others, how these areas are identified, and what can be done to reduce the level of crime and deviance in such areas.

Chapter 2

Positivism, Social Ecology, and the Chicago School

Early in the 20th Century, a diverse group of sociologists found themselves at the University of Chicago. The ideas, method of study, and policy recommendations that grew from their work continue to influence the field of criminology today. While the pioneers of the Chicago School were not the first to study the relationship between crime and neighborhood characteristics, the names of a few of these early thinkers, such as Roger Park, Ernest Burgess, Clifford Shaw, and Henry McKay, have become synonymous with the sociological examination of crime and space. In this chapter, the development of their ideas is traced, the major propositions are presented, some of the critiques of their work are examined, and the continued importance of their theories is discussed.

Setting the Stage: Chicago at the Turn of the 20th Century

In order to better understand the ideas of the early sociologists centered at the University of Chicago, one needs to have a grasp of the historical perspective of the times in which they wrote. The "heyday" of the Chicago School was from 1914–1934 (Martin, Mutchnick & Austin, 1990), an era of great change both in the city of Chicago and the United States. First, the history of the city of Chicago will be introduced. As described by Shaw and McKay (1969), the area that has become the city of Chicago was originally plotted around 1830. At that time, Chicago was less than a square mile of area. By the time the town of Chicago was originally incorporated a few short years later, the territory of the town limits had grown to about 2 ½ square miles and continued to increase as the population of the town grew. While the eastward growth of the city of Chicago was limited by Lake Michigan, by 1889 the city had grown to 170 square miles.

In 1840, the population of Chicago was approximately 4,500 people. The number of people moving to Chicago to seek employment and a better life began to increase dramatically. In only ten years, the number of residents grew to just over 25,000. By 1880, the population had multiplied to about 500,000. The growth had only begun. By 1900, Chicago boasted nearly 1.7 million residents. The population expansion of the city of Chicago based on census data (Gibson & Lennon, 1999) is summarized in Table 2.1.

One of the more dramatic changes in the population composition of the United States as a whole was caused by the large influx of immigrants around the late 19th and early 20th Century. From 1850–1930, the foreign-born population of the United States increased from 2.2 million to 14.2 million (Gibson & Lennon, 1999). Many of these immigrants settled in the growing northern cities, such as New York, Boston, Detroit, Philadelphia, and, of course, Chicago. There was a shortage of labor during this era, and many industrialists actively recruited overseas for cheap labor to work in the factories (Feagin & Feagin, 1993). Table 2.1 summarizes the available data on the number of foreign-born residents in the city of Chicago. In 1870, nearly half of the residents of Chicago were born in other nations. While the proportion of foreign-born residents steadily declined after 1870, the immigrant population in Chicago remained significant especially during the Chicago School era (1914–1934).

Table 2.1. Historical Growth of the City of Chicago

Year	Total Residents	Number Foreign Born	Percent Foreign Born
1870	298,977	144,557	48.4
1880	503,185	204,859	40.7
1890	1,099,850	450,666	41.0
1900	1,698,575	587,112	34.6
1910	2,185,283	783,428	35.9
1920	2,701,705	808,558	29.9
1930	3,376,438	859,409	25.5
1940	3,396,808	675,147	19.9

As the population of the city of Chicago grew by leaps and bounds, the city began absorbing a shifting demographic of new arrivals. Prior to 1880, most of the settlers hailed from England, northwestern European nations, and Scandinavia. After 1880, the immigrant population was largely from southern and eastern European nations. Large numbers of African Americans were leaving the Southern states looking for a better life and greater personal freedoms. In addition to the large number of foreign-born residents settling in the city of Chicago, the African American population of the city grew dramatically from 1880–1920 (Gold, 1987).

In the ethnic and racial mix, not all groups were viewed equally. Immigrants from southern and eastern Europe, such as Italians and Poles, were generally viewed as being inherently inferior to those from northern and western Europe (Gordon, 1964). African Americans experienced a great deal of discrimination and hostility, especially when the economy began to downturn (Feagin & Feagin, 1993). Competition between the various racial and ethnic groups was tight in the city of Chicago, not only for good paying jobs but also for better housing and overall living conditions. Tensions in the city grew, culminating in a serious race riot that broke out in 1919 (Gold, 1987).

The attitude of many native-born Americans and older immigrant groups towards the swelling of the population with more and more new arrivals from Europe began to deteriorate. Immigrants, especially those labeled as "inferior," were no longer viewed as welcome additions to U.S. society. A great debate opened among scientists from various disciplines, including geneticists, anthropologists, sociologists, and psychologists as to whether or not certain groups of immigrants were of poor quality racial "stock" and should therefore be restricted from entering the United States (Gold, 1987).

Are Certain Groups Inherently Inferior? The "Feebleminded" Debate

There was a rather ugly era in United States Immigration Policy and in American society in general which culminated in the passage of the Immigration Act of 1924. A number of "scientists" were affirming the popular but racist beliefs that many social problems that existed in U.S. society, including crime and delinquency, were caused by the moral and intellectual inferiority of certain groups in society. If the growth of these groups were to be reduced or even eliminated, then crime, delinquency, and other social problems would be reduced.

Many of these ideas were not new, but seemed to resurface given the large influx of immigrants and the increased competition among the groups for scarce resources. Charles Darwin argued that in the natural evolution of the species, some were more well adapted to their current environment than others. Certain individuals were born with "good" traits, while other weaker individuals were born with less desirable traits. Through the process of natural selection, the weaker individuals would eventually die out, and only the strong would survive.

Cesare Lombroso and The Criminal Man

The idea that certain individuals were born biologically and/or mentally inferior was picked up by a number of very popular thinkers in criminology, including Cesare Lombroso (1835–1919) and Henry Goddard (1866–1957). Cesare Lombroso has been described as the father of criminology and his work in the area of criminal anthropology remained very popular in the United States until about 1915 (Bohm, 1997). Lombroso was a physician in the Italian army. During this time, there was a general prejudice held by many that people from Southern Italy, including Sicily, were somehow inferior. During an autopsy on a thief who came from Southern Italy, Lombroso discovered what he felt was the key to the problem: The skull of the criminal resembled that of primitive human beings. In effect, the man was not as highly evolved as "normal" human beings (Vold, Bernard, & Snipes, 2002).

Lombroso then set out to develop a list of a number of identifiers, which he called **stigmata,** which could be used to determine whether or not a person was an evolutionary throwback. Lombroso developed a list of a number of stigmata. These included ears that were either too big or too small, abnormal teeth, extra fingers or toes, too much hair or wrinkles, and long arms. If a man had five or more stigmata present, he was labeled as having a condition known as **atavism.** In effect, an atavistic man was more ape-like than human.

Lombroso first published his ideas in 1876 in *L'Uomo delinquente (The Criminal Man)*, and his work set off a heated debate not only among academics, but also among members of the legal and penal communities (Gould, 1981). While many criticized his work, his central idea that the cause of crime was biological in nature remained influential for many years, and was still a very popular theory around the time that the Chicago School sociologists were developing their own ideas about the causes of crime and delinquency.

IQ, Heredity, and Crime: The Thoughts of Henry Goddard

Henry Goddard (1866–1957) focused on the idea that criminals were mentally inferior human beings. In *Feeblemindedness: Its Causes and Consequences* (1914), Goddard argued that criminals were "feebleminded" people who could be identified through the use of an IQ test. Goddard felt that feeblemindedness was genetically based and, through selective breeding, could be eliminated from society. Since all feebleminded people were potential criminals due to their inferior mental capabilities, Goddard advocated either segregating the feebleminded in institutions and not allowing them to breed or forced sterilization.

Goddard was especially concerned with the arrival of immigrants to the United States, especially those from southern and eastern European countries. Goddard and his followers were able to institute the administration of an IQ test to newly arriving immigrants. This test, which was viewed by many as having the ability to measure innate intelligence, included such culturally-specific questions as the following:

Five hundred is played with

a) rackets; b) pins; c) cards; or d) dice

Christe Matthewson is famous as a:

a) writer; b) artist; c) baseball player; d) comedian (quoted from Curran & Renzetti, 1994:98)

Newly arriving immigrants who did not know that five hundred was played with cards or that Christe Matthewson was a famous baseball player would be identified as feebleminded, potential criminals, and innately inferior. Goddard advocated that individuals who did not score well on the IQ test should be barred from entry into the United States.

While in hindsight Goddard's ideas may appear to be almost comical, Goddard was able to "scientifically" validate what many Americans wanted to believe: Certain groups of individuals that would pollute the moral fiber of the country should not be allowed to enter. Goddard's recommendations factored heavily in the development of the Immigration Act of 1924. This Act established quotas limiting the number of people from certain regions from entering the United States. Groups that had arrived prior to 1880 and had demonstrated that they could become "good Americans," such as those from Great Britain, Germany, and Scandinavia, were given large quotas. Quotas for groups from southern and eastern European countries were very small in comparison (Gordon, 1964). For example, in 1929 the annual quota for Great Britain was 65,721 and for Germany it was 25,957. In comparison, the annual quota for Italians was only 5,802 (Feagin & Feagin, 1993).

Many criminologists ultimately dismissed Goddard's assertions that criminals were born feebleminded. However, his ideas were popular until the 1930s (Bohm, 1997). It is important to recognize that the racist, genetically based theories were quite influential among those who studied crime and delinquency at the turn of the 20th Century. The theories of the Chicago School represented a sharp break with the popular thinking of the time, and added even more fuel to the fire in the debates concerning immigration in the United States (Gold, 1987). Instead of looking at the characteristics of the individual as the source of crime and other social problems, the Chicago School thinkers turned to external factors, such as neighborhood characteristics.

Enter the Chicago School

The first sociology program in the United States was established in 1892 at the University of Chicago (Curran & Renzetti, 2001). The early faculty members were most likely shocked by the hustle and bustle of a booming metropolis. Many of the early sociologists had led rather sheltered lives, growing up in small rural communities. Some of their fathers had been ministers, and others were actually ministers themselves (Greek, 1992). Imagine the excitement that these men must have felt as they walked the city streets of downtown Chicago. To say that these early thinkers were immersed in a diverse, rapidly changing society would be an understatement given the demographics of the newly arriving residents and the overwhelming rate of growth in the city. The early faculty members were not tied to a single theoretical perspective or school of thought. Instead, they were willing to draw ideas from a number of different disciplines and theorists. Some of the ideas they incorporated related to human interaction, while others were based on the changing nature of plant and animal life. One of the early thinkers who had a great influence on the theoretical development of the Chicago School was Emile Durkheim, who is credited with being the father of modern sociology.

The Sociology of Emile Durkheim (1858–1917): Societal Growth and Anomie

Just as the theories developed by members of the Chicago School were affected by great changes in the city, the French Revolution of 1789 had an impact on Durkheim's ideas. Nineteenth century French society had undergone very rapid change, both politically and economically. The Industrial Revolution was transforming the way of life that had been in place for centuries. Society was becoming more and more complex. The **norms,** or shared expectations for behavior, that governed the way things had always been no longer applied in this new era, and new norms had yet to be developed.

Durkheim's ideas were centered on the development and evolution of societies. He used the term **mechanical societies** to refer to small, relatively isolated groups of people who are best described as homogeneous in nature. There is very little division of labor among the various members of the group. All share the same religion, values, and beliefs. Durkheim described the members of mechanical societies as sharing the same **collective conscience**, or in his words the "totality of social likenesses" (Durkheim 1965/1893:80). By sharing the same collective conscience, the members have the same idea of what is "right" and what is "wrong." The collective conscience holds members of a society together and serves as a control on behavior. A violation of the norms or rules of a mechanical society is seen as a personal insult to the collective identity of the group. When a crime or act of deviance occurs, the punishments are very harsh.

On a continuum with mechanical societies at one end of the spectrum, **organic societies** would be at the other extreme. Organic societies are marked by an extreme division of labor — people do not share a common identity with their neighbors. Organic societies are generally large, modern, and technologically advanced. Instead of being tied together by a shared collective conscience, the glue that holds the society together is based on the extreme level of interdependence among the members of its society. Essentially, people come to depend on each other because of the diversity of the society. The law in organic societies is needed to regulate all of the various components of the society and enforce interactions or contracts among its members.

Durkheim was concerned with how societies move from mechanical to organic societies. As new members arrive to mechanical societies and the cluster of individuals becomes more diverse, the common identity of the group begins to erode. This can be very problematic, especially if the growth of the society is very rapid. The society may not be able to respond quickly enough to the changes in order to regulate the interactions of the members (Vold et al. 2002). Durkheim used the term **anomie** to describe this condition where the behaviors of the members may not be adequately controlled. For Durkheim, anomie was the end result of rapid industrialization, urbanization, and growth of the population (Curran & Renzetti, 2001). He believed societies experiencing high levels of anomie may experience adverse conditions such as heightened levels of crime, disorder, suicide, and other social problems.

It is easy to see how Durkheim's analysis of how societies grow and change could be applied to the city of Chicago. Large numbers of diverse people from all over the United States as well as European nations were settling in the city on a daily basis. These individuals brought their own religion, customs, norms, and belief systems with them to their new world. Recently arriving immigrants would also bring their language. Under these conditions, a person would not share a common identity with his or her neighbor, and even carrying on a conversation was hard. There would be no collective conscience or shared idea of right and wrong to control people's behavior.

The Invasion, Dominance, and Succession of Robert Ezra Park (1864–1944)

The Chicago School members drew heavily on the ideas of Durkheim, but also added an extra twist: the principles of **social ecology**. Social ecology examines how plant and animal life forms relate to each other in their natural habitat. The Chicago School member who is usually credited with initially integrating the ideas of social ecology with the study of the city is Robert Ezra Park.

Robert Park was a newspaper reporter for 25 years prior to beginning his career as a university professor. During his years as a journalist Park focused on urban problems, especially issues related to housing. Park used the tools of a journalist—personal observations, in-depth interviews, and an immersion in the area being studied—to chronicle the conditions in the city (Taylor et al. 1973). For a while, Park lived in New York City. While working for the *New York Journal*, he was assigned as a police beat reporter. During this time, Park investigated many aspects of urban life, and even managed to infiltrate opium dens (Martin et al. 1990). As a result of his experiences, Park brought a rather unique reality-based perspective to the discipline of sociology.

Today, there are two terms commonly used to describe Park's approach to the analysis of the city: **positivism** and **functionalism**. As a Positivist, Park's work is premised on a few assumptions. First, Positivists assume that human behavior is not a matter of free choice. Instead, a Positivist believes that our actions are, at least to some extent, determined by influences that are beyond our immediate control. Some Positivists adopt a "hard-core" stance on this assumption, maintaining that there is no free will at all—we have no choices and our behaviors are completely determined by these influences. Other Positivists lean toward what Robert Bohm (1997:27) describes as "soft determinism." That is, human beings do have a restricted ability to make choices, but for some people the number of choices may be quite limited.

The second assumption is related to the first. Using the scientific method, Positivists look for behavioral influences either within the constitutional make-up of the person (such as chemical imbalances in the brain or psychological problems) or external to the individual (such as the quality of the home life or other environmental influences). Therefore, a Positivist assumes that there are identifiable differences between criminals and non-criminals, and these differences cause some people to be criminals. As a positivist, Robert Park was looking for clearly identifiable factors that were the root causes of crime and other social problems.

As a functionalist, Park viewed the city as a kind of social organism. When taken together, the various business districts and neighborhoods that make up a city begin to take on the character of a living, breathing organism. Park began to integrate the principles of ecology, which focuses on the interrelationships and interdependencies of plants and animals in their natural environment, with his analysis of the city.

The Development of Natural Areas

If you will, picture a forest. Within this natural habitat, various plants and animals struggle to survive. Every organism is driven by the

Darwinian, evolutionary goal to maximize reproduction of its own species. The plants and animals form symbiotic, cooperative relationships with each other in order to better their chances for life. Competition also exists in this system, as not all areas within the forest are equally beneficial to survival (Gold, 1987).

Park applied a forest model to competition and cooperation between various groups in the city. Within the city, Park was able to identify a number of "**natural areas**," or clusters that were somehow different or set off from the larger organism. These natural areas could be based on the race or ethnicity of those residing within the cluster. For example, in most major U.S. cities, there are areas that are dominated by a different culture, often called China Town, Greek Town, or Little Italy. Park would have described these neighborhoods as natural areas. Some clusters may form based on the income level of the residents, while other natural areas may be based on the concentration of factories or other businesses. Similar to how plants and animals compete in their natural environment, humans residing within these natural areas struggle to survive.

Just as areas of the forest are not all equally conducive to survival, some regions within the city are more desirable to live in than others. Less powerful groups within the racial and ethnic mix of the city are forced to make do with life in the less desirable areas, urban slums, and ghettos (Shaw & McKay, 1969). To better its chances for survival, a group of people "stuck" in a poorer area may seek out a better territory in which to live. To explain this phenomenon, Park applied the ecological concept of invasion, dominance, and succession. Irish people in one neighborhood may begin to invade another natural area dominated by Germans, for example. The Irish may come to dominate this natural area. In time, the Irish may loose control of the natural area as another group, such as the Italians, invades the area. If the Irish were able, then they would move on to invade another even more desirable neighborhood. If the Irish did not have the resources or the power to invade a better neighborhood, then they may be forced to live in a less desirable area. Business and industry, as well as groups of people, can be involved in the pattern of invasion, dominance, and succession as they try to expand and seek out a habitat that is better suited for survival.

Burgess' Contributions:
Life in the Zones

Park had an office mate named Ernest Burgess. Park and Burgess worked very closely together on a number of projects, including the influential book *Introduction to the Science of Sociology* (1921) that was fondly dubbed the "Green Bible" by students at the University of Chicago (Martin et al. 1990). Burgess combined Park's ideas concerning invasion, dominance, and succession with a concentric model of city growth and change.

Burgess recognized that the city of Chicago appeared to expand and grow in a series of concentric circles that moved outward from the central business district. Each circle or Zone had distinct characteristics that set it off from the other zones (Burgess, 1925). Zone I, which was the innermost circle, was the central business district of the city. In Chicago, this area was (and still is) known as the Loop. Few people actually lived in Zone I, as factories and other businesses dominate the area.

Moving outward, Zone II was known as the Zone in Transition. Generally speaking, Zone II was the least desirable area to live in the city. Ever expanding businesses and factories attempted to invade and dominate Zone II from the Loop. Many real estate speculators had purchased housing units and other properties in the area, and as a result most people living in the Zone in Transition were renters (Bursik & Grasmick, 1993). Landlords recognized that the value of their property was not in the housing or rental units that was on the property, but in the commercial value of the land itself (Vold et al. 2002). Factories and businesses had an eye toward buying the property only to tear down the houses and apartment units in order to meet the needs of their expanding businesses. As a result, landlords did not invest a great deal of money into the care and maintenance of the housing units. Properties deteriorated to the point where they were no longer inhabitable. As a result, a family may have resided in a run-down apartment building surrounded by boarded up houses, dilapidated apartment buildings, vacant, overgrown lots, and invading factories and businesses popping up around their home. Only the poorest, least powerful people resided in the Zone in Transition.

As one moved further out into Zone III, housing conditions generally improved. Burgess called this area the Zone of Workingmen's Homes. Second and third generation immigrants and other working class people who had the resources to move out of the Zone in Transition domi-nated the area. Living conditions were better still in Zone IV, or the Residential Zone. Single-family homes and better quality apartments marked this zone. Finally, Zone V, or the Commuter Zone, was made up of the suburban area and surrounding satellite cities and inhabited solidly by members of the middle and upper classes. Burgess noted that the as the city continued to grow and expand in an outward manner, the inner zones would begin to invade, dominate, and succeed into the neighboring zone (Vold et al. 2002).

Clifford Shaw and Henry McKay: Delinquency and Place

The ideas of Robert Park and Ernest Burgess impacted a number of scholars studying and working at the University of Chicago. Few works, however, have had greater impact than the research efforts of Clifford Shaw and Henry McKay. Described as "one of the most funda-mental sociological approaches to the study of crime and delinquency" (Sampson & Groves, 1989:774), Shaw and McKay's work represents a culmination of the foundations set by Park, Burgess, and other sociolo-gists interested in the study of crime and place.

Beginning in 1924, a graduate student of Burgess' by the name of Clifford R. Shaw was interested in the geographic distribution of juve-nile delinquency and other social problems. Shaw, a former probation officer, began to locate the residences of delinquent boys. A few years later, Henry D. McKay, who had just joined the Illinois Institute of Ju-venile Research, worked with Shaw on this tedious, almost overwhelm-ing task (Gold, 1987). Without the use of computers or sophisticated software, the researchers individually plotted the home addresses of male juvenile offenders who had been brought before the Juvenile Court in Cook County. Working with several different waves of data that had been collected over a period spanning four decades, Shaw and McKay manually located the home addresses of nearly 25,000 youths!

Shaw and McKay set out to answer a number of key questions in their influential book *Juvenile Delinquency in Urban Areas* (1942/1969). These questions included the following:

- How are the rates of delinquents in particular areas affected over a period of time by successive changes in the nativity and nationality composition of the population?

- To what extent are the observed differences in the rates of delinquents between children of foreign and native parentage due to a differential geographic distribution of these two groups in the city?

- Under what economic and social conditions does crime develop as a social tradition and become embodied in a system of criminal values? (Shaw & McKay, 1969:4)

The questions that Shaw and McKay set out to answer were a sharp break from the popular thinking of the times. Recall that there was a great deal of political and scientific debate concerning whether or not many of the newly arriving immigrants were of inferior stock and ultimately potential criminals. Shaw and McKay did not focus on genetic causes of crime, delinquency, and other social problems, but instead looked at social and environmental influences on human behavior. Essentially, Shaw and McKay viewed juvenile delinquents not as evolutionary throwbacks or inherently inferior beings, but as "normal" kids whose behavior was somehow tied to the environment in which they lived.

The Data: Official Delinquency Reports

In order to answer their research questions, the homes of the juvenile delinquents had to be identified. For the purposes of their study, Shaw and McKay defined a "juvenile delinquent" as a youth under the age of 17 who was brought before the Cook County Juvenile Court (or other courts having jurisdiction over the case) on a petition of delinquency or whose case was dealt with by an officer of the law without the need of a court appearance. Shaw and McKay note that a better term for this group would be "alleged delinquents," as in many cases the charges against the youth were not sustained. It should be noted that Shaw and McKay studied only male juvenile delinquents. Shaw and McKay looked at the geographic distribution of three different waves of data from the Juvenile Court: 8,056 juveniles from 1900–1906; 8,141 juveniles from 1917–1923; and 8,411 juveniles from 1927–1933.

In addition to the juvenile court referral data, Shaw and McKay also included two other sources of information in their analysis: the home addresses of juvenile delinquents who had been committed to correctional institutions by the Juvenile Court of Cook County and the home addresses of alleged delinquent boys who had been dealt with by a police probation officer. The time span for the data concerning the number of residential commitments mirrored the three waves for the Juvenile Court referrals. With respect to the allegedly delinquent boys who had been dealt with by a juvenile probation officer, only three years of data were used: 1926, 1927, and 1931. While this may not sound like a great deal of information when compared to the other data sources Shaw and McKay used, in each of the three years the police probation officers saw nearly 10,000 boys. In the city of Chicago, any youth who was arrested or somehow came to the attention of the police was automatically referred to a juvenile probation officer for screening. Based on the evaluation made by the probation officer, the vast majority of the cases (85 percent) was disposed of without any further referral to the juvenile court.

Spot, Rate, and Zone Map Construction

Shaw and McKay then set out to create a number of maps based on their various data sources. A **spot map** was based on the place of residence for the alleged juvenile delinquents. In a spot map the homes of the alleged juvenile delinquents were identified using a dot. The information in these spot maps was then converted into rate maps. In order to create the **rate maps**, Shaw and McKay broke the city of Chicago down into 140 different, basically square mile, areas. Using census data, Shaw and McKay calculated the number of alleged delinquents based on the number of 10–16 year old males in the square mile area, so that a rate of x number of delinquents (for example, 5.8) per 100 boys residing in the area was reported. Finally, Shaw and McKay plotted a series of **zone maps** based on their various data sources. In a zone map, the number of alleged male juvenile delinquents was converted to a rate based on the juvenile population residing in each of Burgess' five zones. Separate spot, rate, and zone maps were created for each of the various types of data (police contacts, juvenile court referrals, and commitments) and for each time period of data.

The Distribution of Delinquency and Other Social Conditions by Zones

An analysis of the various map types revealed that juvenile delinquency was not evenly distributed throughout the city of Chicago. Shaw and McKay found a regular decrease in the level of juvenile delinquency as one moved outward from the center of the city. This pattern was consistent for all types of data examined—the number of court referrals, number of juvenile commitments, or police contacts—or even the time period in which the data was collected. A compilation of the zone rates reported by Shaw and McKay is presented in Table 2.2.

As can be seen, the zones with the highest rates of delinquency were Zone I, or the Loop, and Zone II, the Zone in Transition. In some cases,

Table 2.2. Zone Rates for Court Referrals,
Juvenile Commitments, and Police Contacts

Data Source	Zone I	Zone II	Zone III	Zone IV	Zone V
Court Referrals					
1900–1906	16.3	9.1	6.2	4.4	5.6
1917–1923	10.3	7.3	4.4	3.3	3.0
1927–1933	9.8	6.7	4.5	2.5	1.8
Committed Youths					
1900–1906	7.0	3.6	2.4	1.6	2.1
1917–1923	3.5	2.5	1.4	0.9	0.9
1927–1933	3.4	2.2	1.4	0.6	0.4
Police Contacts					
1926 series	10.9	8.2	5.0	2.0	2.2
1927 series	9.9	7.8	4.3	2.4	2.2
1931 series	9.6	7.8	5.3	3.9	3.2

Adapted from Shaw and McKay, 1969.

the difference between the rates for the inner zones and the outer zones was quite dramatic. For example, in 1926, the zone rate for police contacts in the Loop was 10.9. This means that for every 100 male youths aged 10–16, nearly 11 juveniles had a police contact. In the Residential Zone (Zone IV) or the Commuter Zone (Zone V), the rate of juvenile-police contacts dropped to around 2 contacts per 100 youths.

Shaw and McKay set out to explain this pattern. Shaw and McKay viewed juvenile delinquency as indicative of some degree of pathology or "sickness" within a neighborhood. Of course, juvenile delinquency and crime are not the only problematic conditions a neighborhood may experience. Neighborhoods with high levels of unemployment, sickness, death, and poverty would be considered by most to possess less desirable living conditions. Shaw and McKay explored for relationships (or correlations) between the distributions of juvenile delinquency and other social problems, including infant mortality, tuberculosis, and mental disorders within each of the five zones.

Additionally, Shaw and McKay also examined other neighborhood characteristics that existed in the various zones, such as the economic conditions, community stability, and racial or ethnic composition. Economic conditions were measured by the percentage of families receiving welfare enhancements and the median rent paid per month. The level of neighborhood stability was measured by the percentage of homeowners living in a particular zone and the population increase or decrease from

1920–1930. Also, Shaw and McKay included a number of measures of the racial or ethnic composition in a zone, including the percentage of foreign-born and African American heads of household. The neighborhood characteristics by zone as well as the delinquency measures for comparable time periods are presented in Table 2.3.

As can be seen in Table 2.3, living conditions generally improved as one moved outward from the center of the city of Chicago. The infant mortality rate, which was based on the number of infant deaths per 1,000 live births, was over twice as high in the Zone I Loop as compared to the Zone V Commuter Zone. The tuberculosis rate was calculated based on the average number of cases reported annually from 1931–1937. There was a dramatic decrease in the rate as one move from the inner city zones to the suburban areas. A similar pattern was found with respect to the mental disorder rate, as fewer individuals in the outer

Table 2.3. Neighborhood Characteristics by Zone

Neighborhood Characteristic	Zone I	Zone II	Zone III	Zone IV	Zone V
Infant Mortality Rate (1928–1933)	86.7	67.5	54.7	45.9	41.3
Tuberculosis Rate (1931–1937)	33.5	25.0	18.4	12.5	9.2
Mental Disorder Rate (1922–1934)	32.0	18.8	13.2	10.1	8.4
Percentage of Families on Welfare Relief (1934)	27.9	24.0	14.8	8.6	5.9
Median Monthly Rent (1930)	$38.08	$36.51	$53.08	$65.38	$73.51
Percentage of Home Owners (1930)	12.8	21.8	26.2	32.8	47.2
Percentage of Foreign-Born and African American Family Heads (1934)	62.3	64.9	55.9	40.4	39.4
Percent Population Increase or Decrease (1920–1930	-21.3	-9.3	12.3	42.9	140.8
Delinquency Measures Court Referrals (1927–1933)	9.8	6.7	4.5	2.5	1.8
Committed Youths (1927–1933)	3.4	2.2	1.4	0.6	0.4

Adapted from Shaw and McKay, 1969.

zones were admitted to state and private hospitals for insanity and other mental disorders.

Economic Conditions and Population Shifts

The general economic conditions in the outer zones were much better than those found in the inner city areas. If one compared the living conditions in Zone II to Zone V, there were nearly four times as many families receiving welfare in the inner city than in the outer zone. Further, the median rental amount was much lower in the inner zones. It would cost a family nearly half as much to live in the Zone in Transition than it would to live in the Commuter Zone.

With respect to neighborhood stability, homeownership was much higher in the outer zones than in the inner city zones. It should not be inferred that people who rent are the cause of criminal activity. Most people will rent a home or apartment at some point in our lives. However, if a person is renting their home, their living arrangement is by definition temporary in nature. Generally speaking, renters do not share the same stake in the community as homeowners do. Renters come and go at the end of their lease, while homeowners tend to reside in neighborhoods for a longer period of time and therefore tend to identify with their community to a greater extent. Homeowners are more likely to get involved in their local community institutions, such as churches, schools, and various local clubs and organizations than are renters. Neighborhoods with high numbers of rental units tend to be less stable and socially organized than areas with fewer rental units.

Shaw and McKay also found that the population in the inner city zones was decreasing. In Zone I, there was a 21 percent decrease while the Zone in Transition experienced a nine percent population decline. In contrast, the outer zones were growing, in some cases dramatically so. Shaw and McKay noted that business and industry were engaging in the pattern of invasion, dominance and succession in the innermost zones. Not only were the numbers of available housing units reduced by the expanding businesses, but also as commercial development expanded into these inner zones the number of condemned buildings increased. The invasion of business and industry into these residential areas contributed to the instability and lack of social cohesion in the inner most zones.

Finally, Shaw and McKay found that the percentage of African American and foreign-born heads of households was much higher in the inner zones than in the outer zones. As can be seen in Table 2.3, the inner zones were also associated with the highest rates of alleged juvenile delinquency.

Given the era in which Shaw and McKay were writing it would have been very easy for them to use this finding to support the popular racist ideas of their times. Shaw and McKay could have argued that the higher rate of delinquency in the inner zones was due to the fact that these areas were populated by inherently inferior beings. However, Shaw and McKay broke with the thinking of the times, instead focusing on the characteristics of the neighborhoods and not the groups that inhabited them.

Arguably, the most important finding reported by Shaw and McKay was related to the fact that even though the types of immigrant groups residing in the inner city areas had changed dramatically over the years, the delinquency rate remained high. The ethnicity within the inner zones had experienced almost a complete turnover as different groups went through the pattern of invasion, dominance, and succession. It did not matter which racial or ethnic groups resided in the inner zones—delinquency and other social problems remained high. Recall that the popular thinking of the times held that certain groups, such as the Italians, were morally inferior and should be barred from entering the country. What Shaw and McKay were able to demonstrate was that a boy's involvement in delinquency did not depend on *who* the boy was (or which racial or ethnic group he belonged to) but *where* he lived in the city. In effect, no group was found to be inherently more criminogenic than another.

Among the Italians and Poles, for example, Shaw and McKay reported a wide range of delinquency rates that was similar to the range found among native whites. Among Italians, Shaw and McKay found that the rate of juvenile court referrals ranged from 0.89 to 11.76 while the rate for native whites was 0.48 to 14.94. The delinquency rate among Italians youths residing in the outer zones was low. If, in fact, the Italian youths were more likely to become juvenile delinquents than their native white peers due to some sort of in-born deficiency, one would not have found such a pattern. Instead of focusing on biology, Shaw and McKay looked to the characteristics of the community as a contributing factor to the delinquency rate of boys. As stated by Shaw and McKay (1969:154–155):

> While it is apparent from these data that the foreign born and the Negroes are concentrated in the areas of high rates of delinquents, the meaning of this association is not easily determined.... Clearly, one must beware of attaching causal significance to race or nativity. For, in the present social and economic system, it is the Negroes and the foreign born, or at least the newest immigrants, who have the least access to the necessities of life and who are therefore least

prepared for the competitive struggle. It is they who are forced to live in the worst slum areas and who are least able to organize against the effects of such living.

So, What Is Happening in the Inner Zones?

Once Shaw and McKay had determined that juvenile delinquency and other social problems were related more to geography than to biology, they tried to determine how life was different for people living in the inner zones as compared to those residing in the outer zones. Why had delinquency become a popular lifestyle for many of the boys living within these inner zones? To answer this question, Shaw and McKay again demonstrated their willingness to draw on a divergent set of theoretical perspectives.

Shaw and McKay theorized that in the outer zones, residents had adopted a uniform set of conventional norms and values, especially with respect to how children are raised and the importance of respecting the rule of law. In Durkheim's terms, people in the outer zones shared a sort of collective conscience. In the outer zones, a common sense of what is acceptable behavior and what is not is consistently presented to children. Adults serve as role models for law-abiding behavior, and the children are immersed in conventional activities (such as school and church programs) where this same message is provided. This is not to say that no criminals reside in the outer zones. While crime and delinquency do exist, children are not constantly bombarded with peers or adult role models that support a competing set of values. Living according to the conventional, collective conscience is seen as the dominant, desirable way of life by children being raised in the outer zones.

Shaw and McKay felt that life in the innermost zones was quite different. Instead of being presented with consistent messages supporting a conventional moral order, children were instead immersed in a society marked by extreme diversity. While some children were presented with messages that were consistent with the dominant values of society, other children were exposed to messages that stood in stark contrast to what are commonly referred to as "middle class values." Instead of being raised to think that success was achieved through hard work, honesty, and delayed gratification, children in the inner zones may have grown up to believe that lying, stealing, and seeking pathways to easy money was the only way of getting ahead.

As such, the inner zones also had higher concentrations of adult criminals. Children growing up in the inner zones learned to emulate the behaviors and values of the adult criminals. Shaw and McKay noted that these deviant role models existed not only in the neighborhood, but also within the immediate families of some of the children. In such areas, criminal and/or delinquent subcultures could develop and thrive. Gangs of juvenile delinquents were found to be common within the inner zones, each with their own distinct and often deviant expectations for behavior.

Social Disorganization and Juvenile Delinquency

Oftentimes, the term **social disorganization** is used in conjunction with the work of Shaw and McKay and the other Chicago School theorists. According to Sampson and Groves (1989:777), social disorganization may be defined as the "inability of a community structure to realize the common values of its residents and maintain effective social controls." The inner zones were marked by a high level of social disorganization. There was little residential stability in the inner city zones. Renters came and went within the neighborhoods. New immigrant groups and Southern blacks arrived on a daily basis and, since they tended to be poor and relatively powerless, ultimately settled in the cheaper inner zones. As new people came into the neighborhood, the stabilizing ties that had been established prior to their arrival were destroyed. Children did not identify with a single over-arching conventional order. Instead, the high degree of neighborhood diversity and heterogeneity led to the growth and development of competing moral orders. The high level of population turnover and community heterogeneity hindered the ability of the family and other primary groups to control the behavior of the children and local residents (Bursik & Grasmick, 1993). As argued by Sampson (1995), one of the major problems associated with socially disorganized areas is the inability to control the behavior of teenage peer groups, especially gangs.

In this type of socially disorganized environment, norms and values that support criminal and delinquent behaviors develop. Left unchecked, these alternative norms and values may come to support a subculture of delinquency. As the local residents came and went, the subcultural values remained in the neighborhoods and were passed along to the new residents in a process called **cultural transmission** (Eistadter & Henry, 1995; Kornhauser, 1978). Whatever social organization existed in these areas had the tendency to be supportive of delinquent and criminal norms and values (Gold, 1987).

Critiques of Social Disorganization Theory

A number of critiques have been raised against Shaw and McKay's work. Arguably, the most serious charge has been leveled against the data sources that were used to build their theory. Data based on court referrals, police contacts, and juvenile commitments to residential institutions are often called **official records**. In order for a boy to make his way into the spot maps of Shaw and McKay, his alleged misconduct had to be "officially" identified by the police or other agent of the criminal justice system. A popular theory in criminology called **labeling theory** argues that less powerful people in society, such as the poor and members of racial and ethnic minority groups, are more likely to be apprehended by the police and subsequently processed through the criminal justice system (Becker, 1970). Because of the seriousness of this particular critique (as well as the continued reliance upon official records as a source of data both in research and in practical law enforcement applications) more time will be spend discussing this assessment in the following example.

The Saints and the Roughnecks: A Lesson in Labeling

Noted critical sociologist William Chambliss used labeling theory in his classic study of the Saints and the Roughnecks, two groups of delinquent boys who attended the same high school. The Saints were a popular group of white, upper-middle-class youths. All were active in school activities and all but one of the seven boys eventually went on to college. In contrast, the Roughnecks were a group of lower class white boys who were not as well polished as the Saints. Their clothes were not as nice as the Saints' apparel, and their mannerisms were not as polite and deferential. Despite the fact that the Saints committed more acts of delinquency than the Roughnecks, not one of the Saints was ever arrested or taken to the precinct house during the two years that Chambliss observed them. While the delinquent acts of the upper middle class Saints were viewed as "good kids just sowing some wild oats," the delinquency of the Roughnecks was perceived as much more serious. The Roughnecks were viewed as bad kids headed for nothing but trouble. The police targeted the Roughnecks for sporadic harassment and arrested the boys if given any hint that they had been involved in a delinquent act. As a result, each of the members was arrested at least once during the period that Chambliss was studying the boys, and a few of them accumulated a number of arrests. Several had spent a night or two in jail and two of the six Roughnecks were sentenced to a residential commitment in a boys' home for their deviant acts.

If one relied solely upon the use of official data, such as the number of arrests, police contacts, or juvenile commitments, one would conclude that the Roughnecks were much more delinquent than the Saints. This was simply not the case. Chambliss discussed the impact of the social class structure on the behavior and bias of the police and the community. More powerful individuals in our society hold control of our legal institutions. When an upper class boy was delinquent, his parents would be more likely to dismiss the act as a momentary lapse in judgment and berate the police for arresting their son. In effect, upper class parents would not accept the law's definition of their son's behavior as delinquent or problematic. As a result, officers would be less likely to arrest or officially process a youth from an upper socioeconomic class home.

In contrast, when a lower class boy was arrested, an officer would be met with either a cooperative parent or a parent who was indifferent to the actions of the police. The authority of the police would not be challenged in such incidents, and the officers would then be more likely to make arrests in the future. As phrased by Chambliss (1996:54):

> Selective perception and labeling—finding, processing and punishing some kinds of criminality and not others—means that visible, poor, nonmobile, out-spoken, undiplomatic "tough" kids will be noticed, whether their actions are seriously delinquent or not. Other kids, who have established a reputation for being bright (even though underachieving), disciplined and involved in respectable activities, who are mobile and monied, will be invisible when they deviate from sanctioned activities. They'll sow their wild oats—perhaps even wider and thicker than their lower-class cohorts—but they won't be noticed.

Essentially, what Chambliss and others found is that lower class youths are more likely to be arrested and officially processed through the criminal justice system than youths from middle and upper class homes. This means that as Shaw and McKay were looking at their spot maps of where the alleged juvenile delinquents lived, they pondered why so many boys from poorer areas were more likely to be delinquent than boys who lived in the more affluent outer zones. Critics have argued that their entire theory was based on a biased data set. Boys in the outer zone may have been committing just as many delinquent acts, but their actions never showed up in the official statistics used by Shaw and McKay.

As described in the first chapter, there are alternative means of gathering data on the level of crime, including self-report surveys. It has been argued that official data are more reflective of the behavior of the police and the criminal justice system than the behavior of the person apprehended. Self-reports were designed to gather information concerning the behavior of the individual actor and not the behavior of the police. In using self-report data, some researchers have argued that there are no differences in the delinquent involvement of lower and middle and upper class youths (see, for example, Tittle, Villemez, & Smith, 1978) while others would disagree (Elliott & Huizinga, 1983).

A thorough discussion of the debate centering on the accuracy of self-report versus official data is beyond the scope of this text. However, it should be mentioned that there is some debate over whether or not the use of official records provides a "true" measure of the level of criminal activity in a community. This is especially important in light of the fact that the vast majority of research studies exploring the social ecology of crime continue to use official data, such as police reports and the Uniform Crime Reports put out by the FBI, in their analyses (Byrne & Sampson, 1986). Certainly, Shaw and McKay are not the only theorists who are "guilty" of using official data sources.

Other Critiques of Social Disorganization

A second critique of social disorganization theory that has commonly been raised concerns the **ecological fallacy**. Maxfield and Babbie (1995:77) define the ecological fallacy as "the danger of making assertions about individuals as the unit of analysis based on the examination of groups or other aggregations." In their analysis, Shaw and McKay noted that delinquency was highest in the inner zones of the city. Based on that observation, one cannot assume that an individual young boy growing up in Zone II would then be a delinquent. Just because a higher level of delinquency was found in Zone II does not automatically imply that an individual growing up in this area would be delinquent. One cannot make individual predictions based on group level data. Because of the lack of ability to predict the behavior of individuals, it has been argued that the social disorganization theory is relatively weak and its usefulness has been questioned (Bohm, 1997; Einstadter & Henry, 1995).

A third critique that has been raised asserts that the theory is **tautological** in nature. If a theory is tautological, it suffers from circular reasoning. As noted by Akers (1994), this problem has arisen when researchers have tested social disorganization theory in other settings. In order to test Shaw and McKay's theory, the researchers must identify an area as socially disorganized. Oftentimes, an area is defined as "socially disorganized" because of its high level of crime and delinquency. Why is crime high in this area? Crime is high because the area is socially disorganized.

The Legacy of The Chicago School

Despite the critiques of their ideas, the legacy of Shaw, McKay, and the Chicago School continues on. Described by Vold et al. (2002:133) as a "gold mine that continues to enrich criminology today," the ecological approach has experienced a great resurgence in interest and influence. The popularity and influence of social ecology is not confined to academic debates concerning the effectiveness of the theory. As presented in Chapter 4, a number of practical policy suggestions and programs have developed based on the theories of the Chicago School.

Crime and Community-Level Factors

Before leaving our discussion of social ecology, we will briefly examine some of the contemporary applications and empirical tests of the Chicago School's principles. Most notable in the advancement of social ecology has been Robert J. Sampson and his colleagues (see, for example, Byrne & Sampson, 1986; Sampson, 1995; Sampson & Groves, 1989; Sampson & Raudenbush, 1999; Sampson, Raudenbush, & Earls, 1997).

In the essay "The Community," Sampson (1995) summarized the research that has explored variations in crime rates across communities. Shaw and McKay had noted three factors that ultimately led to the deterioration of social organization in a community: low economic status, ethnic heterogeneity, and residential instability. Juvenile delinquency was found to be highest in the poorest areas that also had higher levels of ethnic and racial diversity and residential turnover. As noted by Sampson, contemporary researchers have explored these issues in depth, and a number of other community factors, such as family structure and the level of housing and population density, have been added to the mix.

Crime and Poverty

Many applications of social disorganization theory have focused on the use of one variable: economic status (Byrne & Sampson, 1986). While there has been some debate on the issue, a consistent finding has been that communities with the highest levels of crime also have the highest rates of poverty (Kornhauser, 1978; McGahey, 1986). Some have argued that it is not poverty in and of itself that causes crime, but inequality (Rosenfeld, 1986). As phrased by Michalowski (1985:407), "Poverty is the condition of having little. Inequality is the condition of having less than others, and it is this condition more than poverty itself that serves to stimulate crime." Inequality can lead to heightened levels of social disorganization by highlighting the differences between various racial and ethnic groups as well as further delineating social class lines (Blau & Blau, 1982). Sampson (1995) further elaborated on the nature of the relationship between poverty and crime, adding the concept of mobility. Citing the work of Smith and Jarjoura (1988), Sampson concluded that poverty alone does not cause crime—areas with high levels of population turnover combined with poverty have higher levels of violent crime than high poverty areas with stable residential patterns.

Crime and Ethnic/Racial Heterogeneity

As noted by Sampson, a great deal of research has focused on the relationship between community racial composition and violent crime. A consistent finding of these studies has been that areas with higher numbers of African American residents tend to have higher levels of violent crime. For example, Moore and Tonry (1998), in a discussion of the growing number of violent incidents involving American youths, noted that the epidemic of youth violence has been concentrated among inner city minority males. Why? Is race the sole cause? Few, if any, would answer this question with yes.

The relationship between race and crime is highly complex. Part of the problem is that it is very difficult to completely isolate the sole contributing effects of race. In our society, race is closely tied to other important factors, such as income, unemployment rates, educational attainment, school quality, divorce, and number of single-parent homes. Some have argued that the effect of race on crime, delinquency and other social problems is declining in its significance (Wilson, 1980;

1987). While community racial composition continues to be examined by those interested in social ecology theories, Sampson argues that it is debatable whether or not race adds anything new and distinct to the explanation of crime and delinquency, especially if poverty, mobility, and other related factors are already included in the discussion.

Crime and Population Density

In his review of the literature, Sampson also discussed the influence of housing density on crime. Citing the work of Roncek (1981), Sampson argued that the most dangerous places to live were those areas with large numbers of people living in apartment housing or multi-unit structures. As more and more people share the same living space, interactions become less frequent and more impersonal. Neighbors do not recognize each other, nor do they watch out for each other. This effect may be intensified in densely populated public housing units, where high concentrations of poor oftentimes minority residents reside. William J. Wilson (1987) discussed life in Robert Taylor Homes, which was the largest public housing project in the city of Chicago in the early 1980s. The complex was comprised of twenty-eight sixteen-story buildings that covered a landmass of ninety-two acres. While the official population neared 20,000 residents, it was expected that up to 27,000 residents actually lived in the complex. In 1980, less than one percent of the city's population lived in Robert Taylor Homes. However, 11 percent of the city's murders, 9 percent of the rapes, and 10 percent of the aggravated assaults occurred within the complex.

Crime and Instability

Contemporary social ecologists have expanded the definition of community instability beyond a simple analysis of residential turnover. Recall that Shaw and McKay (1969) noted that social disorganization was closely linked to the concept of invasion, dominance, and succession. Groups of people or businesses displaced previous residents in an area, and these invading forces competed for scarce resources. Ultimately, the shared sense of community that had existed prior to the residential turnover would be lost, resulting in social disorganization. Social ecologists have continued to examine the issue of residential mobility, and have expanded the examination of changes in a city's residential turnover to include the rapid growth of suburban areas (Bursik, 1986).

While community instability is an important factor in the discussion of crime and delinquency, instability within the family has also been explored. Sampson (1985; 1986) has investigated the impact of family structure on crime and delinquency, noting that there is a strong relationship between family disruption and rates of violent crime. There are a number of reasons that such a relationship exists. First, neighborhoods with higher rates of divorced, separated, and female-headed families have lower levels of formal and informal social control. Formal social control is derived from participation in community institutions and local affairs, such as clubs and committees that may be promoted through local churches, volunteer organizations, schools, or sporting events. Involvement in formal community institutions has several advantages. Participants may have a higher degree of integration and identification with their local community, thereby reducing the feelings of social isolation. Communities whose members have high levels of participation in formal organizations are better able to take charge of the destiny of their own neighborhoods. For example, residents may pursue what Bursik and Grasmick (1993) call extra-local resources, such as block grants and other additional municipal services to better their own living conditions and increase the level of crime control. The involvement of local residents in these organized efforts is related to family structure, as divorced, separated, and unmarried people are less likely to participate in formal community institutions than married-couple families.

Informal social control is derived from neighbors watching out for the well being of each other. Sampson (1986:27) provides the following examples of informal social control: "neighbors taking note of and/or questioning strangers, watching over each other's property, assuming responsibility for supervision of general youth activities, and intervening in local disturbances." In order for these informal control mechanisms to exist, neighbors must know each other and feel comfortable taking action when a potential problem occurs, such as a group of neighborhood youths hanging around on a street corner drinking beer and vandalizing buildings. Adults assume responsibility not only for the behavior of their own children, but also for the behavior of their neighbors' children. Sampson maintains that areas with higher numbers of intact families will also have higher levels of informal social control.

Sampson's Concept of Collective Efficacy and Crime

Most recently, Sampson and his coauthors have explored the effects of **collective efficacy** on the level of crime and disorder in a community. Collective efficacy has been defined as "social cohesion among neighbors combined with their willingness to intervene on behalf of the common good (Sampson et al. 1997:918)." In order for communities to have a high level of collective efficacy, there must be a high level of mutual trust among the neighbors. High levels of trust can only result when people know their neighbors and can anticipate their reactions. In addition to fostering trust, social cohesion in neighborhoods leads to the development of shared expectations for behavior. People know what the rules are and respect them. Because of the mutual trust and knowledge and appreciation of the neighborhood rules, if an adult observed a violation of the neighborhood norms then he or she would feel comfortable stepping in to correct the situation.

The level of collective efficacy in a neighborhood depends on a number of factors. These include population change and residential mobility, the concentration of lower-income residents, racial segregation, and the number of female-headed households. In effect, collective efficacy may be thought of as the opposite of social disorganization (Vold et al. 2002). Sampson and his coauthors have found support for the effects of collective efficacy on crime and disorder using a number of methods, including videotaping and categorizing more than 23,000 street segments within the city of Chicago (Sampson & Raudenbush, 1999).

Summary

The work of the Chicago School continues to be an influential area of criminological thought. Prior to the development of their theories of social ecology, the popular thinking of the time focused attention on various characteristics of the individual as the root cause of human behavior. The Chicago School theorists argued that individual characteristics, such as race or IQ, were not of great importance in the study of crime and delinquency. Instead, they focused on the characteristics of the neighborhoods in which a person lived as an influential factor in whether or not a person became involved in crime and delinquency.

Crime, delinquency, and other social problems tended to be concentrated in social disorganized areas marked by low economic status, ethnic heterogeneity, and residential instability. Contemporary social ecologists have also added the influences of family structure, formal and informal social control, and community cohesion. Together, these various influences impact the socialization of youths as they grow up and learn to function as members of society.

In the Chicago School Tradition...

We will close this chapter with an excerpt from a participant observation study conducted by Elijah Anderson, a prominent sociologist. While the theories of the Chicago School continue to be highly influential, others would argue that the greatest contribution to criminology was their use of participant observation as a research technique. As you read the first Spotlight on Research, I hope you can appreciate the richness of this type of data. Participant observation provides a much different picture of the everyday life of the local residents than could ever be provided by an examination by more traditional "official statistics," such as the FBI UCR. While Professor Anderson's study was conducted on the streets of Philadelphia, many of the same sights, sounds, and neighborhood transitions could easily be seen in any older large urban area.

Spotlight on Research I

From "The social ecology of youth violence"
Elijah Anderson, Ph.D.*

This spotlight on research features an excerpt from one of the many outstanding works of Elijah Anderson, professor of sociology in the Department of Sociology at the University of Pennsylvania. In this essay, Professor Anderson takes us for a walk down Germantown Avenue, richly describing the sights and sounds we encounter along the way. As you read this passage, pay careful attention to the various perceptual cues that signal that the neighborhood is changing as one moves

* Reprinted with permission from Anderson, E. (1998). The social ecology of youth violence. In M. Tonry & M. Moore (eds.) *Youth Violence* (pp. 68-79). Chicago: University of Chicago Press. Copyright University of Chicago Press.

down the avenue. Can you visualize the various zones? How would life be different for a child growing up in the various neighborhoods along the Avenue? Why have the neighborhoods changed? What, if anything, can be done to improve the quality of life for the residents living in the impoverished areas? These are the types of issues we will be exploring in this text. So, sit back, relax, and enjoy your stroll down Germantown Avenue with our host Elijah Anderson.

Down Germantown Avenue

Germantown Avenue is a major Philadelphia artery that goes back to colonial days. Eight and a half miles long, it links the northwest suburbs with the heart of inner-city Philadelphia. It traverses a varied social terrain as well. Germantown Avenue provides an excellent cross-section of the social ecology of a major American city. Along this artery live the well-to-do, the middle classes, the working poor, and the very poor. The story of Germantown Avenue with its wide social and class variations can serve in many respects as a metaphor for the whole city. This essay about the "code of the street" begins with an introduction to the world of the streets, by way of a tour down Germantown Avenue.

One of the most salient features of urban life, in the minds of many people today, is the relative prevalence of violence. Our tour down Germantown Avenue will focus on the role of violence in the social organization of the communities through which the avenue passes, and on how violence is revealed in the interactions of people up and down the street. The avenue, we will see, is a natural continuum characterized by a code of civility at one end and a code of conduct regulated by the threat of violence — the code of the street — at the other. But the people living along this continuum make their own claims on civility and the streets as well.

We begin at the top of the hill that gives Chestnut Hill its name. Chestnut Hill is the first neighborhood within the city of Philadelphia as you come into town from the northwest. Often called the "suburb in the city," it is a predominantly residential community of mostly white, affluent, educated people, which is becoming increasingly racially and ethnically mixed. The houses are mostly large single buildings, surrounded by lawns and trees. The business and shopping district along Germantown Avenue draws shoppers from all over the city. At the very top of the hill is a large Borders Bookstore. Across the street is the regional rail train station, with the local library in close proximity. Moving southeast down the avenue, you pass a variety of mostly small, up-scale businesses: gourmet food shops, a camera shop, an optician's, a sporting goods store, a bank, jewelry stores, clothing boutiques. Many of the buildings are old or built to look old and are made of fieldstone with slanted slate roofs, giving the area a quaint appearance. You see many different kinds of people — old and young, black and white, afflu-ent, middle- and working-class, women (some of them black) pushing babies who are white. Couples stroll hand in hand. Everyone is polite and seems relaxed. When people pass one another on the sidewalk, they may make eye contact. People stand about nonchalantly on the side-walk, sometimes with their backs to the street. You do not get the feel-ing that there is any hostility or that people are on guard against being compromised or insulted or robbed. There is a pleasant ambience — an air of civility.

One of the things you see at this end of Germantown Avenue is that relations in public appear racially integrated, perhaps self-consciously so. There are integrated play groups among small children on the play-grounds. At the bank, there is relaxed interaction between a black teller and a white client. There are biracial friendship groups. At the Boston Market restaurant blacks and whites sit and eat together or simply share the restaurant. A black man drives by in a Range Rover; two well-dressed black women pull up in a black Lexus. In their clothing and cars, the black middle class choose styles and colors that stand out and are noticed as expensive; they are quite expressive in laying claim to middle-class status.

In the upscale stores here, there is not usually a great concern for se-curity. During the day the plate-glass windows have appealing displays; some shops even have unguarded merchandise out on the sidewalk.

Once in a while, however, a violent incident does occur. There was a holdup at the bank in the middle of the day not long ago, ending in a shoot-out on the sidewalk. The perpetrators were black. Such incidents give the residents here the overly simplistic yet persistent view that blacks commit crime and white people do not. That does not mean that the white people here think that the black people they ordinarily see on the streets are bound to rob them: many of these people are too sophis-ticated to believe that all blacks are inclined to criminality. But the fact that black people robbed the bank does give a peculiar edge to race re-lations, and the racial reality of street crime speaks to the relations be-tween blacks and whites. Because everybody knows that the simplistic view does exist, even middle-class blacks, as well as whites, have to work against that stereotype. Both groups know that the reality is that crime is likely to be perpetrated by young black males. While both black and whites behave as though they deny it, this background knowledge threatens the civility of the neighborhood. The cleavages of wealth, and the fact that black people are generally disenfranchised and white people are not, operate in the back of the minds of people here.

Once can see this as a black male walking into the stores, especially the jewelry store. The sales personnel pay particular attention to people until they feel they have passed inspection, and black males almost always are given extra scrutiny. Most blacks in Chestnut Hill are middle-class or even wealthy, although some come into the neighborhood as day workers, and many are disturbed by the inability of some whites to make distinctions between middle- and lower-class blacks or between people who are out to commit crime and those who are not.

The knowledge that there are poor blacks further down the avenue also results in people "here" being on guard against people from "there." Security guards may follow young black males around stores, looking for the emblems and signs that they are from there and not from here. And at night the stores do have interior security devices, although they are outwardly decorative. These elements can, but most often do not, compromise civility between the races in Chestnut Hill; in fact, people generally "get along."

Down the hill, beyond the Boston Market, is Cresheim Valley Road, a neighborhood boundary. On the other side, we are in Mount Airy, a different social milieu. Here there are more black homeowners, interspersed among white ones, and there is more black street traffic on Germantown Avenue. Mount Airy is a much more integrated neighborhood than Chestnut Hill, and the black people who live here are mostly middle class. But Germantown Avenue in Mount Airy and the shops and stores along it are disproportionately used by blacks rather than whites and by poorer blacks rather than middle-class blacks. Whites and middle-class black adults tend to use the stores in Chestnut Hill, finding them more consistent with their tastes. As a result, the shops here are blacker, even though they may be middle class.

A sign that we are in a different social milieu is that exterior bars begin to appear on the store windows and riot gates on the doors, at first on businesses such as the liquor store. Pizza parlors, karate shops, take-out stores that sell beer, and storefront organizations such as neighborhood health care centers appear—establishments that are not present in Chestnut Hill. There are discount stores of various sorts, black barbershops, and other businesses that cater to the black middle class but also to employed working-class and poorer blacks. Many of the black middle-class youths use the streets as a place to gather and talk with their friends, and they adopt the clothing styles of the poorer people further down the avenue. So people who are not familiar with social types sometimes cannot distinguish between who is middle class and who is not. This confusion appears to be a standing problem for store owners and managers, and may lead to a sense of defensiveness among middle-class people who do not want to be violated or robbed. But it is a confusion that the youth tend not to mind.

Continuing down the avenue, we pass the Mount Airy playground with its basketball court, which is always buzzing. Evenings and weekends it is full of young black men playing pick-up games. There is a real social mix here, with kids from middle-class, working-class, and poor black families all coming together in this spot, creating a staging area. The urban uniform of sneakers and baggy jeans is much in evidence, which gives pause to other people, particularly whites (many of whom avoid the area). In many ways, however, the atmosphere is easygoing. The place is not crime-ridden or necessarily feared by most blacks, but there is a certain edge to it compared with similar but less racially complex settings further up the avenue. Here it is prudent to be wary—not everyone on the street here recognizes and respects the rule of law, the law that is encoded in the criminal statutes and enforced by the police.

Yet next to the playground is a branch of the Free Library, one of the best in the city, which caters mainly to literate people of Mount Airy, both black and white. Indeed, the social and racial mix of the community is sometimes more visible in the library than on the street itself.

There are many beautiful old buildings in Mount Airy. But the piano repair shops, sandwich stores, and plumbing-supply companies tend to have exterior bars and riot gates, which militates against the notion of civility as the dominant theme of the place. A competing notion crystallizes, and that is the prevalence of crime, the perpetrators of which are more often concerned not with legality but with feasibility. Ten years ago there were fewer bars on the windows and the buildings were better maintained. Today more relatively poor people are occupying the public space. There are still whites among the storekeepers and managers of various establishments, but whites have been displaced in the outdoor public spaces by poorer blacks. Moreover, the further down the avenue we go, the less well maintained the buildings are. Even when they are painted, for example, the painting tends to be done haphazardly, without great regard for architectural detail.

In this section, a billboard warns that those who commit insurance fraud go to jail. (No such signs appear in Chestnut Hill). There is graffiti — or signs that it has recently been removed. More dilapidated buildings appear, looking as though they receive no maintenance. Yet among them are historic buildings, some of which are cared for for just that reason. One of them is the house where the Battle of Germantown was fought during the Revolutionary War. Another was a stop on the underground railroad.

As Mount Airy gives way to Germantown, check-cashing agencies and beeper stores appear, as well as more small take-out stores selling beer, cheese steaks, and other snack food. More of the windows are boarded up, and riot gates and exterior bars become the norm, evoking in the user of the street a certain wariness.

Germantown appears to be a more solidly black working-class neighborhood. Whites, including middle-class whites, do live here, but they either tend to avoid the business district or the stores simply do not attract them. On Germantown Avenue, discount stores of all sorts appear — supermarkets, furniture stores, and clothing stores. Of the people you pass, many more are part of the street element. Here people watch their backs, and more care is given to one's presentation of self. It is not that you are worried every moment that somebody might violate you, but people are more aware of others who are sharing the space with them, some of whom may be looking for an easy target to rob or just intimidate.

Germantown High School, once a model of racially integrated high-quality education, is almost all black, a shadow of its former academic self. Resources have declined and many of the students are now impoverished and associated with the street element, and most of those who are not still have a need to show themselves as being capable of dealing with the street. In fact, the hallways of the school are in some ways an extension of the streets. Across the street from the high school is a store selling beer. Continuing down the avenue, we pass blocks of small businesses: taverns, Chinese take-out places, barbershops and hair salons, laundromats, storefront churches, pawnshops. Groups of young people loiter on street corners. We also begin to see boarded-up buildings, some of them obviously quite grand at one time, and empty lots. A charred McDonald's sign rises above a weed-covered lot. A police car is parked at the corner, its occupants keeping a watchful eye on the street activity. After a time, they begin to drive slowly down the street.

Just before Chelten Avenue, a major artery that intersects Germantown Avenue, is Vernon Park. The park has a caretaker who is trying to keep it maintained despite the carelessness and even vandalism of the people who like to gather there. A mural has been painted on the side of an adjacent building. Flowers have been planted. On warm days, couples "making time" sit about on the benches, on the steps of statues, and on the hoods of cars parked along the park's edge. But even during the day you can see men drinking alcohol out of paper sacks, and at night the park is a dangerous place where drug dealing and other shadowy business is conducted. This is what I call a major "staging area," because the activity that occurs here sets the stage for other activity, which may either be played out on the spot, in front of an audience of people who have congregated here, or in less conspicuous locations. An altercation in Vernon Park may be settled with a fight, with or without gunplay, down a side street. People come here to see and be seen, to "profile" and "represent," presenting the image of themselves by which they would like to be known — who they are and how they stand in relation to whom. The streets are buzzing with activity, both legal and illegal. In fact, a certain flagrant disregard for the law is visible. We see a teenage boy walk by with an open bottle of beer in his hand, taking a swig when he wants to.

A young man in his twenties crosses the street after taking care of some sort of business with another young man, gets into his brand-new black BMW Sidekick, and slides up next to his girlfriend who has been waiting there for him. He is dressed in a crisp white T-shirt with Hilfiger emblazoned across the back, black satin shorts with bright red stripes on the sides, and expensive white sneakers. He makes a striking figure as he slides into his vehicle, and others take note. He moves with aplomb, well aware that he is where he wants to be and, for that moment at least, where some others want to be as well. His presentation of self announces that he can take care of himself should someone choose to tangle with him.

Here in Germantown, especially in some pockets, there is less respect for the code of civility, and that fact necessitates a whole way of moving, of acting, of getting up and down the streets, which suggests that violence is just below the surface. The people of Germantown are overwhelmingly decent and committed to civility, yet there is something about the avenue, especially at night, that attracts the street element. When that element is present in numbers, there is a sense that you are on your own, that what protects you from being violated is your own body, your own ability to behave the right way, to look as though you can handle yourself, and even to be able to defend yourself. While it is not always necessary to throw down the gauntlet, so to speak, and be ready to punch someone out, it is important, as people here say, to "know what time it is." It is this form of regulation of social interaction in public that I call the "code of the street" in contrast to the "code of civility," based on trust and the rule of law, that strongly prevails up the avenue. You are not always tested, but you have to be ready for the test if you are. Mr. Don Moses, an old head of the black community, described the code this way: "Keep your eyes and ears open at all times. Walk two steps forward and look back. Watch your back. Prepare yourself verbally and physically. Even if you have a cane, carry something. The older people do carry something, guns in sheaths. The can't physically fight no more so they carry a gun." People here feel they must watch their backs, because everything happens here. And if the police are called, they may not arrive in time. People get killed here, they get stabbed, but they also relax and have a good time. In general, there is an edge to public life that you do not find in Chestnut Hill.

Chelten Avenue is lined with discount stores and fast-food restaurants. Yet just around the corner and two blocks down is a middle-class residential area. Most people here are black, but there are representatives of the wider society here, as well, including the police, the welfare office, the fast-food and clothing store chains. On Tuesday mornings, food-stamp lines snake around Greene Street at Chelten. There are also little people running small, sometimes fly-by-night businesses. Hustlers and small-time money men canvas the food stamp line with wads of cash — ready to buy discounted food stamps. It is this lack of resources that encourages a dog-eat-dog mentality that is concentrated at Chelten Avenue. Yet there is a great deal of other activity too. Especially during the summer, there is sometimes a carnival atmosphere. And the fact that the general area is diverse both racially and socially works to offset the feeling of social isolation that the poor black residents of Germantown have.

Occasionally, residents of Chestnut Hill drive this far down Germantown Avenue, and seeing what this neighborhood looks like has an impact on their consciousness. But they do not see below the surface. Mainly, they take in the noise and the seeming disorder, the poverty, and the incivility and when raving about urban violence they associate it with places like this, when in fact this neighborhood may not be as violent as they assume. To be sure, welfare mothers, prostitutes, and drug dealers are in evidence, but they coexist with—and are in fact outnumbered by—working people in legitimate jobs who are trying to avoid trouble.

As you move on past Chelten Avenue, you pass through quieter stretches colored by the residential nature of the surrounding streets, alternating with concentrated business strips. Many of the businesses are skin, hair, and nail salons. A common aspiration of the poorer girls in these neighborhoods is to go to beauty school and become cosmetologists.

We pass by the old town square of Germantown, which is surrounded by old, "historically certified" houses. Such houses appear sporadically for a long way down the avenue. Unfortunately, some are badly in need of maintenance. Just beyond the square is Germantown Friends School, a private school founded 150 years ago on what was then the outskirts of town but is now surrounded by the city.

Further down Germantown Avenue, thrift shops and discount stores predominate. Most are equipped with window bars and riot gates. Both the bars and the residents' understanding proclaim that this is a tough place. Some people can be counted on to behave according to the laws of force, not those of civility. Many people have to be forced to behave in a law-abiding way. The code has violence, or the possibility of violence, to back it up, and the bars on the windows signify the same thing—a lack of trust, a feeling that without the bars the establishment would be vulnerable. The code of the street has emerged.

The further we go down the avenue, the more boarded-up buildings there are, and more and more empty lots. In fact, certain areas give the impression of no-man's-lands, with empty overgrown or dirt lots, a few isolated buildings here and there, few cars on the street, and almost no people on the sidewalks. We pass billboards advertising "forties" (forty-ounce malt liquor) and other kinds of liquor. Churches are a prominent feature of the cityscape as a whole. Along this part of Germantown Avenue some of them are very large and well known, with a rich history, and are architecturally like those in Chestnut Hill and Mount Airy, but others are storefront churches that sometimes come and go with the founding pastor.

People move up and down the street. Even in the middle of the morning, groups of young men can be seen standing on corners, eyeing the street traffic. Yet the morning is the safest time of day. As evening approaches, the possibility of violence increases, and after nightfall the rule of the code of the street is being enforced all along the lower section of the avenue. Under that rule, the toughest, the biggest, the boldest prevail. We pass a school at recess. Kids are crowding into a makeshift store where someone is barbecuing hot dogs and ribs. Even at play, they hone their physical skills, punching each other lightly but seriously, sizing each other up. This sort of play-fighting, playing with the code, is commonplace.

Continuing, we pass collision shops — former gas stations surrounded by many cars in various states of disrepair — music stores, and nightclubs. We arrive at Broad Street, Philadelphia's major north-south artery, where Germantown Avenue also intersects Erie Avenue, forming a large triangle that is one of the centers of the ghetto of North Philadelphia. It is a staging area that is racially diverse, drawing all kinds of people from adjacent areas that are extremely poor. In Germantown there are a fair number of working people. In North Philly there is extensive concentrated poverty. North Philly is in the depths of the inner city — the so-called hyperghetto — and people here are more isolated from others who are unlike themselves in terms of both class and race (Massey and Denton 1993).

Just beyond Broad Street is a business strip with the same sort of establishments we saw further up the avenue — clothing stores, sneaker stores, furniture stores, electronics stores. Many offer layaway plans. In addition, there are businesses that cater mostly to the criminal class, such as pawnshops and beeper stores. Pawnshops are in a sense banks for thieves; they are places where stolen goods can be traded for cash, few questions asked. Check-cashing exchanges, which continue to be a common sight, also ask few questions, but they charge exorbitant fees for cashing a check. As in Chestnut Hill, merchandise is displayed on the sidewalk, but here it is under the watchful eye of unsmiling security guards. The noise level here is also much louder. Cars drive by with their stereo systems blaring. A young man wearing headphones saunters down the street. On the adjacent streets, open-air drug deals occur, prostitutes ply their trade, and boys shoot craps, while small children play in trash-strewn abandoned lots. This is the face of persistent urban poverty.

This is another staging area. People profile and represent here, standing around, "looking things over," concerned with who is where, but also aware of others "checking them out." Here, phrases like "watch your back," or as friends reassure their friends, "I got your back," takes on meaning, for some people are looking for opportunities to violate others, or simply to get away with something. A man opens his car door despite approaching traffic, seeming to dare someone to hit him. Further down the block a woman simply stops her car in the middle of the street, waiting for her husband or boyfriend to emerge from a barbershop. She waits for about ten minutes, holding up traffic. No one complains, no one honks his horn; they simply go around her, for they know that to complain is to risk an altercation, or at least heated words. They prefer not to incur this woman's wrath, which could escalate to warfare. In Chestnut Hill, where civility and "limited" warfare are generally the orders of the day, people might call others on such behavior, but here the general level of violence can keep irritation in check. In this way, the code of the street provides social organization and actually lessens the probability of random violence. When the woman's man arrives, he simply steps around to the passenger side and, without showing any concern for others, gets into the car. The pair drive off, apparently believing it to be their right to do what they just did.

At Tioga Street and Temple University Hospital, whose emergency room sees gunshot and stabbing victims just about every night, the code of the street is much in evidence. In the morning and early afternoon, the surrounding neighborhood is peaceful enough, but in the evening the danger level rises. Tensions spill over, drug deals go bad, fights materialize seemingly out of nowhere, and the emergency room becomes a hub of activity. Sometimes the victim bypasses the hospital: by the time he is found, there is no place to take him but the morgue. Nearby there is a liquor store and a place selling cold beer. People buy liquor there and drink it on the street, adding to the volatility of the street scene.

More and more gaps in the rows of houses appear, where buildings have burned down, been torn down, or simply collapsed. Others are shells, their windows and large parts of their walls gone, leaving beams exposed. Still others are boarded up, perhaps eventually to collapse, perhaps to be rebuilt. Indeed there are signs of regeneration among those of destruction. Here and there a house is well-maintained, even freshly painted. Some of the exposed outer walls of standing structures have colorful, upbeat murals painted on them, often with religious themes. We pass a large building a car repair shop, gaily decorated with graffiti art. Further down we pass a hotel that rents rooms by the hour.

There continue to be signs of the avenue's past life — large churches built by European immigrants at the turn of the century, an old cemetery, an occasional historic building. The many open areas — empty lots, little overgrown parks — underline the winding character of this old highway as it cuts through the grid pattern of streets formally laid out well after this became an established thoroughfare.

We drive through another business district with the usual stores catering to the very poor. Two policemen pass by on foot patrol. This is another staging area. The concentration of people drawn by the businesses increases the chance of violence breaking out. A lot of people are out, not just women and children but a conspicuous number of young men as well, even though it is still morning. Practically all of them are black, with just an occasional Asian and even rarer white face among them.

We enter an area where there seem to be more empty lots and houses you can see right through than solidly standing buildings. Some of the lots are a heap of rubble. Others are overgrown with weeds or littered with abandoned cars. This is a spot where the idea of a war zone comes to mind. Indeed, gunshot marks are visible on some of the buildings. The black ghetto here gives way to the Hispanic ghetto. The faces are different but the behavior is similar. Yet in the midst of this desolation there is a newly built gated community in the Spanish style. Just beyond it, we reach Norris Street; at this intersection three of the four corners are large empty lots. But we also pass an open area that has been transformed into a community garden. Now, in late spring, vegetables in the early stages of growth are visible.

We are now just north of Philadelphia's center city area. This used to be a bustling commercial area, with factories producing everything from beer to lace and huge warehouses in which the goods were stored before being shipped out either by rail, traces of which are still visible, or through a nearby port on the Delaware River. Here and there some of the behemoths are still standing, although one by one they are falling victim to arson.

And so we reach the other end of Germantown Avenue, in the midst of a leveled area about a block from the river and overshadowed by the elevated interstate highway that now allows motorists to drive over North Philadelphia rather than through it, thereby ignoring its street life, its inhabitants, and its problems.

Works Cited

Massey, Douglas S., and Nancy A. Denton. 1993. *American Apartheid: Segregation and the making of the underclass.* Cambridge, Mass.: Harvard University Press.

Chapter 3

Choosing Crime

Theories based on the Positivists' perspective, described in Chapter 2, are not the only methods to explain a person's involvement in crime and deviance. In this chapter theories that are based on the idea of crime as a matter of choice are explored. According to proponents of choice-based theories, people are involved in crime because they have carefully weighed the pros and cons of criminal activity and have made a rational decision to get involved in crime. This chapter begins with a discussion of the historical roots of this alternative perspective, a school of thought commonly known as **Classical criminology**.

The Evolution of the Classical School of Criminology

The ideas, assumptions, and policy recommendations of Classical criminologists were a sharp break with the popular thinking of the times. For over a thousand years in Europe, spiritual explanations of crime were the driving force behind the criminal justice system. These spiritual explanations, sometimes called **demonology**, were based on the assumption that crime and deviance were the result of possession by demons or temptation at the hands of the Devil (Einstadter & Henry, 1995). Demonologists assumed that human beings were essentially good people. This natural tendency to do good was constantly under attack by demons and the forces of evil. It was only through strong faith in God that one could resist the temptation of Satan.

Because of the strong influence of the church, these theologically based theories of crime did not include a distinction between "crime" and "sin." The writings of St. Thomas Aquinas (1225–1274) were very influential in this era. Aquinas argued that crime violated the natural law, which was derived from the law of God himself. If a person committed a crime, then he or she also committed a sin. Violations of the law were taken very seriously, since the criminal had broken not just the law of humans, but also the law of God. As a result, punishments for criminal acts were horrific (Vold, Bernard, & Snipes, 2002). The state had a divine right to exercise moral authority and inflict painful punishments on the accused. Consider, for example, the fate of Damiens, who was convicted of stabbing King Louis XV of France:

> On 2 March 1757 Damiens the regicide was condemned 'to make the *amende honorable* before the main door of the Church of Paris', where he was to be 'taken and conveyed in a car, wearing nothing but a shirt, holding a torch of burning wax weighing two pounds'; then, 'in the said cart, to the Place de Greve, where on a scaffold that will be erected there, the flesh will be torn from his breasts, arms, thighs and calves with red-hot pincers, his right hand, holding the knife with which he committed the said parricide, burnt with sulphur, and, on those places where the flesh will be torn away, poured molten lead, boiling oil, burning resin, wax and sulphur melted together and then his body drawn and quartered by four horses and his limbs and body consumed by fire, reduced to ashes and his ashes thrown to the winds' (Foucault 1979:3).

In addition the use of brutal public punishments, the criminal justice system also regularly made use of trials by ordeal and torture to elicit confessions for alleged crimes (Hibbert, 1966). For example, if you were accused of being a witch, you might be tied up and thrown into a lake. If the water would not accept you and you floated, this would indicate that you were indeed a witch and you would then face punishment (torture, burning at the stake, etc.) for this crime. If the water accepted you, then this was seen as an indication that you were pure and therefore innocent of the charges. Of course, you would also be dead.

Many times, these "trials" resulted in convictions of the weak. Physically strong individuals who were able to endure the rack and other forms of torture had a better chance of being found innocent of the charges, regardless of whether or not they had actually committed the crime for which they were accused. As stated by Beccaria (1764/1963:32–33):

> Of two men, equally innocent or equally guilty, the strong and courageous will be acquitted, and weak and timid condemned, by virtue of this rigorous rational argument: "I, the judge, was supposed to find you guilty of such and such a crime; you, the strong,

have been able to resist the pain, and I therefore absolve you; you the weak, have yielded, and I therefore condemn you. I am aware that a confession wrenched forth by torments ought to be of no weight whatsoever, but I'll torment you again if you don't confirm what you have confessed."

In this system of justice, judges had unlimited discretion to make laws, decide guilt or innocence, and impose whatever punishment was felt to be appropriate. Oftentimes, the harshness of the punishment was determined not by the severity of the crime, but by the status, power, and influence of the convicted person (Monachesi, 1955). The end result was that the laws, convictions, and punishments were completely arbitrary.

There was a wave of growing dissatisfaction with the criminal justice system of the time, and many philosophers and critical thinkers began to search for a system that would be more effective. These social theorists were part of a larger movement called the Enlightenment, which sharply disagreed with the authority and dominance of the church in all aspects of life. It was out of this revolutionary philosophy that Cesare Bonesana, Marquis of Beccaria wrote a highly influential essay, *On Crimes and Punishments* (1764). Beccaria's reforms greatly impacted the development of the criminal justice system in the United States and other western societies (Curran & Renzetti, 2001). Even in contemporary times, his ideas continue to have a significant influence on the way we view crimes and punishments.

Cesare Beccaria
On Crimes and Punishments *(1764)*

The name Cesare Beccaria is often synonymous with the school of Classical criminology. Beccaria built on the ideas of several philosophers, including Hobbes (1588–1678), Locke (1632–1704), and Rousseau (1712–1778). The general philosophy of these thinkers was that crime was not a result of satanic influence or demonic possession, but rather an issue of rationality.

You might recall that the theologically based theorists assumed human beings were essentially "good" people who were under an attack of sorts by the forces of evil. Beccaria and other Classical theorists assumed the opposite. At their very core, people were seen as hedonistic, self-serving, and interested only in the pursuit of their own selfish pleasures without any regard for the feelings of other people. If left to their own devices, humans always revert back to this selfish tendency.

While Beccaria and other Classical theorists assumed that humans were hedonistic by nature, they also argued that humans were rational beings. If everyone did what he or she wanted to do whenever they wanted to do it, the result would be total chaos. Society could not function under such circumstances. To avoid what Hobbes called a "war of each against all," Classical theorists proposed that we enter into a **social contract** with each other. All members of a society come together and form an understanding that certain types of behavior are acceptable, while other actions are not. Since this social contract limits personal freedoms, people do not really want to enter into this contract. However, they recognize the need for it.

Punishments are necessary to enforce the social contract. If there were no penalties associated with violations of the social contract, all would revert back to their selfish nature. Beccaria assumed that human beings exercise free will in deciding on a course of action. Before engaging in a criminal act, humans carefully weigh the consequences and rewards associated with their behavior. Because humans are rational beings, punishments need only be harsh enough to convince a person that more harm than good would come from violating the law.

The Keys to Deterrence: Certain, Swift, and Proportionate Punishments

Reacting against the popular use of horrific punishments as well as the arbitrary nature of their application, Beccaria made a number of assertions regarding the effective use of punishment to deter crime. In order for punishments to reduce crime, Beccaria argued that punishments should be **certain, swift, and proportionate** to the severity of the crime.

Certainty refers to the inescapable application of the punishment. In the case of a bank robber, Beccaria would assume that prior to the commission of the robbery, the robber would carefully weigh out the pros and cons of such an action. How much money would be gained? How much prison time would be mandated for this crime? Beccaria would argue that it is not so much the number of years of prison time but the fact that the prison term could not be avoided that would influence the decision. In the criminal's rational deliberations, it would not be a question of "What will I get *if* I get caught" but "What will I get *when* I get caught."

The punishment must also fit the severity of the crime. The punishment should be punitive enough to make a person think twice about committing a crime. Punishments that are too severe for a specific offense may actually lead to the commission of more serious criminal acts. For example, for a moment assume that the punishment associated with conviction for armed robbery is the death penalty. If an individual has made up her mind up that she is going to rob the local 7-11, she might ask, "Why not shoot everyone in the store while I am at it? There would be no witnesses who could identify me, and since the punishment is the same for both, why not?" In this example, the application of the death penalty for the armed robbery would be too severe a punishment, since the would-be robber would not be deterred from committing the more serious offense of mass murder.

The application of the punishment must be closely linked in time to the commission of the crime. Being rational human beings, we would not associate the pain of conviction and punishment with the commission of the crime if there were a long period of time between the criminal act and the consequences. This is especially true given that in many cases the rewards of criminal activity are immediate. If a man robs the convenience store, he would not have to wait to get the money—when he walked out of the store, he would have his reward. If he were to be identified as a suspect, the process of investigation, arrest, trial, and sentencing (if he was actually convicted) could take months, and even years.

In addition to his revolutionary ideas concerning the application of punishments, Beccaria also called for judicial reform. Beccaria wanted to limit the role of judges in the criminal justice system. In his opinion, it should be the job of the legislatures, not the judges, to define what actions constituted a crime and then to define the appropriate punishments for such an action (Beccaria, 1764/1963). Judges should only be concerned with determining whether or not a person was guilty of an offense. Once guilt had been determined, the judge would have no alternative but to assign the pre-determined sanction for the act. Since all people were equal under the law regardless of their power and influence, there would be no mitigating circumstances or other excuses for criminal behavior. Everyone was responsible for his or her behavior, and there were no allowances for individual differences between those convicted of crimes.

From Classical to Neoclassical and Beyond

While Beccaria's ideas were extremely influential in modifying the criminal justice system, in practice there was some difficulty in implementing his model, especially with respect to the equal application of punishments regardless of the characteristics of the offender (Taylor, Walton, & Young, 1973). If one adopted a pure classical philosophy, all individuals convicted of a similar offense, such as murder, would be given the same punishment. It would not matter if the convicted person was a juvenile, mentally ill, or if the offense was considered a crime of passion. Under a pure classical interpretation, all individuals have roughly the same capacity to make a rational choice regarding whether or not to engage in a criminal activity.

The recognition that certain individuals were incapable of making rational decisions and exercising full freedom of choice led to the development of **Neoclassical criminology**. In this school of thought, free choice and individual accountability are still important elements. However, neoclassicists began to take adopt a "softer" approach when presented with certain types of offenders. Children, the elderly, mentally ill, or those suffering from conditions like Down's Syndrome or other challenging conditions just did not seem to fit in well with the basic assumptions upon which Classical criminology was built. Neoclassical criminologists began to recognize that there were individual differences between criminals, and that these differences may have an impact on the type of reaction that would be appropriate. As phrased by Taylor et al. (1973:9, emphasis in original):

> The criminal had to be punished in an environment conducive to his making the correct moral decisions. Choice was (and still is) seen to be a characteristic of the individual actor—but there is now a recognition that certain structures are more conducive to free choice than others.

In effect, Neoclassicists began to recognize that the ability of many offenders to exercise free will was constrained by factors that were beyond their immediate control. Because of their inability to make a rational choice, convicted offenders who fell into one of these classifications should receive special treatment at the hands of the criminal justice system. Instead of a "one-size-fits-all" punishment, sentences for criminal behavior should be tailored to meet the needs of the individual offender.

Some may not see a great deal of difference between the Neoclassical school and Positivism, discussed in Chapter 2. Imagining a continuum with Classical criminology on one extreme end and Positivism on the other may help. Classical criminology assumes that crime is a matter of free choice. After carefully weighing the punishments and rewards, people freely choose crime as a rational means to a desired end. There are no excuses or justifications for criminal behavior. Poverty, peer influence, biology, psychiatric disorders, or neighborhood characteristics should not be considered. Crime is a matter of individual choice.

At the other end of the spectrum is Positivism. In its most extreme form, a hard core Positivist would argue that there is no free choice at all. Our behavior is determined by factors beyond our immediate control. Even those adopting a softer approach would hold that our behavior is strongly influenced by various societal structures and individual differences.

Between these two extremes lies the Neoclassical school. Proponents of this tradition began to open up the door to the notion that perhaps for some people, their ability to make a rational decision is somehow affected by their individual life circumstances. Choice is still recognized as a powerful element of the Neoclassical school, as most criminals have the ability to exercise their free will in choosing crime.

So What Works?
The Never Ending Debate

Understanding the underlying assumptions of various schools of thought is important, since the perspective that an individual subscribes to with respect to the root cause of crime has an impact on what he or she feels is the best response to criminal activity. If one adopts the Classical criminology perspective, then the policy recommendations for curbing crime would include the use of certain, swift, and proportionate punishments. Criminals freely choose crime knowing full well that the act is wrong. In order to keep a person on the straight and narrow path, the perceived pain associated with commission of a criminal act must outweigh the perceived benefits.

A Positivist, on the other hand, would argue that the use of punishment as a deterrent to criminal behavior would have little if any impact on the behavior of the offender. Crime is not a matter of choice. A person engages in criminal activity for a variety of reasons — inadequate socialization, poor role models, neighborhood influences, psychological imbalances, etc. Law violators need treatment for their condition, not punishment. Proponents of a Positivistic orientation would advocate the use of various reformation and rehabilitation programs, including education, vocational training, and behavior modification therapy.

Consider, for a moment, the case of Darryl Strawberry, a former star baseball player for the New York Yankees. Strawberry has had a highly publicized struggle with drug use over the past decade. He has been in and out of various treatment centers for drug and alcohol addiction. In April 1999, Strawberry was arrested in Tampa, Florida for soliciting a prostitute and possession of cocaine. He was given a sentence of probation, but was caught violating the restrictions on five separate occasions. In the fifth violation, Strawberry disappeared for four days on a cocaine binge. He was again arrested and faced a possible prison sentence for his actions (Karp, 2001). There was a great deal of national interest in the case as Americans debated the issue of what should be an appropriate response for his behavior: punishment or treatment?

Ultimately, the judge in the case ruled that Strawberry needed treatment in a residential drug rehabilitation program more than the 18-month prison term he was facing. Strawberry was ordered to attend a drug rehab program and complete 100 hours of community service. While some agreed with the judge's decision, others were outraged by what appeared to be a lenient sentence given to a repeat offender who had demonstrated his complete lack of respect for the law and the criminal justice system. Those who agreed with the judge's decision felt that Strawberry's criminal acts were the result of an illness. Punishment would not cure his disease; treatment was the best option to modify his behavior. Those who disagreed with the judge viewed Strawberry's behavior as a matter of choice. How is Strawberry ever going to learn if he simply receives another slap on the wrist for his actions? A lengthy prison term would be the only appropriate reaction to his criminal behavior.

The debate between Positivists and Classical criminologists regarding the appropriate response to criminal behavior has been going on throughout the history of crimes and punishments. The pendulum swings back and forth between punishment and treatment as the appropriate response to criminal behavior. The most recent philosophical shift began in the late 1940s. Prior to World War II, America's correctional system was punitive in nature. Large maximum security institutions were popular and administrators were too fearful of escapes to incorporate rehabilitation treatments into their institutions (Barnes & Teeters, 1959). After World War II, a Positivistic philosophy took hold, as rehabilitation and reintegration were the driving principles. Individual and group therapy sessions were commonplace in prisons as psychologists and other professionals attempted to identify and correct problems within the individual offender.

Beginning in the 1970s, a growing wave of dissatisfaction with the rehabilitation and treatment ideal began to take hold. The country was in the midst of a dramatic increase in the crime rate, and rehabilitation programs began to be viewed as part of the problem. Public skepticism was validated in a report released by Robert Martinson in 1974. Martinson reviewed 231 research studies that had been conducted to evaluate the effectiveness of rehabilitation programs. Martinson limited his review to studies that had a sound evaluation research design with treatment and control groups and valid outcome measures that could be directly linked to the rehabilitation program. What Martinson found was devastating: No one program had any appreciable effect on the recidivism rate. This report, coupled with a number of studies that reported high recidivism rates for repeat offenders, effectively ended the treatment and rehabilitation era. The pendulum began to shift from a more liberal Positivistic philosophy back to a more conservative stance based on Classical criminology.

Contemporary Applications of Classical Criminology

The resurgence in popularity of the Classical criminology perspective in the 1970's spawned the growth of a number of related theories and crime prevention strategies. These contemporary applications of Classical criminology have been developed across a number of disciplines, including economics, sociology, psychology, victimology, and geography. While a number of theories may be included under this umbrella, rational choice theory, routine activities theory, and crime pattern theory are discussed.

Rational Choice

The names most closely associated with the development of rational choice theory are Derek Cornish and Ronald Clarke (see, generally, Clarke & Cornish, 1985; Cornish & Clarke, 1986; Clarke & Felson, 1993). In the 1960s and 1970s, Cornish and Clarke worked on a research project that involved an examination of the effects of institutional treatments on juvenile delinquents. Cornish and Clarke began to question whether or not the treatments had any long-term impact on the behavior of the juveniles. Furthermore, when they compared the rates of running away and other forms of misconduct that occurred at the various treatment centers, Cornish and Clarke found that even though the centers serviced the same types of delinquents, some of the treatment centers had more problems than others. Cornish and Clarke began to develop the idea that something about the specific environmental characteristics in some of the treatment centers provided greater opportunities for misconduct than in centers with fewer problematic incidents. In effect, some situations provided greater opportunities for deviant behavior than others (Cornish and Clarke, 1986).

Cornish and Clarke's model rests on the assumption of a rational offender making decisions about whether or not to commit a crime. Would-be criminals process available information from their physical and social environment. Prior to the commission of a crime, an individual assesses his or her personal needs and wants; evaluates the risk of apprehension, the severity of the expected punishments, and the expected gain; and reacts selectively to the specific situational factors, such as whether or not a target is well guarded. Criminals make rational decisions about when and where to commit their crimes, carefully selecting targets that offer the highest probability for pleasure with the lowest probability for pain (Clarke & Cornish, 1985; Cornish & Clarke, 1986; Lab, 2000).

Cornish and Clarke's Decision Models

Rational choice theorists differentiate between several different types of criminal decisions, not all of which are directly related to the crime itself. Cornish and Clarke (1985; 1986) have developed a rather complex model to explain the decision-making process a potential offender goes through in deciding whether or not to commit a specific type of crime, in this case burglary in a middle-class residential suburb. The first phase of this model is described as the initial involvement model. According to Cornish and Clarke (1986:2), "Criminal involvement refers to the processes through which individuals choose to become initially involved in particular forms of crime, to continue, and to desist." These involvement decisions are affected by a number of factors, outlined below.

1. Background factors: This includes the individual characteristics of the would-be offender, including their gender, temperament, intelligence, and cognitive decision-making style as well as the characteristics of their family life, available role models, social class, and educational level.

2. Previous Experience and Learning: Potential offenders evaluate their direct and indirect experiences with crime and the police and assess their conscience and moral attitudes towards criminal activity.

3. Assessment of Generalized Needs: The needs of the individual may center on money and the attainment of material goods, or may be driven by sex, enhanced status within the peer group, or simply excitement.

4. Solutions Evaluated: This involves the weighing of perceived risks and punishment versus potential gains. Would-be offenders also consider the degree of effort required in the commission of the crime as well as the moral costs of their actions.

5. Perceived Solutions: Would-be offenders must consider their options. "Should I pursue a legitimate job in order to get what I want, or should I commit a crime? If crime is the answer, what type of criminal behavior should I engage in? Would burglary meet my needs (and suite my personal strengths), or is robbery a better personal choice?"

6. Chance Event: As the would-be offender goes through their daily life, he or she eventually will encounter an event that will force them to make a decision. This chance event may involve being presented with an easy opportunity to commit a crime, peer pressure, or an urgent need for money.

7. Readiness: This is described as the first decision point. At this stage, the individual makes a conscious decision, recognizing that he or she is ready to commit a specific type of crime.

8. Decision: This is the second decision point. When confronted with a chance event, the offender makes a decision to commit the crime.

Event Decisions

While involvement decisions may be made over an extended period of time, event decisions are made quickly using information based on the characteristics of the specific situation. Once the decision has been made to commit a residential burglary, the offender must select a specific target. A neighborhood must be selected that offers the lowest level of risk, and within this neighborhood the burglar must choose which home will be attacked. These choices will be based on the burglar's assessment of opportunity, required effort, and risk. For example, neighborhoods that have organized crime watches or large numbers of stay-at-home mothers may be avoided due to the heightened perception of risk of detection. Once a neighborhood has been selected, homes with obvious displays of wealth, overgrown shrubs, or high privacy fences may be more attractive targets than homes with large dogs or visible alarm systems.

Persistence and Desistence

Once an individual has made the choice to become involved in crime, the decision making process is not over. The offender constantly re-evaluates the decision of whether or not to continue his or her involvement not only in crime, but also in this particular form of crime. Cornish and Clarke argue that with continued success, a burglar will increase the frequency of offending until he or she attains a level that is personally judged to be the most favorable. Decisions to persist in this chosen area of crime will be enhanced by a number of factors, including increased professionalism, changes in life style and values, and changes in the peer group. Increased professionalism is marked by better skills in the planning and selection of targets, larger gains from criminal activities, better skills in talking with the police and dealing with the court system, and heightened levels of pride taken in one's work. Changes in life style and values include choosing legitimate occupations to enhance burglary opportunities, such as working for a delivery service in order to gain a better view of the insides of people's homes; placing greater value on illegitimate enterprises and less importance on legitimate avenues for success; and enjoying "life in the fast lane." Changes in the peer group that facilitate criminal involvement include losing contact with non-criminal friends and disagreeing with "straight" family members.

Finally, there are also decisions that must be made in order for a criminal to choose to stop committing crimes. In the case of a residential burglar, events may occur during the commission of a burglary that may cause the individual to reassess their level of readiness to commit further burglaries, such as getting apprehended by the police, being surprised by a homeowner, getting bitten by the family's dog, or reduced profit from the burglary. Other life events may also occur, such as getting married or having a child, having friends or co-offenders get arrested for their criminal involvement, being offered suitable legitimate employment, or running out of available targets in the neighborhood. These events present the burglar with decision-making opportunities to persist with the chosen criminal path, desist and choose legitimate employment, or perhaps even choose other forms of criminal activity that may be more attractive, such as commercial burglary, becoming a fence for stolen goods, or perhaps burglarizing a different type of residence.

As you can see, the process developed by Cornish and Clarke is highly complex. The would-be offender as well as the active offender constantly evaluate and re-assess their level of readiness, personal abilities, individual needs, and the target attractiveness based on the information available to them. This is a rational process in which offenders try to benefit themselves by choosing the best course of action, be it to get involved in crime, persist in criminal activities, or instead to engage in legitimate pathways to success.

Summary: Rational Choice Theory

Rational choice theory is based on the assumption of a rational offender carefully weighing out the risks, perceived punishments, and perceived gains in a decision making process. This decision-making process needs to be assessed with respect to both the individual offense (for instance, why a burglary has been committed of a middle class residence versus a low-income public housing unit) as well as the individual offender, as he or she assess his or her own motivations, skills, and prior learning experiences.

Proponents of this perspective do not focus on trying to identify individual differences between criminals and non-criminals the way Positivists do. Rational choice theorists argue that this practice of dividing the world into two groups—criminals versus non-criminals—lumps all criminals together in a homogenous group and makes the assumption that all criminal behaviors and all motives to commit crimes are essentially the same. Rational choice theorists argue that what is really needed is a closer examination of specific types of crimes, as well as the motives for that particular crime and the methods used. In order to reduce crime, the focus needs to be on the criminal event itself and the situational factors that contribute to the commission of the crime.

Routine Activities

Routine activities theory was initially proposed by Lawrence Cohen and Marcus Felson (1979). Proponents of routine activities theory hold many of the assumptions held by supporters of rational choice theory. In fact, many times the theories are presented as complimentary perspectives, offering both a macro and **micro**-level analysis. Routine activities theory is said to be oriented at the **macro**-level. Macro level theories focus on broad changes across societies or populations. Conversely, the decision models implicit within rational choice theory are at a more individual, micro level (Clarke & Felson, 1993). Taken together, these theories examine how work, recreation, spending patterns, and our every day involvement in "routine activities" can contribute to the likelihood of converging in time, space, and place with a rational motivated offender, thereby increasing the opportunity for a crime to occur.

When Cohen and Felson initially developed routine activities theory, a number of rather interesting changes had been occurring in American society. First, as previously noted, the crime rate had experienced a rather dramatic upsurge. Citing the most recently available FBI Uniform Crime Reports, Cohen and Felson pointed out that from 1960–1975 the robbery rate had increased 263 percent, the forcible rape rate had increased 174 percent, and the homicide rate had gone up 188 percent. Similar increases were also found with respect to property crimes, with the burglary rate experiencing an increase of 200 percent (FBI, 1975).

What was somewhat perplexing was that the crime wave had occurred in spite of the fact that other pathological social conditions that are often tied to crime rates, such as poverty and unemployment, had actually been on the decline. One would expect that when the general social conditions in metropolitan areas experience improvement then the crime rate in these areas would decrease. This was not the case — in fact, just the opposite had happened. The crime rate had experienced a dramatic increase despite substantial improvement in the educational levels, median incomes, and employment rates in our cities and surrounding metropolitan areas.

Cohen and Felson set out to explain these seemingly incompatible trends by focusing on structural changes in the way Americans lived their lives. In a nutshell, changes in the routine activities of everyday life increased the opportunity for crimes to occur. Cohen and Felson focused on illegal activities (termed **direct contact predatory violations**) in which a perpetrator intentionally takes or otherwise harms a target. In their definition, at least one criminal must come into direct physical contact with at least one target, which could include people or their property. Cohen and Felson argued that changes in life patterns had occurred after World War II that had contributed to the increase in direct contact predatory violations. People were spending less time at home with family members and more time outside of the home with non-family members — either at work, school, recreation or other activities.

According to Cohen and Felson, in order for a direct contact predatory violation to occur, three elements needed to converge in space and time: **motivated offenders, suitable targets, and the absence of capable guardians.** At the heart of the theory was the notion that the shift in routine activities that occurred after World War II increased the likelihood that a motivated offender would come together in time and space with a suitable target in the absence of a capable guardian.

The Crime Triangle

The three elements essential for the occurrence of a crime — motivated offenders, suitable targets, and the absence of capable guardians — are sometimes referred to as "the crime triangle." In Cohen and Felson's model, motivated offenders were a given — in their theory, it was not really relevant to explore whether an individual person or group was more or less criminally inclined than another. What was important was to examine the circumstances that provide the opportunity for criminally motivated people to translate their inclinations into action.

At the time, the availability of suitable targets had also increased since World War II. Cohen and Felson noted marked increases in consumer spending patterns from 1960–1970. Americans were accumulating more and more possessions, which translated into more property available for theft. Along with the change in quantity of potential targets, Cohen and Felson also noticed a change in the size and weight of many products. For example, in 1960 the lightest television listed in the Sears catalog weighed in at 38 pounds. By 1970, the lightest television available weighed only 15 pounds. Similar reductions in size and weight were also noted in radios, record players, toasters, and other small electrical products. Smaller, lighter items make better targets for illegal removal, since they are easier to conceal and carry off. Of course, this trend of smaller, more expensive, lightweight gadgets did not stop in 1970. Think of all of the items that have become commonplace in the past decade; — cell phones, lap top computers, walkmans, Palm Pilots, Gameboys, etc. — that make very suitable targets for a motivated offender.

When you hear the phrase "absence of capable guardians," you might think of the police (or lack thereof). The police are only one type of capable guardian, and some would argue that their level of effectiveness in crime prevention is questionable. In what has become a classic study on the effectiveness of random patrol activities on crime, data from the Kansas City Preventive Patrol Experiment indicated that substantial increases in the normal level of patrol had no significant effect on the level of criminal activity reported in the area (Kelling, et al. 1974). This study will be discussed in greater detail in Chapter 4.

This point should not be taken as an attack on the effectiveness of the police. The police are simply outnumbered and over-extended. For example, a popular measure of the level of police protection is the police-population ratio, which is defined as the number of sworn officers per 1,000 citizens. According to the Bureau of Justice Statistics, in 1999, the average national ratio was 1.5 sworn officers per 1,000 citizens. It should also be pointed out that not all of these sworn officers were assigned to full time patrol activities. Some of the sworn officers included in the ratio were administrators, while others may have been assigned to special units such as school resource officers, traffic duty, detectives, or desk duties. This would mean that the ratio of *patrol officers* per 1,000 citizens was actually much lower.

Further, as discussed by Felson (1998a), the actual time that a patrol officer can devote to guarding your home against crime is minimal. Few patrol officers are assigned to large geographic areas with many suitable targets that must be protected over a 24-hour period. Felson estimated that an individual home will lack the capable guardianship of the police 99.98 percent of the time. Even if a patrol officer happens to be driving by a home, the likelihood is very low that a particular patrol officer would be familiar enough with the residents and routine activities of the home to recognize that the person carrying a brand new color television out of the front door is not authorized to do so. Felson (1998a) estimates that less than 1 percent of criminal offenders are "caught in the act" by a patrol officer who happens to be driving through a neighborhood at the right place and the right time.

For Cohen and Felson, the more effective capable guardians were ordinary citizens, moving through the routine activities of their daily lives all the while keeping an eye out for the safety of others and their property. The availability of capable guardians also changed after World War II. For example, consider the crime of residential burglary. Since the 1960s, the proportion of residential burglaries that have occurred during the day has increased dramatically (Miethe & McCorkle, 2001). Why?

Consider an episode of Happy Days, a television series based on the life of the Cunningham family in the 1950s. Both parents resided in their home, and Mrs. Cunningham was a stay-at-home mom who took care of their two children. In Cohen and Felson's terminology, Mrs. Cunningham was a capable guardian. Her presence in the home was a strong deterrent to a would-be rational offender assessing the suitability of her home and the homes of her neighbors as potential targets. Compare life at the Cunningham's home to the type of life most experience today. More than likely, kids come home to an empty house after school. Even if living in a two-parent household (which is becoming more and more of a rare event), it is likely that a mother works outside of the home. Many of the neighborhood children return to empty homes as well. Structural changes in our society — such as the increase of women entering the workplace and the decrease in two parent homes — alter our routine activities and decrease the availability of capable guardians, thereby increasing the likelihood for crime to occur.

Cohen and Felson maintained that the lack of any one of the three elements — motivated offenders, suitable targets, or absence of capable guardians — was enough to prevent the successful completion of a direct contact predatory crime. Furthermore, Cohen and Felson made the argument that even if the number of motivated offenders or suitable targets were to remain the same in a community, changes in the routine activities of residents could lead to greater opportunities for criminal acts to occur.

Advances in Routine Activities Theory: The Addition of Social Control

In his later writings, Felson (1986; 1998a; 1998b; Felson & Clarke 1995) began to incorporate the ideas of social control theorist Travis

Hirschi with routine activities theory. According to Hirschi (1969), an individual's involvement in crime and delinquency was dependent upon his or her bond to society. If an individual had a strong bond with society, then he or she would be more likely to lead a life of conformity. If, however, the bond to society had been weakened, then an individual would choose crime as a reasonable alternative.

For Hirschi, the social bond is made up of four components: attachment, commitment, involvement, and belief. **Attachment** refers to a person's ties with others, specifically whether or not the person cares about the opinions of other people. In the misfortunate of living with a roommate from hell, does one care to wash the dishes, take phone messages, vacuum, or otherwise follow the rules of the house? Probably not. Without attachment, a person does not feel bound by the norms of society (or the apartment). A person with strong attachment to others has internalized the norms of society and developed a strong sense of conscience (Curran & Renzetti, 2001).

Hirschi described **commitment** as the rational element of his theory. For example, by simply reading this book a strong commitment to conformity is indicated. You are enrolled in college and are actually taking the time to read your assigned materials. You have made an investment in your future and have much to lose if you do not play by the rules. When the weekend comes up and your friends encourage you to go out for a wild night of drinking on the town, chances are you will weigh your commitment to conventional society. If you go out and get stupid-drunk and get arrested, what will happen? Will you lose everything you worked for? According to Hirschi, because of the investment of time and effort in the pursuit of conventional activities, the rules of society will be followed.

Involvement refers to the amount of time a person spends engaged in conventional activities. If a teenager plays on sports teams, has an after school job, takes trumpet lessons, attends church activities, and spends a great deal of time doing homework there simply are not enough hours in the day to get into trouble. Opportunities for criminal involvement are limited because of the person's involvement in conventional activities. Finally, **belief** has to do with whether or not a person believes that the rules of society are "good," necessary, and should be followed. If a person does not believe that the rules of society apply to him or her, then he or she will not feel any pressure to follow them.

In tying Hirschi's ideas with routine activities theory, Felson compares the elements of the social bond to handles on a suitcase. According to Felson (1998a:44):

Social bonds are like the handles on a suitcase: The more handles, the easier it is to carry. The more bonds you have to society, the easier it is for society to carry you along. This does not mean you have no free will; it only means you will *choose* to go along with the rules because the price you pay for not doing so is too high. This is why control theory has a strong 'rational' component and is consistent with the offender decision-making perspective...(emphasis in original)

Felson argues that almost everyone has a handle, and the handle is necessary in order for informal social control to occur. If a child does not care about what other people think, does not feel that the rules apply to him, is not involved in any conventional activities, and has no stake in conformity then the child does not have a "handle" by which society can grab onto and keep the child's behavior controlled by informal means.

Felson uses the term **"intimate handler"** to describe parents or other adults who are both physically and emotionally close to the child. Everyone's handle is a bit different, so if an adult is going to effectively control the behavior of a child, then the adult must know the child well enough to grab onto his or her unique handle. What works to shame and control one child may be completely ineffective with another — it takes intimate knowledge of the child to know what words or actions will get the child back on track.

Due to their closeness with the child, intimate handlers are also able to recognize if items that are entering the home are of questionable origin — for example, if a child is caught wearing a new pair of expensive pants that the parent did not purchase for the child. An intimate handler will be able to recognize that the pants were probably stolen and be able to grab onto the appropriate handle to correct the behavior, such as making the child return the stolen pants and apologize to the store manager.

Even the best parent cannot monitor the actions of the child 24 hours a day, 7 days a week. This is where **informants** become an important element of informal social control. If you grew up in a tightly knit community where everyone knew everyone, then you may have experienced this form of informal social control. A neighbor may have seen you doing something wrong, like skipping school, and reported your actions to your parents. While this may seem like a "normal" thing for the neighbor to do, in contemporary societies this type of informal social control is on the wane. This type of intervention requires that the neighbor have intimate knowledge of you and your family. The neighbor must 1) recognize you; 2) be familiar enough with the routine activities of your life to know that on Tuesdays at 11:00 a.m. you should be in school; 3) know who your parents are, 4) and feel comfortable enough calling your parents to let them know what you had been up to.

Felson argues that changes in contemporary society have reduced our ability to exert informal social control. These changes include the increase in the number of working mothers, the movement towards larger schools, greater distances between one's home and place of work, lower fertility rates, greater geographic mobility, higher rates of divorce, blended families, and even wide-spread use of the automobile. These changes reduce the likelihood that an individual child engaging in a criminal act will be detected, recognized, and either handled appropriately or reported to the proper intimate handler.

This advancement in routine activities theory is quite similar to many of the ideas discussed in chapter 2 with respect to social disorganization, collective efficacy, and the importance of informal social control. Communities with high levels of social disorganization (in the words of Shaw and McKay) will tend to have higher numbers of children with weak bonds to society whose behavior is monitored by few intimate handlers and informants. Strengthening the bonds that both children and adults have with their neighbors may ultimately reduce crime. In chapter 4, a number of policy recommendations based on re-building communities and enhancing informal social control will be discussed.

Summary: Routine Activities

Like rational choice theory, routine activities theory is premised on the basic assumption of a rational offender carefully weighing the costs and benefits of his or her actions. While rational choice theory is focused on the individual offender, routine activities theory takes more of a macro level, incorporating broad changes in contemporary society and the way these changes have impacted how we live our every day lives. In order for crime to occur, three elements need to converge in space and time: motivated offenders, suitable targets, and the absence of capable guardians. Changes in American society have increased the likelihood that a motivated offender will come together in time and space with a suitable target in the absence of a capable guardian.

Since its inception, routine activities theory has had a great impact on crime prevention strategies. Practical applications of Cohen and Felson's ideas will be covered in the next unit. For now, the last choice-based theory, crime pattern theory, will be introduced.

Crime Pattern Theory

Crime pattern theory may be viewed as a combination platter of rational choice, routine activities, and environmental principles (Rossmo, 2000). Crime pattern theory begins with the assumption of a rational offender. During the course of everyday movements through time and space, suitable targets may be brought to the attention of a motivated offender. So far, nothing new. The added twist of crime pattern theory is that the level and the type of criminal activity can be predicted through an analysis of a city's geographic environment, such as land use patterns, street networks, and transportation systems. Proponents of crime pattern theory hold that crimes do not occur randomly in time or space, but are influenced greatly by the physical movements of offenders and victims.

The criminologists most closely associated with the development of crime pattern theory are Paul and Patricia Brantingham. Their theoretical orientation is a marriage (in more ways than one) between traditional criminology (Paul) and training in urban planning and mathematics (Patricia). The pair has written extensively in the area of environmental criminology, of which crime pattern theory is a principle component (see, for example, Brantingham & Brantingham, 1981; 1991, 1998a; 1999). According to the Brantinghams (1991), environmental criminology is the study of the spatio-temporal or locational dimension of crime. Environmental criminologists are concerned with answering questions such as where and when crimes will occur; what the movements are that bring the offender and the target together at the location of the crime; what is involved in the thought processes that lead to the selection of the crime location; and how targets and offenders are distributed spatially in urban, suburban, and rural settings.

The Language of Crime Pattern Theory: Nodes, Paths, and Edges

Crime pattern theory introduces us to a number of new vocabulary terms. First is the idea of **action space**. As potential offenders live their daily lives, they travel throughout their city conducting both legitimate and illegitimate activities. These activities may include going to the mall or shopping district, going to work, to attend classes, and down to the entertainment district on the weekends. These areas—shopping, work, school, or entertainment areas—are referred to as **nodes,** or the areas that people travel to and from. The movements between these various nodes form an **awareness space**, or the parts of the city that an individual has at least some information about. Since the awareness space requires only minimal knowledge, the awareness space is larger than (and completely contains) the action space (Rossmo, 2000).

Chances are, most people are not intimately familiar with their entire city. In fact, in a large city, there are more than likely areas that they have never been to and, in some respects, do not really even exist to them. However, most are intimately familiar with the travel **paths** that they take between their personal activity nodes—the path from home to work to school and so forth. A path can follow any form of transportation: highways, streets, sidewalks, mass transit lines, or even a footpath from a dorm to classroom buildings.

Based on the movements along the paths between personal activity nodes a **cognitive map** or mental image of the environment is formed. In addition to personal activity nodes and highly familiar paths, a cognitive map may also include various special locations within the environment, like tourist attractions or necessary places of business (like the county courthouse). Cognitive maps may be different depending upon the time of day or day of the week—a mental image of the entertainment district node and the path to it may be very different on Friday nights at 11:00 p.m. than on Sunday mornings.

Moving along the paths between various personal activity nodes introduces **edges**. According to the Brantinghams (1998:33), an edge is a "sharp visual break between different types of land use, between different socioeconomic and demographic residential and commercial areas. Edges are clearly apparent along major parks, next to single-family areas, and surrounding high-activity shopping centers." Edges can be quite striking. I recall driving into Detroit with some friends from high school to go to a Tigers baseball game. We got off at the wrong interstate exit and ended up right next to a large university campus. The sharp visual break was quite dramatic: On one side of the street was a beautiful well groomed urban campus, while on the other side of the street was a string of dilapidated vacant homes with broken windows and overgrown, littered lawns. Edges can be high crime areas. Within a node, people have a sense of who belongs and who does not. This is not the case with an edge where strangers come and go, moving with relative anonymity.

As long as people remain in the areas defined by your cognitive map, they feel safe. When they travel off of the beaten path, so to speak, they may feel some anxiety. Landmarks are no longer recognized and strangers are all around. It is difficult to tell who belongs and who does not. Furthermore, people tend to be creatures of habit. The routine activities of daily life rarely require ventures into unchartered territory. As a result, people may rarely leave their awareness space.

Crimes and Cognitive Maps

Just as college students have a cognitive map based on their awareness space, so do criminals. At the heart of crime pattern theory is the assumption that crimes will occur in the areas where suitable targets intersect an offender's awareness space. A burglar will tend to search out suitable targets during the course of his or her routine movements through time and space. Since both criminals and non-criminals rarely venture away from their regular awareness space, most offenses will occur close to the home, workplace, shopping centers, or entertainment areas frequented by the offender or along the paths between these activity nodes. Offenders search for suitable targets outward from the nodes and paths, following what has been called a **distance decay function:** The further offenders move away from the comfort zone of their cognitive maps, the less likely they will be to search for targets in the area.

In studies of offender mobility, a number of interesting trends have been noted. In general, the distance between an offender's home and the location of the crime tends to be relatively short, with a sharp drop off in the number of crimes as one moves further and further from the offender's home (Eck & Weisburd, 1995). However, the distance decay function may vary based on the type of offense, whether expressive or instrumental in nature.

Expressive crimes (or **affective crimes**) are more spontaneous, emotional, and impulsive crimes that are done in anger. These include domestic violence, some forms of rape, and assaults. **Instrumental crimes** are crimes committed in order to achieve a goal, such as money, status, or other personal gain (Miethe & McCorkle, 2001). Examples of instrumental crimes include burglary and robbery. In general, expressive crimes are committed closer to home than instrumental crimes (Eck &

Weisburd, 1995; Phillips, 1980; Rossmo, 2000). For predatory instrumental crimes, there appears to be a sort of "buffer zone" located
around the home of the offender. In this buffer zone, targets may be
viewed as being too risky because of the likelihood of being recognized
and ultimately arrested. Because expressive crimes by definition are
more emotional (and hence less rational) in nature, the buffer zone does
not seem to be as important in the selection of an appropriate target
(Brantingham & Brantingham, 1981; Rossmo, 2000).

Cognitive Maps and Urban Development

As noted previously, one added component of crime pattern theory is
the study of the relationship between a city's geographic environment
and the level and type of criminal activity. As argued by the Brantinghams (1991), the awareness spaces and cognitive maps for both offenders and non-offenders will vary based on the actual structure of the city
and its transportation system. For example, in a major city that has a
thriving mass transit system, awareness spaces are more nodal in nature—most are very familiar with their end location (shopping node,
entertainment node, etc.) but not so familiar with the actual paths to get
between the nodes. Criminals living in this type of city have the same
cognitive maps. Therefore, criminal activity is expected to be higher in
and near the major nodes along the transportation network than along
the paths (which may not cognitively exist).

In newer cities or cities without mass transit, the prediction of high
crime areas is different. For example, in newer cities with sprawling strip
malls for shopping, dispersed entertainment centers, and separate residential and commercial areas, crime is expected to be more spread out
than in older, more densely concentrated cities. This has to do with the
size of the awareness spaces and cognitive maps of potential offenders.
Because the nodes are so spread out, extensive travel is necessary in order
to conduct the routine activities of life. More travel translates into larger
search areas for potential targets. Since the targets are not concentrated,
it follows that the level of criminal activity is not concentrated either.

The relationship between urban design, traffic patterns, and criminal
activity has important considerations for real estate developers and city
planners (for a more in-depth discussion of these issues, see generally
Felson, 1998b). For example, in the development of a new suburban

housing development, a number of residential streets may be designated as major traffic routes for the subdivision. Since the volume of traffic is expected to be higher along these paths, houses along these arteries will be exposed to a greater number of motivated offenders who will incorporate the road into their awareness space. Planners and developers should take steps to reduce the likelihood that one of these homes would become a target for criminal activity, such as incorporating landscaping or architectural designs to enhance visibility and guardianship of the homes along this major path.

Additionally, the physical layout of the streets in a neighborhood can also have an impact on the level of criminal activity. Brantingham and Brantingham (1991; 1998) have noted that neighborhoods with highly predictable street grid networks will more than likely have higher crime rates than areas with more "organic" street layouts. In a city based on a grid system, it is very easy to get around. For a number of years, I lived in St. Petersburg, Florida, which is based on a grid system. In St. Pete, all streets run north and south and all avenues run east and west in a highly predictable manner. I used to own a pizza shop that was located at 5570 4th Street North. Based solely on the address a person even remotely familiar with the city would know exactly where the business was located: on 4th Street North about midway between 55th and 56th Avenues.

The problem with this type of layout is that people feel very comfortable venturing into unknown parts of the city. Cognitive maps become very large because the city is so predictable. If a person needed to go to 9810 66th Street South, the journey would not be difficult. This place could easily be located within a cognitive map even if an individual had never been in the area. For criminals, larger cognitive maps and larger awareness spaces translate into larger search areas for potential targets. Therefore, to design a neighborhood for safety, a number of winding roads, dead-end streets, or cul-de-sacs that lend a bit of uncertainty to those unfamiliar with the neighborhood should be included. A number of crime prevention strategies based on rational choice, routine activities, and crime pattern theories will be explored in the next unit.

Target Selection and the Rational Offender

It is important to stress the basic assumption upon which crime pattern theory is based: a rational motivated offender searching for suitable targets within his or her awareness space. Brantingham and Brantingham (1991:28) have proposed the following outline that describes the process of crime site selection:

(1) Individuals exist who are motivated to commit specific offenses.

(a) The sources of motivation are diverse. Different etiological models or theories may appropriately be invoked to explain the motivation of different individuals or groups.

(b) The strength of such motivation varies.

(c) The character of such motivation varies from affective to instrumental.

(2) Given the motivation of an individual to commit an offense, the actual commission of an offense is the end result of a multistaged decision process which seeks out and identifies, within the general environment, a target or victim positioned in time and space.

(a) In the case of high affect motivation, the decision process will probably involve a minimal number of stages.

(b) In the case of high instrumental motivation, the decision process locating a target or victim may include many stages and much careful searching.

(3) The environment emits many signals, or cues, about its physical, spatial, cultural, legal, and psychological characteristics.

(a) These cues can vary from generalized to detailed.

(4) An individual who is motivated to commit a crime uses cues (either learned through experience or learned through social transmission) from the environment to locate and identify targets or victims.

(5) As experiential knowledge grows, an individual who is motivated to commit a crime learns which individual cues, clusters of cues, and sequences of cues are associated with "good" victims or targets. These cues, cue clusters, and cue sequences can be considered a template which is used in victim or target selection. Potential victims or targets are compared to the template and either rejected or accepted depending on the congruence.

(a) The process of template construction and the search process may be consciously conducted, or these processes may occur in an unconscious, cybernetic fashion so that the individual cannot articulate how they are done.

(6) Once the template is established, it becomes relatively fixed and influenced future search behavior, thereby becoming self-reinforcing.

(7) Because of the multiplicity of targets and victims, many potential crime selection templates could be constructed. But because the spatial and temporal distribution of offenders, targets, and victims is not regular, but clustered or patterned, and because human environmental perception has some universal properties, individual templates have similarities which can be identified.

For purposes of this discussion, the point made in (2) is most relevant: Given the fact that he or she is motivated, the offender carefully and rationally searches out an appropriate target or victim. For certain types of crimes, this decision making process can be quite involved. For other types of crimes, the process can be much shorter. The important point is that there is a decision making process by which crime victims are rationally selected by offenders as both the hunted (targets) and hunters (offenders) move through time and space.

Also of interest in this decision making model is the idea of a **template,** or a mental image of a "good" target. Information used to build this template comes from a variety of sources, and the offender may not even consciously be aware of some of the criteria. For example, in a large university with a diverse number of course offerings, students may hunt for a "good" course. Based on their own experiences and discussions with peers, they have a mental image or template of what the perfect course would be. During drop-add week, they may shop various sections comparing the instructor, course content, and requirements laid out in the syllabus to their template. When comparing potential courses to the template, some rejections are easy to articulate (no 8:00 a.m. classes!), while other reasons for not taking a course are a bit "fuzzy," such as a "bad" feeling from the instructor on the first day. The general argument here is that criminals select "good" targets in the same manner that students choose a "good" course—through a rational decision making process based on a variety of data available. Students might also have different templates constructed for courses in their major versus elective courses, day classes versus night, etc., much the same way that a criminal will have different templates for different potential targets. Rational decision making processes follow the same general path, whether a person is choosing a suitable course or a suitable target.

Summary: Crime Pattern Theory

Crime pattern theory incorporates elements of both rational choice and routine activities theory. Through the course of the routine activities of daily life, rational motivated offenders are exposed geographically and temporally with rather limited portions of a city. It is along the pathways, edges, and within the nodes of their awareness space that offenders select appropriate targets or victims through a multistage decision making process. The actual occurrence of crimes in a city will by affected by the geographic structure of the city's land use patterns, transportation system, and street networks.

The Bottom Line:
Is Crime Rational?

It appears now that we have come full circle. We began this chapter with a discussion of Classical criminology, which was based on the assumption of a rational, hedonistic offender whose behavior can only be kept in check through the careful application of certain, swift, and proportionate punishments. We then learned of rational choice theory, which explored the decision making processes through which would-be offenders try to benefit themselves by carefully choosing the best course of action, whether it be to get involved in crime, persist in criminal activities, or to, instead, desist and engage in legitimate pathways to success. Routine activities theory presented us with the notion of motivated offenders, suitable targets, and the lack of capable guardians converging in time and place as we conduct the business of our everyday lives. Finally, crime pattern theory incorporated the notion of a rational, motivated offender with an analysis of city's geographic environment in order to predict the level and type of criminal activities that would be most likely to occur. If you can pick up on a common thread in this various theories, it would be the idea of a rational offender. So, the question remains: Is crime rational?

If you are looking for a simple yes or no answer to this question, then you will be sadly disappointed. I've taught Theories of Criminal Behavior courses more times than I care to admit, and one of the most consistent complaints that I hear from students is that you never get a definite answer. Half of the empirical research studies seem to support a theory, while an equal number of studies refute the propositions. Research studies testing choice theories are no different. While a number of studies have found support for the idea of a rational offender carefully assessing the potential gains against perceived certainty and severity of punishment (see, generally, Cornish & Clarke, 1986; Cromwell, Olson,

& Avery, 1991; Katz, 1988; Tunnell, 1992) others have not (see, for example, Paternoster, 1987). The issue is even more complicated when one considers the type of crime (either expressive or instrumental, white collar crime versus street crimes) as well as various offender characteristics (like adults versus juveniles).

For example, consider the crime of auto theft. As noted by Miethe and McCorkle (2001), there are two very different images of a typical car thief. On one extreme, there are professional car thieves who carefully seek out targets that will provide the greatest profit. Clarke and Harris (1992) found that certain types of cars are targeted for stripping for their parts, like Volkswagens or Saabs. Professional auto thieves engage in more elaborate decision-making processes, from learning which cars have the most marketable parts to acquiring more sophisticated equipment to increase the likelihood of success in their thefts.

At the other end of the spectrum is the image of juvenile joy riders that happen to stumble across opportunities (like a motorist leaving the keys in the ignition) with no planning or foresight, stealing the car simply for the fun of it. While it may appear that juvenile auto thieves are less rational in their criminal involvement, Fleming (1999) found that juvenile auto thieves voiced a number of motivations for committing their crimes. Some of the most active juvenile offenders described motivations that were instrumental (for profit) in nature, while others were categorized as irrational and immature in their thinking. However, even among the joy riders and thrill-seekers, there may have been some level of rationality on the part of the offenders. Fleming argued that for teens and pre-teens, thrill and excitement might be as rational a goal as money and economic gain for older offenders.

Part of the issue in trying to assess whether or not an offender behaved rationally is trying to tease out the meaning of "rationality." In a study of active residential burglars, Cromwell, Olson and Avery (1991) found evidence that the offenders did engage in a rather simple decision making process in which they assessed the risk of apprehension based on a number of environmental cues. In effect, the burglars exercised a sort of "limited rationality," where long term costs, risks, or gains were not heavily weighted in the decision making process. The concept of limited rationality recognizes that most people are unwilling or unable to completely assess every minute detail prior to making a decision. Instead, offenders develop what Cook (1980) called a "standing decision" to commit crimes if a certain type of opportunity presents itself. The idea is that given a certain set of environmental cues, a burglar may decide to select a particular target. This target may not be the *best* (or most rational) choice, but it may be a satisfactory choice.

Decisions do not have to be completely rational in order to fit in with the assumptions of choice theories. The theories only require that a minimal degree of planning and deliberation has occurred prior to the commission of a crime (Hirschi, 1986; Cromwell, Parker, & Mobley, 1999). This concept of limited rationality should also be considered in light of the fact that many offenders are under the influence of drugs or alcohol at the time the decision was made to commit their crimes. According to the Bureau of Justice Statistics (1999b), 51 percent of surveyed inmates were under such an influence at the time that their crime was committed. This was especially true for violent offenses, such as assault, murder, manslaughter, and sexual assaults. The ingestion of certain types of drugs and/or alcohol may lower inhibitions, reduce fear and perception of risk, and increase aggression (Akers, 1992). Under these circumstances, the concept of limited rationality may become even more limited.

Summary

The resurgence in interest in Classical criminology has brought about a number of interesting changes in the way we think about crime, criminals, and what to do about the crime problem. While all begin with the concept of a rational offender, the choice theories that we have explored in this unit—rational choice, routine activities, and crime pattern theory—each add their own unique contributions to or understanding of crime. In chapter 5, some of the practical applications of choice theories in crime prevention and crime reduction strategies are examined.

Choosing Pathways to Success:
Street Level Drug Sales in Detroit

We close our discussion of choice-based theories with a reprint of a qualitative study conducted by Tom Mieczkowski, a colleague and friend. As part of his dissertation research, Professor Mieczkowski spent several months on the streets of Detroit, observing and talking with heroin dealers. The results of his study were quite dramatic and supported a strong sense of rationality among the crew bosses and the runners. In this Detroit neighborhood, the drug distribution networks conducted sales in highly organized manner that would be similar in many respects to legitimate business operations. As you read the passage, consider which aspects of the operation were conducted in a rational manner. How were the runners selected? Did the runners consider various options available to them with respect to reducing their risk of apprehension by both the police and their crew boss for their actions? Could you find any evidence that decisions were made in an irrational manner?

Spotlight on Research II

Geeking Up and Throwing Down: Heroin Street Life in Detroit[*]
Thomas Mieczkowski, PhD.

When I carried out this research I entered the experience only with a sense of curiosity and with the paradigmatic vision of a person interested in organized crime. My mentor Joe Albini had long before disabused me of moralistic notions of crime, or even pathological ones at least when one was examining "vice" as he liked to call it with a smile. These were activities that were only possible because the very same citizenry that condemned them in the daylight indulged in them in the dark. And why? Because these activities brought excitement, pleasure, release, relief, or other satisfactions to those who indulged in them.

This view certainly made sense to me. And I had seen it in many places before I began to look at the heroin trade on the streets of Detroit. Merton, to my mind, had explained the basic dynamics in his means/ends conceptualization. My research wasn't something that revealed the mystery of motive; it revealed the mystery of method. My research was designed to find out something about the method by which these things were done. We don't wonder why the bank was robbed. We

* Source: Mieczkowski, T. (1986). Geeking up and throwing down: Heroin street life in Detroit. *Criminology*, 24, 645–666. Reprinted with permission.

are curious about how it was done, because we know banks try to be very secure places.

What I found about the method of selling heroin on the street of Detroit is expressed in this article. And it was a fascinating discovery for me. It was a demonstration of both the rational, strategic and utterly comprehendable world of drug selling and the shape of the drug-selling milieu as a competitive market. I was not by conscious commitment a "rational choice" theorist. Indeed, I've never thought of myself as a theorist of any kind. I wrote what I saw, as I comprehended it. And it seems, now looking, back that nothing I saw would surprise many from a "theoretical perspective". My hat is off to you, Mr. Bentham, for even amidst the most "disorganized" of communities there are sterling examples of the rational thinking mediated by the hedonistic calculus you identified so long ago. Why people sell heroin is no mystery. How they sell it, on the other hand, is a great curiosity!

Tom Mieczkowski
December 5, 2002

Over the last two decades there have been a number of ethnographic studies of the heroin subculture. Especially since the work of Preeble (Preeble and Casey, 1969) a committed group of anthropologists, sociologists, and criminologists have investigated and reported upon the life and activities of the "street people" who make up the urban heroin world. Feldman (1977), Agar (1977), Gould, Walker, Crane, and Litz (1974), Hanson, Beschner, Walters, and Bovelle (1985), and Johnson, Goldstein, Preeble, Schmeidler, Lipton, and Spunt (1985) are some of the more recent examples of this research activity. Generally, these efforts have provided criminologists with a clearer picture of the world of the heroin user and have provided insight into the concept of the drug subculture. They have almost universally concentrated on the life of the addict, even when recognizing both that the concept of addiction is complex and that the complications of polydrug use make labels like "heroin addict" somewhat misleading (Johnson et. al., 1985: 3–4).

This paper reports ethnographic data on the street life of individuals involved in the heroin subculture. It represents, therefore, an extension of these already existing studies. But it also views the heroin world from a somewhat specialized perspective. This study concentrates exclusively on the heroin seller and the social organization of selling (typically called "dealing") at the retail level. It is typical of earlier studies to view dealing as an adjunct activity to maintaining a heroin habit (Redlinger, 1975: 331–332). Alternately, these studies view dealing heroin as one of many activities comprising what is generally referred to as a "hustle" or "hustling" style of life (Goldstein, 1981; Smith and Stephens, 1976). The "hustle" is any opportunistic activity which can generate income. It characterizes the street addict, who then on an ad hoc basis may become involved in distribution of drugs. For instance, he may function as a "touter", a "cop man", or engage in a variety of property or predatory crimes (Hanson, et. al., 1985: 49–74). This study reports on activity which does not closely conform to the traditional "hustling" model, since the operatives who distribute heroin are not loosely connected as day-to-day improvisational entrepreneurs. They do not engage in entrepreneurial activity in order to fund their own heroin habit. In contrast, they are really more accurately described as quasi-bureaucratic functionaries in a well-defined social system. Furthermore, there are several other important differences in regards to the subjects of this study: (1) The drug retailers in this study do not use heroin; (2) the system of social organization of the sellers is relatively well-defined and does not conform well with a "loose" hustling or opportunistic model; and (3) the operatives in this study are surprisingly young and report that the use of young operatives is common and is based upon legal considerations.

During the years 1982 and 1983, the author conducted a research project concerning teenage-dominated heroin selling syndicates in the city of Detroit, Michigan. This project was undertaken with two aims: the first was to produce an ethnography of such a group, and the second was to test certain aspects of criminal organization as they have been argued in the literature of organized crime (Mieczkowski, 1983; 1985). This paper is offered as a brief summary and overview of the results of that research. It will mainly concentrate on the ethnographic data, presenting a portrait of the sales syndicate techniques and the various roles which exist within the syndicates.

The research effort presented herein examines heroin retailing syndicates as they appeared to function in two major inner-city housing projects in Detroit. As an ethnography, this effort is a compilation of information about the style of life of the operatives of these subcultural groups. The terms in the title are used to introduce this dimension of interest. These two words are bits of the argot of this heroin subculture. "Geeking up" is an expression meaning "getting high," that is, taking an intoxicant. "Throwing down" is an expression of physical confrontation, "street fighting". The heroin world has its own daily social realities. The terms used in this paper, such as "runner," "crew boss,"

"Young Boy, Inc." (YBI), are terms which are used by the informants and which are part of the argot of this drug subculture.

Methodology

The data of this study comes from the interviews and observations of heroin dealers in the field. This study took place in the streets of the inner city of Detroit. The data base is a series of interviews with 15 heroin dealers. Also included are the observations made by the author over the course of three months spent on site with these individuals. It is supplemented with information gathered by the author during the course of many years residence in the city and many years of teaching and interacting in the city with a variety of individuals whose experience is relevant to the topic. Here included are police officers, probation and parole officers, health care workers, social workers, and many others who daily life brings them into continuing contact with the heroin subculture. (See Note 1.)

In general, the sale of heroin was organized by a simple syndication process. It involved the formation of patron-client networks centered around the pragmatic goal of selling drugs for financial profit. This financial motivation is noteworthy because syndicate members did not hold or employ any approving ideology of heroin use. Rather, by contrast, most sellers expressed considerable contempt towards the heroin user. Each of these syndicates (and there appear to be many of them) operates independently or only with very loose associations with other groups. They range in size from small to "mega-syndicates" employing perhaps a hundred or more operatives. But even though some mega-syndicates achieve wide public recognition, there does not appear to be a monopoly of the heroin trade. It seems that such a monopoly would be hard to create even though powerful operatives may wish to do so. The trade is simply too broad and entrepreneurial participation too easy to accomplish. The entrance and exit of individuals, at least at the lower echelon of the syndicate, occur at a high rate. Participation appears often short-lived and sporadic. Little importance seems to be invested in longevity or high degrees of abstraction regarding the organization itself.

Findings: The Heroin Scene in Detroit

Heroin use has long been a part of the Detroit community. Medical personnel knowledgeable regarding local addict populations report individual users whose heroin history goes back more than 30 years. Also, in Detroit—as is argued for the urban centers of the country in general—it appears that over the last two decades drug use is more prolific, that heroin is more widely used, that the number of users in all social categories is increasing, and that the mean age of drug users is dropping (Detroit Health Department Bureau of Substance Abuse, 1983).

According to the statements of older addict/informants, post-World War II drug trafficking in the Detroit community appears to have been based upon the "Dope Pad System." These retail selling operations used a rather conventional and simple strategy to distribute heroin. A fixed physical location was used as a base. Heroin was secured and "broken down" from wholesale to retail quantities. It was both diluted with fillers ("stepped on," "cut") and repackaged in small retail units of sale. There were several operatives typically present in the dope pad. A boss of sorts was in charge of two or three other functionaries. These other functionaries provided security and acted as business assistants. Sometimes operatives would run a "shooting gallery." They would either provide the necessary accessories to the retail customer—a syringe, a needle, a spoon or heat source—or they would actually inject the chronic addict who was unsuccessful in finding a vein into which they could inject their narcotics. All of these "services" were rendered for a fee. Also operating as employees of the dope pad were advertisers ("steerers"), who would circulate on the streets and advertise the location of the dope pad, sometimes offering testimony about the superior quality of the product.

In the early 1980's the dope pad, while still an operating entity in the heroin subculture, has been in many areas of the city superseded by a new style of retail operation. This system is personified in Detroit by the Young Boys, Inc.(YBI), and uses a technique of retail sales which is called the runner technique. The intentions here are to present a description of the runner technique and then offer an interpretation of why this transformation took place.

The Young Boys Technique and the Runner System

The Young Boys, Inc. utilize a technique of criminal organization called the runner system. The runner system is an organized, cooperative strategy for the selling of heroin. It is designed to market heroin in public places, most typically either at the curbside of public roads or other open locales such as areas in front of shops and stores, playgrounds, parks, and schoolyards. Running heroin does not require a highly controlled and conventionally secure location or place of business (as does the dope pad system). Instead the runner system uses individual participants who are organized into a rational division of labor. Interacting cooperatively in accordance with accepted rules, they direct their attention to the successful exchange of heroin for money.

The runner system is a multi-tiered, task-directed organizational system which serves a heroin-consuming clientele. The direct and actual sale of heroin is the role of a street-level actor who is called a runner. The runners in this study had the following general attributes: (1) all the runners were male; (2) all the runners were black; (3) all the runners were relatively young; (4) runners were not, generally, chronic users of "hard" drugs, and none were heroin addicts; (5) all runners, with a single exception, were recreational users of some drug or drugs. A general profile of runner characteristics is presented in Table 3.1.

It is interesting to note that, although runners appear by and large to be recreational drug users, they are not addicted to heroin. Typically, however, they have tried heroin at some point in their lives. The data indicates that 9 out of 15 dealers in the informant group had tried narcotics and that 4 of the15 had considered themselves addicted at some point. Only one informant admitted to using narcotics during the time period of the study. The 12 who considered themselves "recreational"

Table 3.1. A Profile of Runners

Informant	Current Age	Age Began Selling	Ever Used Heroin	Ever Addicted	Currently Use Heroin	Never Use Other Drugs
K.	21	20	Yes	Yes	Yes	Yes
L.	19	17	No	No	No	No
T.	17	16	Yes	No	No	Yes
F.	18	16	Yes	No	No	Yes
Bo.	22	20	Yes	Yes	No	Yes
D.	20	19	Yes	No	No	Yes
I.	19	17	Yes	No	No	Yes
Bu.	20	16	Yes	Yes	No	Yes
N.	19	14	No	No	No	Yes
Bn.	18	16	Yes	No	No	Yes
P.	23	NA	Yes	Yes	No	Yes
E.	16	14	No	No	No	Yes
G.	19	16	No	No	No	Yes
Tk.	19	17	No	No	No	Yes
C.	20	17	No	No	No	Yes
Mean Values	19.3	16.6				

users of drugs cited marijuana and cocaine as their substances of choice, with some also periodically taking pharmaceuticals like Dilaudid, Percodan, Valium, Talwin, barbiturates, and other psychoactive agents.

It was reported by almost every informant (14 out of 15) that drug use of any kind "on the job" is strongly disapproved. Being intoxicated in the course of dealing is considered a very dangerous condition. If one is not "straight," the risks and dangers of selling drugs are augmented. The runner role precludes any form of "high" while working. All runners reported that their immediate superior, the crew boss, would enforce this drug prohibition by denying a drug consignment (the "front" or "stash") to a runner if he suspected that the runner was "high." This is a potent sanction. It results in no income for the runner.

The "front"—a consignment of heroin packets—is given to the runner to sell. If a runner can not obtain such a consignment, he is effectively unemployed. It is to be noted that the crew boss is not stigmatizing the use of drugs per se, but rather the irresponsibility of a runner who would be intoxicated when time had come for his "shift". Some of the parameters of the retail trade are demonstrated in Table 3.2. All earnings and costs are in dollars. It is important to comment on some of the earning data in Table 3.2. The data are not annualized or otherwise projected. This is because runners worked irregularly over the course of the conventional time frames used to measure earnings (yearly,

Table 3.2. The Runner's Retail Activity

Informant	Daily Earnings	Hours Worked Per Day	Retail Unit Sold	Retail Cost Per Unit
K.	$100–150	8–12	Tablet	$15–25
L.	$300	16–18	Bag	$7–8
T.	$3,000	16–17	Bag	$11–12
F.	$3,000	12–16	Bag	$11–12
Bo.	$25–50	6–12	Bag	$11–12
D.	$100	4–12	Bag	$12
I.	$200–300	9–19	Pack	$10–12
Bu.	$300–400	8–12	Pack	$10–12
N.	$25–200	10–11	Pack	$10
Bn.	$200	8–12	Pack	$10
P.	$100	2–8	Pack	$10
E.	$100	12	Pack	$10
G.	NA	2–8	Pack	$10–12
Tk.	$50–100	12–14	Pack	$12
C.	$25–150	8–12	Pack	$10

monthly). These earnings (see Table 3.2) are essentially "peak" earnings. Informants themselves did not have accurate data in regard to their earnings on an annual basis. Wide varieties of income and irregularity in the rate of income earnings are not unusual of drug subcultures. Johnson et al. (1985: 81–82), for example, report variations of as high as 300%. This variability is not outside the range of incomes projected from Table 3.2. (See Note 2.)

The heroin consignment is given to the runner by the crew boss in the form of bags, packs, or packets. Runners reported the use of all three terms. Generally, these were small, white or brown hard paper envelopes, or sometimes homemade envelopes culled from hard magazine newsprint. Often they were labeled with either a brand name or they were marked on the pack with a graphic logo. The packets were broken down by the crew boss from a bundle. The bundle is the heroin unit which is consigned to the crew boss and consists of 10 to 12 packets, packs, or bags. Each runner receives a small number of packs (usually two to three) to hold in his pocket as an inventory. The runner, after receiving his merchandise, takes up his station or selling position on the street. This is typically on the sidewalk or easement area immediately adjacent to a public roadway. This permits clients who are in vehicles to make purchases with relative ease and convenience.

The Role of the Runner

The art and strategy of selling heroin is a skill that has to be successfully mastered by the runner. It should be noted here that the "challenge" of heroin life-style has been recognized and described by several researchers (Preeble and Casey, 1969; Sutter, 1970; Sutker, 1974; Smith and Stephens, 1976). The runner's critical role is selling the heroin to the customer in face-to-face interaction and collecting the money from the customer generated by the sale. The runner is thus confronted by several challenges in his work. The first challenge is that his behavior is illegal, and it is necessary for the runner to carefully consider his customers. Runners generally report that they are reluctant to sell to anyone who is not an established and recognized customer or, in their perception, someone who is not an obvious addict. Four informants reported that they would not hesitate, for example, to ask a customer to role up their sleeves in order to examine their arms for "tracks," marks and scars left by the repeated usage of a hypodermic syringe. Runners also indicated that in general they preferred to acquire new customers by introduction through established customers.

In general, runners prefer to do repeat business with customers with which they have established fairly enduring trade relationships. But this is not always possible and is even more difficult in the case of public selling on the streets, since by its very nature it prompts contact with strangers. As a consequence, and in spite of their preference, runners often have to deal with strangers about whom they know nothing. Moreover, an established customer is no guarantee of safety in any event, for an old customer may pose threats for a variety of reasons. For instance, he may be recruited by the police to make a "set-up" purchase, or introduce an undercover agent as an "old friend" who wants to buy some heroin.

A third challenge the runner faces is the possibility of a "rip off" or robbery, from both strangers and old customers. Also the customer may not pay the money after receiving his drugs, or he may try to short-change or "shuffle" the money by a complex con which involves alternately changing orders for drugs and amounts paid out until the runner is so confused that he is "hustled" out of some of his "stash." Runners reported occasional straightforward armed robberies of both their stash of drugs and their cash-on-hand. Since the runner's basic labor task is to hold, deliver, and collect for drugs traded, these activities by customers all represent threats and risks which the runner must anticipate and avoid.

The skillful runner learns to reduce risks whenever possible. This risk reduction is a function of the experience and mental acuity of a runner and is also related to the interaction of the crew unit as a whole. In large crews of 8 to 12 runners, certain members of the crew serve strictly in the role of guns while the remaining members devote all their time to sales. The guns are armed and stationed around the main site of sales. The guns serve as a security presence for the exposed runners. Guns observe and monitor the street transactions. Should anything go awry, guns are expected to intervene. In smaller crews of 3 to 5 members, the crew boss also serves in the role of gun. In small crews, then, there is usually only a single gun—the crew boss. In large crews it is reported that out of 12 runners, as many as 8 may be guns.

To deal with police, runners usually rely on a simple flight strategy—they run away. A crew of teenage runners, informants reported, is believed to be generally immune from being shot by police for fleeing the scene of dope dealing. In general, they believe that community sanctions and reactions would be extreme if such an event were to occur, and therefore the police are somewhat inhibited from using this form of control. Considering this belief, flight then is a reasonable strategy for dealing with confrontations with the police in the marketplace. Three to

25 crew members simultaneously fleeing into the surrounding neighborhood means that, in reality, police using a classical "raid" maneuver would likely only catch a few individuals, each with an inconsequential amount of heroin. These dealers are often juveniles as well, and therefore legal sanctions against them are restricted, so this makes enforcement of the law even more discouraging to the police.

The runner is primarily held to his responsibilities by his immediate supervisor, the crew boss. As noted earlier, the crew boss dispenses heroin consignments to the runners under his charge. The crew boss is also the collector of funds which are acquired by the runners in the course of their work. Periodically, during the course of business hours, all runners either report to the crew boss, or the crew boss goes into the field and, making rounds, collects the accumulated revenues. This does not usually entail taking all the money held by the runner, but rather varying amounts. This variation occurs because there are several different methods by which the runner is paid for his work. In smaller crews, the crew boss himself pays the runner on a daily basis. This is typically done at the end of a "shift," when the runner receives either a flat, prearranged amount, or, more likely, a payment in cash based on the volume of his sales during the shift. Runners reported receiving about $2 per pack of heroin sold. While the wage ranges reported were rather large (from $25 to $3,000 per shift), the range in per-pack profit was not. Reports from runners, crew bosses, and lieutenants were all consistent in this regard. When runners alone are considered, the daily reported wage is around $160. This money is earned during an average ten-and-a-half-hour work day, thus indicating a wage of about $14 per hour for the average runner in this study.

Supplemental income was available to the runner in a number of ways. Runners reported periodically receiving "tips" from customers as a token of appreciation for services rendered. One informant reported that unless he received a tip for carside service from a customer, the next time that customer wished to make a purchase, he would not go up to the car, but rather make the customer exit the auto and walk up to the runner. Tips were not reported with sufficient frequency or volume to constitute a significant percentage of the runners' income, however. In order to generate substantial additional income, runners would resort to a number of "scams" or "hustles." These strategies were either directed at the customer or at the crew boss. Generally, they reflect the reality that interaction relative to income was a zero-sum game within the crew. The amount of money available to the crew is finite, in that it is a function of the amount of heroin that the crew boss can secure from his supplier. This determines what is available to the runners in the form of consignments. This factor, once fixed, is inelastic and determines the total money volume the crew can generate (by selling 100% of the supply). If the runner is to boost his income level, it must come by reducing the income of some other participant in the system. Later it will be noted that there is some relational ambiguity reported by syndicate operatives. This "zero-sum" economic reality may be one of the factors which contribute to this sentiment.

Customers are exposed to exploitation in several ways, and runners take advantage of this vulnerability. The crudest such strategy is the "rip off," where the runner secures the client's money before producing the drug and then refuses to produce the drug while keeping the customers money. Also, there are two variations on this rip-off. One is to not only effectively steal the customer's money by withholding the paid-for drug, but by threat or force of arms to rob him or her of all the money in his or her possession. Also, the runner may carry in his pocket a set of envelopes or packs identical to the packs of heroin, only these packs have in them some impotent substance like flour or sugar. The runner may "sell a dummy" to the customer by slipping him such a pack instead of an envelope containing the heroin that he thinks he is buying. A limitation on these scams is that they are not very subtle, and are effective for only one time, at least typically. Once a customer is exploited in this manner, he is unlikely to return, except for revenge. In order to be successful scamming must be more subtle, for it must permit the runner to gather more income without at the same time destroying the basis for his livelihood.

A scam which reflects a bit more sophistication is the "staged rip-off," a scam in which a runner, cooperating with an accomplice, participates in a fake robbery in the role of a victim. The runner can then report to his crew boss that he was robbed, and thus ought to be held blameless. He can even call on the corroborating testimony of his fellow crew members who may have witnessed the "rip-off." Later, the conspiring pair will share the loot from the scam. Although this is a more sophisticated strategy than overtly defrauding the customer, it can only last for one or two performances. A runner who reports chronic rip-offs will at the least be dismissed from his position, and more than likely the sharp crew boss will suspect complicity. The crew boss may make his feeling known by administering a good beating to the "victim" of the rip-off, and making up the proceeds lost to the theft by withholding a portion of the entire crew's wages.

Other crew members are likely to punish the "victimized" runner as well. This is because cheating the crew boss also lowers the general wages paid on volume. The crew boss is often required to pay "in front" for his heroin consignment or "stash." Therefore all losses have to be recovered from the crew's gross earnings. Thus, rip-offs reduce their net earnings and motivate a style of self-policing that is frequently found in labor groups who collectively produce their wages.

The most sophisticated of all the runner's scams for generating additional income is the practice of pinching. Pinching is the skimming off of small quantities of heroin from each bag that the runner receives as his consignment. A runner will open each packet and remove a small quantity of the heroin, which he then collects until he has a sufficient amount to sell as a whole pack. This money goes directly into his pocket. The nature of the street sale is such that the customer does not normally have a lot of time to assess and judge the condition and contents of the packs he is purchasing. He is generally unlikely to notice a small loss because the actual exchange of the drugs is quite furtive. Some runners actually effect a "cut" of the bag by not only removing some of the heroin but also replacing the weight with a filler of some kind. Although these cuts are small, in the course of a work day they can amount to a significant quantity of heroin, since runners see a substantial number of customers in the course of a normal shift. Table 3.3 gives an indication of the nature and the volume of the trade reported by the runners in this study.

It is noteworthy in examining the table to comment on the rather substantial difference in crew sizes reported by informants. This is explained by reference to the fact that some crews were small, "self-starter" units while others were appendages of mega-syndicates which employed large numbers of operatives. This will be further explained in some detail in the section devoted to the role of crew boss.

The mean overall figure for the average number of customers is around 135 per shift per runner. Thus, if a runner can effect a 1/25th cut, he can generate three packs of heroin per shift for his own personal profit. Such a scam, then, might improve his daily income by as much as 50%. According to the crew bosses and lieutenants, this strategy, the pinch, represents the most serious and costly violation of work rules by runners, and probably the most effective and profitable long term scam available to them. If a runner wishes to secure an income which goes very far beyond the $100 to $200 per day income level, including eliminating the risk of being disciplined by a superior, he must aspire to a different role. In order to do that, he must gather together some patronage

Table 3.3. The Heroin Trade for Runners

Informant	Career Length (Months)	Size of Crew	Chief Item Sold	Clients Per Day
K.	12	Solo	Dilaudid	25–50
L.	24	Dope Pad	Heroin	300–400
T.	12	5–6	Heroin	300–400
F.	24	3–6	Heroin	400–500
Bo.	24	2–3	Heroin	20–25
D.	8	3–6	Heroin	NA
I.	24	5–7	Heroin	20–50
Bu.	48	2–3	Heroin	20–25
N.	60	3–7	Heroin	50–60
Bn.	24	2–3	Heroin	20–40
P.	NA	3–4	Heroin	NA
E.	24	1–25	Heroin	20–50
G.	NA	6–8	Heroin	NA
Tk.	24	5–12	Heroin	20–30
C.	36	2–3	Heroin	50–60
Mean Values	26	5.1		136

power. Typically, a runner who was diligent and ambitious could, with effort, move up to the next level, the crew boss. The mobility-conscious runner who wanted to build a career aspired to that role.

The Crew Boss

The role of the crew boss was uniformly reported to be the most demanding and dangerous of all roles within the runner system. The crew boss is the immediate organizer and supervisor of the crew of runners selling "his" heroin. The crew boss has two primary sets of responsibilities: (1) he acts as the on-site manager and operator of his crew; and (2) he acts as the source of heroin, and therefore must maintain "contacts" either with independent suppliers or with a lieutenant in the organization. For the assumption of these increased duties and subsequent risks, the crew boss receives a substantially higher wage for his labor. The crew boss, additionally, does not have to work so visibly and openly on the street as do the runners. Nor does the crew boss have to deal directly with the consuming public. Table 3.4 gives some basic dimensions of the role of the crew boss. (See Note 3.)

The management and operation of the crew itself is a considerable responsibility. Among the duties of the crew boss are the following: (1)

Table 3.4. Characteristics of the Crew Boss

Informant	Age at Attainment to Crew Boss	Crew Size	Daily Sales Transactions	Earnings ($'s per day)
Bo.	21	2–3	250	600–700
Bn.	18	3–4	360	750–1000
E.	16	8–10	850	1000–1200
C.	19	6–7	850	800–900
N.	18	3–7	600	1200
Tk.	19	5–12	950	3000
F.	18	3–6	400	3000
T.	17	5–6	400	3000
Mean Values	18.25	5.5	582	1484

the crew boss has to locate and hire the runners; that is, he is the effective manager of personnel for the street operation; (2) he must serve in a protective role for the crew by organizing and planning for their security; (3) he must act as an internal discipline and control force between and among runners; (4) he acts in the role of accountant and treasurer; in this capacity he arranges for the drugs which are to be sold, and he deals with the financial matters pertaining to this; (5) he collects the money which the crew accrues through its sales activities; and (6) he determines the profit of the crew and serves in the role of paymaster in his relationship to the runners. These disbursements include not only payment to the crew of wages and commissions, but also payment for the cost of the heroin. These heroin costs were alternately reported as sometimes due "in front" (must be prepaid in full), or else consigned to the crew boss (who could pay after sales were completed). The crew boss held absolute responsibility in these areas.

An additional responsibility of the crew boss is the security not only of the crew itself, but the cache or "stash" of heroin, which is a valuable commodity itself. In smaller organizations, with less than five or six runners, the crew boss himself acted as the "gun" or protector and security agent in the runner operations. In this role the armed crew boss monitored the street sales area and the customer-runner interaction, keeping his runners and their inventory under surveillance. This, of course, also permitted him to observe the crew and discourage its members from any scams which they may be contemplating in the course of their work. When engaged as a security agent the crew boss typically left the heroin "stash" hidden in some physical location which permitted him to keep it under direct observation, but which made it unnecessary to actually keep it on his person. With this arrangement he could both keep himself and the heroin cache fairly secure and also conveniently re-supply the runners as they required new during their shift.

Crew runners who sold out their pocket inventory reported to the crew boss who either went to or sent them to the "stash" to restock the runner with more merchandise. During the course of these resupply efforts, it was also customary for the crew boss to collect the accumulated cash the runner was holding from his sales. The crew boss either held the money on his immediate person or would place it in the cache where he would keep it under observation. Crew bosses were, in this regard, tempting targets for predatory criminals. Crew bosses inevitably held a substantial amount of cash and/or drugs in their custody. The crew boss needed to always bear in mind this reality. This situation was further complicated by the fact that he might be "fingered" or deliberately targeted by a crew runner desiring to set him up for a "hit" or armed robbery.

The strategy of setting up a fellow syndicate member was reported as a risk of the role of crew boss. For example, it sometimes occurred when a runner was engaged in the scam of staging a robbery by cooperating with predators from outside the syndicate. Crew bosses all confirmed that such a set up was a hazard of the job. In a busy operation, the runner is important because he is a person who can locate or lure the crew boss into a vulnerable position where he may be the victim of waiting predators. Also, the runner is very likely to know or have a very good idea about the locale of the "stash" of money and heroin. The conspiring runner then can not only finger the crew boss, but he can often finger the stash as well.

It appears that when syndicate operations go awry, conspiracies take place among members of the syndicate who finger each other for various reasons. The kinds of events which appear to lead to these conspiratorial activities fall into three general categories: the breakdown of trust relationships among syndicate operatives, traumatic experiences in the sale operations, or the loss of or inability to account for money or drugs which have been extended on consignment to operatives by superiors or creditors. One interesting report in this regard concerns the setting up of an allegedly innocent runner as the explanation for the failure of a crew boss to pay off a lieutenant for a consignment of heroin. The crew boss has absolute responsibility for paying for heroin received by the crew. Loss of heroin on the street for any reason must be made good by the crew boss. This is especially critical when the heroin has been consigned in advance of cash payment, as is typical of bigger syndicate operations. Failure to pay cash for the consignment is the biggest or most extreme crisis a crew boss can face. In this instance the crew boss had used a large section of the cash proceeds from runners' sales to pay off a personal debt. When the lieutenant came around to collect the outstanding balance due, the crew boss could neither pay the cash nor return the merchandise. In an effort to save himself from the wrath of his superior, he explained the shortage of cash by claiming a particular runner had "set him up" by cooperating with some robbers who had stolen his money. The crew boss was able to convince the lieutenant of the truth of the incident, and as a consequence the lieutenant went out into the street where he killed the runner identified by the crew boss as the betrayer. The runner died with no knowledge of why he had been condemned.

Other such intrigues were reported by both runners and crew bosses, but not all so extreme as this case. Since money is the primary motive for participation in the syndicate, conspiracies inevitably revolve around financial gain. There is a certain ambivalent quality in the expressions of syndicate participants, who alternately talk in terms of tightly bonded social relationships with their syndicate "brothers," and then refer to the lack of trust and solidarity as reflected in the scams runners and crew bosses pull on each other. This variation in the emotional or affective expressions about syndicate relationships is interesting. The single major factor that was cited by syndicate members, in terms of what brought them into the syndicate, was some very close primary relation. One, for instance, would be brought to a crew boss by a close friend, or sibling, in order to "hire on" as a runner. There was not a single report of an individual being recruited into a syndicate of social strangers with whom he had no previous personal and generally positive social contact. To the extent there was social distance in the syndicate, it did not appear to extend beyond social knowledge through sibling or friendship contact.

Accounting for this ambivalence is problematic. It has been noted earlier that economic competition is one of the factors which contribute to this sentiment. It is also reasonable to argue that all illicit syndicates face this contradiction as a consequence of the illegality of their operation. The inability to have normal recourse to third-party resolution may contribute to the tension in such system, and exert a sort of "Hobbesian effect" upon social relationships (Albini and Mieczkowski, 1985).

Additionally, contradictory traits may be in operation in this system. The crew boss desires, of course, loyalty and obedience from his subordinates. But at the same time the nature of the work also require assertiveness, boldness, and "street smarts" in order to do a good a job. Thus, Tk. related the following as we sat one day in a car surveying the street scene in the neighborhood, watching the heroin traffic and right in its midst kids playing a roughhouse game of some sort. Tk. looked over to me and said, "You see that nigger over there, the big one?" I looked and saw a sturdy and boisterous 12-year-old. He was clearly the dominant child in a play group of 10 or 15. I nodded my head. "That's the kind I want. That's the kind I look for. See how smart he is? He's got them all under him, man. They afraid of him."

The crew boss was a patron to the runners who worked for him. Typically bosses were expected to actively manage the team effort of runners, much as any entrepreneurial business required management. Runners who performed exceptionally well expected to receive appropriate bonuses for their performances. The good crew boss provides these bonuses. They were sometimes outright cash payments, or sometimes expensive gifts, especially shoes, clothes, and jewelry. Sometimes, in cases where the crew boss owned an expensive and appealing automobile, the runner might receive the use of the car for a day or a weekend. The crew boss is also required periodically required to recruit new runners and integrate new and old runners into a harmonious whole. In the managerial role, the crew boss acts as a discipline agent, social regulator, arbiter, and reference.

In matters of controversy, the crew boss is judge and jury. It is absolutely essential that a crew boss have the respect and preferably the fear of the runners on his crew. Crew bosses generally reflected a managerial philosophy in regards to discipline that is typical of pragmatic business management. If a crew boss is good at his job, discipline is not a serious problem. This is because a well-operated crew is a self-disciplining mechanism. By gearing earning to sales in the form of wages plus bonuses, a motive is provided for the individual to have initiative in selling. By taking losses, such as result when an individual is "scamming" on the crew out of the gross earning before wages are paid or bonuses offered, the cost of any individual's cheating is felt in all wages. The crew boss then gets the runners to generate their own internal pressure towards conformity and away from perfidy. Of course, these techniques have the effect of reducing cheating, but not eliminating it entirely.

It is necessary for the crew boss to resort at times to other methods to maintain the syndicate organization, including active disciplining of runners who violate operational norms. Chiefly, in these cases, the crew boss relies upon the following mechanism (order reflects approximate frequency of use): (1) threats of violence; (2) active intimidation; (3) inflicting a beating without weapons; (4) inflicting a beating with a weapon; (5) wounding with a gunshot; and (5) killing with a gunshot. None of the informants who had functioned as crew bosses claimed to have committed a homicide against one of their own runners. But all crew bosses reported using some degree of physical violence in the course of their work. Crew bosses generally characterized the use of violence as a regrettable but necessary aspect of their role. They chiefly stressed the tactic of dramatic confrontation, displays of bravado (acting "wild"), and threats of violence. A typical illustration of this is the report of informant Bo. Bo. had a confrontation with a runner on his crew whom he had accused of "pinching" on his heroin consignment. In this case Bo. had drawn a gun, placed it against the runner's chest, and, cocking the hammer, threatened to "blow the motherfucker away." Bo. later told me he had no intention of really killing the runner for the offense, which he felt was minor. But he wished everyone, including the offending runner, to think he would kill for such an offense. The crew boss felt he had a lot to gain from having a "scandalous" reputation. This meant that the boss wanted the crew to think that, in anger, he became wild and impulsive and was capable of "anything".

It was not uncommon for a crew boss to express some consciousness of group identity in a positive light. For instance, he might typically refer to "us" in reference to the crew, or talk about his "brothers" who were the runners. Clearly, there was some feeling of a group identity, and a "we" consciousness that was an aspect of the syndicate. But this development was relatively subdued and arrested in comparison to the kind of identity that surrounds groups like the youth gang, or motorcycle groups like Hell's Angels. All informants replied negatively, for instance, when asked about their crew having a name for themselves. Likewise, they replied negatively when asked if the syndicate had a feeling of membership that was pronounced or formalized comparable to the street gangs typical of the city, like the B.K.'s or the Flynns. Crews were not very long-lived. They considered themselves an "old" organization if they operated continuously for a month. And it was not unusual for crew members who commented upon how "tight" or "together" the "brothers" on their crew were to immediately respond "crew" when asked if customers, police, or crew members represented the biggest source of operational problems for the boss.

Rip-offs were seen as dramatic and always a possibility, but the crew boss consistently blamed "scamming" by their own crew members as the single biggest financial loss in their operations. This was especially true of pinching, which crew bosses felt drove customers into the arms of competitors.

One crew boss described the dramatic disciplining of a runner who worked for him and who had pinched a pack of heroin a little too strongly. The customer, who had purchased several packs, returned complaining about the "count" he had received, especially in one of the packs. The crew boss examined the packs, and concurred with the customer that they indeed were short. The crew boss immediately laid the blame on the runner. He confronted the runner in the presence of the customer, who fingered the runner as the salesman he had bought from earlier. The crew boss then, in the customer's presence, "beat the shit out of" the runner to put it in the crew boss's terms. He then made good on the short-volume packs by exchanging them for new ones, and sent the now-satisfied customer on his way. The crew boss recounted that his performance in this matter was governed by a strategy with three aims. He wished to punish the runner for trying to scam on him. This, in turn, could be used as an example to the other runners who would be deterred from similar activity. Finally, this would not only produce a happy customer, but attract future customers, since this incident might be seen as a commitment to quality and integrity in the marketplace. For instance, it was alleged that one of the reasons for the original popularity of the early Young Boys, Inc., operatives was their "money-back guarantee" on the heroin they marketed. If you didn't like it you could bring back the remaining merchandise for a refund! Of the seven crew bosses in this study, only two indicated that they would outright refuse any reimbursement, exchange, or other arrangement in regard to customer claims on merchandise they were not satisfied with. Five of the informants who had experience as crew bosses took the position that should a customer provide reasonable evidence that the heroin had been tampered with or shorted by the crew runners, they would provide alternative merchandise.

In this study the crew bosses were, on the average, older than runners and were also uniformly experienced as runners themselves (see Tables 3.1 and 3.4). This experience of having started out as a runner gives the crew bosses an increased ability to manage and operate a crew of their own. Most informants responded to queries about their days as a runner in the form of treating it like an apprenticeship. Interestingly, individuals who were runners at the time of the study often talked of "learning" the technique of working a crew, and frequently expressed the overt desire to become a crew boss as soon as they had secured the necessary funds for a stash and the necessary expertise to cultivate both a following of runners and a source of heroin in quantity. The crew boss had to look in two directions. He had to look towards the crew as a responsibility, but he also had to look outward and/or upward in order to secure the quantity of heroin required to keep the crew busy and profitable. This brings the crew boss into contact with individuals who are more powerful than himself, in the patron-client meaning of that term. The crew boss requires either the patronage of a supplier or a lieutenant, just as the runner requires the patronage of the crew, and the addict requires the patronage of the runner.

Becoming a Crew Boss

Securing these patron-client contacts is an important prerequisite to becoming a crew boss, and represents a restricting requirement to securing this position for oneself. While attaining the patronage of a "big man" or "lieutenant" who can provide substantial quantities of heroin on a regular basis is essential in terms of the crew boss creating his patronage capabilities, it also represents some liabilities and costs.

To achieve patronage means one has a "big man" from whom one can secure heroin on a scale consistent with the requirements of the crew of runners. To acquire this patronage means the individual has the potential to receive substantially higher levels of income than any runner. For a runner to achieve this represents a major act of mobility and of "moving up" in the system. A runner who can accumulate enough savings from his earnings to make an initial purchase from a "big man" and who has garnered enough organizational experience and respect from his own activities as a runner stands a good chance of improving his income anywhere from three- to ten-fold.

To succeed on a large scale, the aspiring crew boss must have more than a substantial sum with which to pay for his initial investment expenses. A really big operation turns over large quantities of heroin, and the quick and efficient supplies which runners require make a line of credit from a supplier nearly mandatory. If cash on demand is the sole form of acceptable payment for heroin, the volume possibilities of the business are reduced tremendously. This is because sales are restricted by cash flow limitations rather than actual market demands. It is in the interest of both the syndicate patron and client to create a credit system to permit quick and maximal movement of heroin into the consumer market. The establishment of credit arrangements to accomplish this signifies the true establishment of the crew boss and a real career turning point.

For a runner to move into the role of crew boss it is essential that a complex series of patron-client relationships be cultivated. Crew bosses unanimously agreed with the assessment that contacts, in the form of finding patrons, are more difficult to establish than is the problem of raising the required cash for a purchase. A good contact is an individual who will provide heroin in large quantities on a regular and dependable basis. The best sort of contact is one that will do this on credit as well, being content to wait until the crew boss has sold the drugs and collected the cash from the consumer before receiving payment.

In this study, the crew bosses reported two routes by which they came to achieve their role position. These are the self-started mode and the recruited mode. Self-starters are highly motivated, entrepreneurially oriented individuals who are ambitious in their pursuit of wealth and participate in syndicate operations of their own making. Starting as runners, they come to realize by experience the income possibilities available to them if they can create for themselves high levels of patronage power. They seek to attain patronage power to build a syndicate. By saving their earnings as runners, and by seeking out contacts with independent wholesalers of heroin, self-starters begin their climb by securing several ounces of heroin in a cash purchase. This quantity will be inflated by the purchaser by a "cut." It will then be packaged and consigned to a crew of assembled runners. This crew of runners will be made up of very young teenagers, most of whom the aspiring self-starter will know as a former colleague, a social friend, a relative, or so on. This style of operation is for some crew bosses a permanent form of operation. This is especially true of the smaller (two- or three-runner) crews. When crews reach the size of five, six, or seven, a fission process has a tendency to take place, breaking the crew into small units once again. Large crews which persist intact over longer periods appear to be rarer than the smaller entrepreneurial crews of self-starters. Large crews which persist over time are the appendages of a larger style of syndicate, although in terms of retail activity they operate the same as small crews.

These large crews consist of sizable groups of runners (from 6 or 7 up to 20 to 25) who are recruited and managed by crew bosses, who in turn work for a superior official referred to as a "lieutenant." The lieutenant, in turn, works for another superordinate, the "big man." The lieutenant actively manages several crews all of who are "owned" by the "big man." It appears, based on reports from informants, that these big syndicates may have under their control several hundred runners, organized into several crews. These large syndicates appear to be an active and important force in the heroin trade, but they are not capable of monopolizing the trade. The most generous estimate that informants gave in regard to the percentage of supply attributable to the big operations was 60%. The Young Boys, Inc. are an example of one of these large syndicate operations. There appears to be a tendency for the media to focus exclusively on these large operations, and to consider heroin distribution to be nearly single-handedly their domain. Not only does this sort of distortion happen, but through the process of retrospective interpretation, many independent dealers are labeled with the terms applicable to the large syndicate, even when they are not a part of the organization. As one informant put it, "anybody who is Black and young and selling dope is a Young Boy."

Conclusions

This paper reports three interesting and unusual findings. Perhaps most noteworthy is the fact that the street selling network in Detroit is staffed by individuals who do not use heroin, and who in general lack an ideology for the approval of heroin use. Second, these networks are, relative to the "hustler-oriented" models, more structured. In actual operation they are rather bureaucratic in form. It is noted that they are relatively short-lived, however, and therefore bear some resemblance to the more fluid "hustler" conception of drug distribution. Last, these networks are staffed by relatively young operatives, which is also rather rarely reported (Geberth, 1978).

The argument for the runner system's appearance and popularity in Detroit is based upon viewing the heroin distribution mechanism as an evolving social organization which adapts to and exploits advantages afforded to it by the social environment in which it operates. The runner system represents, in this view, an improvement over the older system, the dope-pad style of heroin distribution. The runner system is a superior strategic system. First, it allows the narcotics operatives to escape the disadvantageous confinement of the dope pad and renders police surveillance and control more difficult. A second advantage is that by taking the trade out into the streets directly, a larger volume of sales can be accomplished per unit time, and thus it is a more attractive economic approach to retailing. A third advantage is that the use of minors as street operatives reduces legal difficulties for syndicate executives, who themselves are adults. While the informant population in this study consisted of both adults and minor runners and crew bosses, it was widely reported that minors were actively sought with this conscious purpose in mind. Additionally, not only do crew bosses and other syndicate executives see this legal advantage, but they believe that minors will work more cheaply and are easier to regulate and control than adult operatives.

In this regard it is reasonable to contend that the appearance of YBI-style syndicates is a rational innovation in the Mertonian sense of accomplishing legitimate social goals, the creation of a profit-generating business, by utilizing socially disapproved means (Merton, 1968). Viewed in this fashion it is also reasonable to expect that such a system, if it proves to be a continuing success, will spread as a consequence of it competitive advantages in the heroin-selling subculture. Clearly, such a development is of importance, not only for its criminological interest, but because of the social policy implications it may bring with it. How does such a system fit into the assumptions and operating principles of the juvenile justice system? In what ways will the social views of heroin, heroin abuse, and the role of the state in the regulation of such substances be altered?

Finally, it is worth noting that street ethnography, a genre into which this research effort can be grouped, has been instrumental in clarifying and illuminating the drug subculture and its actual methods of operation. The value of this methodological approach is confirmed once again. Yet, as has been argued, this research is the most difficult and the least supported of all forms of sociological investigation (Shafir, 1980). Perhaps it is feasible that funding, grants, and the kinds of emphasis given to the varieties of sociological method in graduate education could be turned with more intensity towards cultivating such research skills and practices in contemporary sociology.

Notes

1. The interviews were initiated through the help of a volunteer intermediary who was a life-long resident of the community under study. After a period of pre-arranged contacts and some time spent in the field as an observer, a snowball effect began to take hold and informants themselves began to come forward voluntarily. The methodology of this study, and some similar studies, will be presented in greater detail in a paper currently in preparation with Dr. Joseph Albini.

2. As the reader can see, there is substantial variability among some of the reported data in this table, and in some of the others as well. Informants T. and F. consistently reported both dollar and customer figures which the author found to be rather high, relative to other informants. However, their replies are included for the sake of completeness.

3. Again, one notes that T. and F. report figures which seem relatively high.

References

Agar, Michael, 1973. Ripping and Running. New York: Seminar Press.

Albini, Joseph and Tom Mieczkowski, 1985. Vigilantism and homicide. Presented at the annual meetings of the American Society of Criminology.

Detroit Health Department Bureau of Substance Abuse, 1983. Long Range Target Strategy 1983–1988. Detroit: City Coordinating Agency.

Feldman, Harvey, 1977. A neighborhood history of drug switching. In Robert Weppner (ed.), Street Ethnography. Hollywood: Sage.

Geberth, Vernon, 1978. The quarterkids. Law and Order 20, 9: 42–56.

Goldstein, Paul, 1981. Getting over: Economic alternatives to predatory crime among street drug users. In James Inciardi (ed.), The Drugs Crime Connection. Hollywood: Sage.

Gould, Leroy, Andrew Walker, Lansing Crane, and Charles Litz, 1974. Connections: Notes from The Heroin World. New Haven: The Yale Press.

Hanson Bill, George Beschner, James Walters, and Elliot Bovelle, 1985. Life with Heroin: Voices from the Inner City. Lexington, Mass.: Lexington Books.

Johnson, Bruce D., Paul Goldstein, Edward Preeble, James Schmeidler, Douglas Lipton, Barry Spunt, and Thomas Miller, 1985. Taking Care Of Business: The Economics of Crime by Heroin Abusers. Lexington, Mass.: Lexington Books.

Merton, Robert, 1968. Social Theory and Social Structure. New York: The Free Press.

Mieczkowski, Tom, 1983. Syndicated crime in the Caribbean: A case study. In Gordon Waldo (ed.) Career Criminals. Hollywood: Sage.

Mieczkowski, Tom, 1985. Street selling heroin: The Young Boys technique in a Detroit neighborhood. Unpublished doctoral dissertation. Detroit: Wayne State University.

Preeble, Edward and John Casey, 1969. Taking care of business: The heroin user's life on the street. The International Journal of the Addictions 4, 1: 1–24.

Redlinger, Lawrence, 1975. Marketing and distributing heroin: Some sociological observations. Journal of Psychedelic Drugs 7, 4: 331–353.

Shafir, William, 1980. Fieldwork Experience. New York: St. Martin's Press.

Smith, R.B. and Richard Stephens, 1976. Drug Use and hustling: A study of their interrelationship. Criminology 14, 2: 155–175.

Sutker, Patricia, 1974. Field observations of a heroin addict: A case study. American Journal of Community Psychology 2, 1:221–240.

Sutter, Alan, 1969. Worlds of drug use on the street scene. In Donald Cressey and Douglas Ward (eds.) Delinquency, Crime, and Social Process. New York: Harper Row.

Chapter 4

Theory into Practice I: Building Communities

In the previous two chapters, a number of theories that have examined issues related to space, time, and crime have been explored. Chapter 2 introduced the ideas of the Chicago School theorists as they tried to explain crime and other social problems based on neighborhood characteristics. In Chapter 3, a number of choice theories were presented that examined how a motivated rational offender finds and selects suitable targets. The next two chapters move beyond the sometimes-abstract theoretical principles and into practical applications. As discussed in the following chapters, a number of programs stem from the thoughts of Shaw and McKay, Cornish and Clarke, Cohen and Felson, Patricia and Paul Brantingham, and others who have studied the relationship between crime and place. For ease of presentation, the various programs are divided into three general categories: 1) programs designed to build communities; 2) programs designed to prevent crime through target hardening; and 3) programs designed to enhance law enforcement tactics (which will be presented in the third unit on crime analysis and crime mapping). In this chapter, programs designed to build communities will be presented.

Building Communities

As explained in Chapter 2, Shaw and McKay tried to explain why juvenile delinquency and other social problems seemed to be concentrated in certain areas within the city of Chicago. Higher levels of infant mortality, tuberculosis, mental disorders, poverty, and residential turnover were just a few of the conditions facing residents living in the inner city zones. The term social disorganization was used to describe a condition in which neighbors do not know their neighbors, nor do they share a common set of norms and values. Shaw and McKay's theory had very obvious practical implications: In order to reduce crime and improve social conditions in areas marked by social disorganization, programs designed to build community ties and enhance social cohesion were needed. If local residents had a real sense of community, then the mechanisms of informal social control could be used to keep peoples' behavior in check, especially with respect to the monitoring of juveniles growing up in the area.

The Chicago Area Project (CAP)

In 1932, Clifford Shaw took his theoretical ideas to the streets of the city of Chicago in the form of the **Chicago Area Project (CAP)**. The goal of Shaw and CAP was (and continues to be) a noble one: "To work toward the prevention and eradication of juvenile delinquency through the development and support of affiliated local community self-help efforts, in communities where the need is greatest" (http://chicagoareaproject.org). From its humble roots as an experimental program in three low-income areas, the CAP has grown to serve as an umbrella organization with over 40 affiliated social service agencies and various special programs aimed at curbing juvenile delinquency and other social problems through community organization (See Box 4.1 for a further discussion of CAP).

Box 4.1. The Chicago Area Project: The Legacy Lives On

The Chicago Area Project is the longest running community based delinquency prevention program in the United States. The goal of CAP is to develop and oversee special projects and encourage the growth of locally-controlled organizations that seek to improve the quality of life for residents of the city of Chicago and surrounding Cook County. The CAP model is based on the premise that a child has the best opportunity for a successful, productive life when all residents of a community work in a positive, cooperative manner to care for and watch over the children growing up within that community. To achieve the goal of building cooperation among community residents, the CAP has a number of affiliated community organizations, programs, and special projects that fall under its organizational structure. The following is a description of a few of the components of the modern-day CAP:

African American Male Rites of Passage (ROP). This Afrocentrically-based program is designed to assist African American males, ages 14 to 21, in the development of life skills necessary to lead an independent life. Many of the participating youths reside in group homes or foster care. Youths are provided instruction in a number of topical areas, including African and African/American history, financial management and budgeting, problem solving skills, interpersonal relations, conflict resolution, taking responsibility for their actions, and pre-employment training. Participants also attend a two-day retreat and, upon successful completion of the program, attend a graduation ceremony where they are welcomed by members of their community and praised for their commitment to live their life based on the principles taught through the ROP. After graduation, the youths are eligible to receive other CAP services, such as vocational training, job placement, and assistance with housing.

Community Organizing (CO). Community Organizing is a CAP program whose specific charge is community development. Workers and organizers with the CO initiative are assigned to neighborhoods experiencing high rates of delinquency, poverty, and other conditions related to social disorganization. The CO representative provides technical assistance to local residents who are encouraged to participate in the identification of problems and possible solutions. The ultimate goal is to develop a neighborhood-based organized group that can take ownership of their community and maintain its development and continued improvement. CO assists local residents in providing conferences, training, programs and other special events designed to enhance the quality of life for neighborhood youths and adults.

Youth as Resources (YAR).YAR is a program for young people ages 5 to 21. The goal of YAR is to get youths involved in the identification of problems within their own communities and develop solutions. Instead of adults telling the youths what to do, the program asks the youths to take on the responsibility of shaping their own roles in their communities. The underlying philosophy is that if youths know that they can contribute to the improvement of their own neighborhoods, they will be more likely to get involved. YAR includes three components: community service, in which youths identify and implement projects to improve the quality of life in their own communities; service learning, which is a school based component that ties the community projects to academic learning; and violence prevention. Since its inception in 1968, YAR has funded over a hundred different projects that have impacted the lives of thousands of young people in the Chicago area. YAR programs have worked successfully in a variety of environments, including public housing communities such as Robert Taylor Homes, juvenile correctional facilities, and schools. Additionally, YAR works with juvenile female offenders, assisting them with their transition back into the community to ultimately lead productive lives as full participating members of their neighborhoods.

For more information on these and other programs, please see the website for the Chicago Area Project at http://chicagoareaproject.org.

From the inception of CAP, the neighborhood was the focal point of operation. Once a neighborhood was identified for intervention, Shaw and his colleagues set out to identify and draw upon pre-existing community resources: the most influential residents and the most powerful institutions within that particular community (like a church, community center, local businesses, or other central point for local community activities). The overarching philosophy was to bring together community leaders and local resources to achieve three goals: to bring positive adult role models into contact with local juveniles, to provide local residents with resources to assist with child rearing and juvenile delinquency prevention, and to encourage communication between local residents and various institutional representatives who could provide needed benefits and resources to the community (Bursik & Grasmick, 1993). Through these conscious efforts to organize the local residents, Shaw believed that the natural ability of the community to develop and enforce norms of social control would be enhanced (Vold, Bernard, & Snipes, 2002).

One of CAPs more innovative (and controversial) approaches was to recruit local community leaders to serve as "indigenous workers." It was the job of the indigenous worker to organize local residents to achieve the goals of CAP. The utilization of indigenous workers offered a number of benefits. As a local resident, the indigenous worker would already have intimate knowledge of the neighborhood. The indigenous worker would be able to identify the local hangouts for juveniles as well as the kids who were headed for trouble. Additionally, the indigenous worker would be accepted by the local residents, and would not generate the same level of scrutiny, suspicion, and resentment that an outsider would (Kobrin, 1959).

While the idea to use local residents to staff the centers seemed like a good idea, there were some problems. Professional social workers felt that the use of untrained workers was unwise and potentially harmful to the youths (Bennett, 1981; Kobrin, 1959). What made this issue particularly sticky was that the character of some of the indigenous workers was called into question. In some instances, individuals with serious criminal records were placed into positions of authority within the community organizations. The public did not favor such appointments, nor did the professional social workers who felt that their positions were being taken away by ex-convicts with no education or professional experience (Bursik & Grasmick, 1993; Sorrentino & Whittaker, 1994).

Nevertheless, the CAP initiated a number of positive experiences for youths, including sports and recreational programs, summer camps, scouting activities, arts and crafts workshops and other opportunities to engage in legitimate activities. Local youths were encouraged to interact with community adults who would supervise their activities and serve as positive role models for behavior. Detached workers were recruited to work closely with neighborhood kids, especially targeting youths known to be gang members. Much like the indigenous workers, detached workers were often local residents who had little or no formal training in working with juveniles. Detached workers were expected to work with gang members during after school and evening hours, providing "curbside counseling," supervision, and to serve as stable, positive role models for conventional behavior (Bursik & Grasmick, 1993; Schlossman & Sedlak, 1983).

The CAP was truly a noble effort to reduce juvenile delinquency in the city of Chicago's socially disorganized areas. Unfortunately, the effectiveness of the CAP to reduce the level of juvenile crime has been described as negligible at best (Hope, 1995; Lundman, 1993). Schlossman, Zellman & Shavelson (1984) noted that as time passed Shaw himself relied less and less on official statistical reports of juvenile delinquency to demonstrate the overall effectiveness of the CAP's efforts. However, in analyses of the overall impact of programs similar to the CAP that were launched in other major cities, evaluators reported a number of positive results. Youths in the similar programs were provided with opportunities to interact with positive adult role models, had structured vocational and recreational activities available to them, and were given the opportunity to learn various problem-solving techniques (Curran & Renzetti, 2001; Miller, 1962).

Despite its shortcomings, the CAP was and continues to be an important community crime prevention strategy. Many of the strategies employed by Shaw, while controversial at the time, have become commonplace in a variety of community outreach programs (Bursik & Grasmick, 1993).

Empowerment Zones and Enterprise Communities

The general guiding principle of reorganizing and rebuilding communities towards the goal of self-help can be found in many contemporary crime prevention efforts, most recently in federal programs designed to assist economically disadvantaged communities designated as Empowerment Zones and Enterprise Communities. Empowerment Zones (EZ) and Enterprise Communities (EC) are large-scale programs funded through the Department of Housing and Urban Development (HUD) of the United States federal government. While the emphasis of many of these programs is on economic development, others focus on promoting social services and overall community improvement (Howell & Hawkins, 1998). This is a relatively new strategy in which tax incentives are offered to businesses willing in invest in geographically small, economically depressed areas (Sherman et al., 1997).

As of 1995, 35 states had adopted EZ/EC legislation that offers incentives to businesses to relocate or expand in economically challenged areas and hire local residents (Wilder & Rubin, 1996). The state of Florida was the first to adopt such legislation, offering a number of tax benefits and financial incentives to businesses that would create jobs in designated EZ/EC zones. The state of Florida offered corporate income tax and sales tax credits for companies that hired individuals living in EZ/EC zones and provided property tax credits for businesses to relocate to designated areas.

Designating an EZ/EC area is dependent upon a number of factors, including unemployment rates, poverty rates, median incomes, number of individuals receiving welfare or other government assistance, level of property abandonment, and level of population decline (Sherman et al., 1997). Today, many of the EZ/EC designated areas are located in high crime inner cities, although the program has expanded to include rural areas with few opportunities for legitimate employment.

Once designated as an EZ/EC area, the local community is eligible to receive a variety of state and federal dollars designed to improve the quality of life in the area. For example, the Youth Out of the Education Mainstream Program provides special assistance to schools located in EZ/EC areas. Training for students and staff is provided in the areas of truancy, school discipline, on-campus violence, and overall school safety. Other programs have provided employment training for public housing residents, youth leadership and development programs, and anti-crime and anti-drug use programs for youths living in EZ/EC designed areas (Coordinating Council and Juvenile Justice Delinquency Prevention, 1996). For a description of a special program used in a Boston, Massachusetts, EZ/EC designated area, see Box 4.2.

Box 4.2. Boston SafeFutures Program

The SafeFutures program is designed to develop and enhance partnerships between public and private agencies, churches, civic and business groups, and local residents to address the special needs of at-risk and delinquent youths. The goal is to coordinate whatever resources are available from the state and federal government as well as the private sector to prevent and intervene in acts of juvenile delinquency. Some of the funding has been specifically earmarked to assist areas designated as Empowerment Zones/Enterprise Communities.

The city of Boston, Massachusetts was awarded funds for a SafeFutures program in the Blue Hill Corridor area, which was previously identified as an EZ/EC area. The economically challenged area has been burdened with high levels of poverty, unemployment, violent criminal activity, and a serious gang problem. The resources from a number of partners are being coordinated in an effort to create a youth-centered services delivery system. These partners include area residents, local schools, the Boston Police Department, the local district attorney's office, various community action groups, and the Boston Coalition, a citywide crime prevention planning process. The Boston SafeFutures Program includes the following components:

Treatment/Enforcement: This component will involve the creation of a day treatment center to serve about 100 youths per year, enhancement of the juvenile justice system and the availability of aftercare services such as counseling and job training, expansion of the availability of mental heath services, and greater enforcement of juvenile probation conditions.

Prevention/Early Intervention: Working with the local schools, health centers, youth programs and other community-based organizations, a number of new delinquency prevention programs will be developed and other pre-existing programs will be enhanced. These programs will involve vocational training, recreational activities, mentoring programs, and family strengthening programs.

At-Risk and Delinquent Girls: This is a comprehensive program designed to meet the special needs of at-risk and delinquent girls. Services will include educational enhancement, recreational activities, mentoring, health education, vocational assistance, and individual, group, and family counseling.

Gang-Free Schools and Communities: A number of community partners will assist in providing educational programs to local residents in reducing gang activities in their neighborhoods. Alternative educational placements will be created for youths at high risk of gang activities. Additionally, job training and vocational assistance will be provided for youths living in federally subsidized housing projects.

For additional information on this and other SafeFutures Communities, see the Office of Juvenile Justice and Delinquency Prevention website at http://ojjdp.ncjrs.org/.

As noted by Sherman et al. (1997), EZ/EC programs are designed to assist local residents and their neighborhoods. By stimulating the local economy, local residents have a variety of legitimate employment opportunities available to them, thereby reducing the pressure to resort to criminal activities in order to earn a living. These new jobs offer hope to the youths growing up in economically depressed areas, and enhance their motivation to learn the skills and training required to perform such jobs. Ultimately, the improved economic conditions lead to increased interactions among local residents and strengthen neighborhood resources, including churches, schools, and other local businesses. Since many business owners avoid high crime areas, the reduction in crime in successful EZ/EC program areas brings new businesses to the community. In the spirit of the CAP, the economic development results in the natural growth of informal social control.

How effective are these programs at building local communities? Sherman et al. (1997) reviewed the evaluations of a number of such initiatives. Since the EZ/EC programs are relatively new, few evaluations of their effectiveness exist. In the eleven studies that were examined, the results were generally positive. Employment opportunities and commercial investments increased in the targeted zones, sometimes dramatically so. Papke (1992) found a long-term decline of 19 percent in the unemployment rates in a number of Indiana cities that had enterprise zones. In contrast, Boarnet and Bogart (1995) found no change in the level of unemployment or property values in areas designated as enterprise zones in the state of New Jersey.

But what about the impact on crime and delinquency? Sherman et al. (1997) concluded that EZ/EC programs are promising as a crime prevention program if the program is designed with that specific goal in mind. The idea behind EZ/EC programs—to rebuild economically depressed areas—may provide a necessary ingredient in the overall plan to reduce crime and improve the overall quality of life in these areas.

In addition to the EZ/EC programs, a number of federal and state agencies have funds set aside specifically for the development and empowerment of local neighborhoods. The Office of Juvenile Justice and Delinquency Prevention (1995) lists over 50 different community based initiatives funded through a variety of federal agencies, including the Department of Justice, the Department of Health and Human Services, the Department of Education, the Department of Labor, the Department of the Interior, as well as a number of private funding agencies.

Building Communities and the Role of Law Enforcement Agencies

In this section, the efforts of the Department of Justice to build communities through partnerships with local law enforcement agencies will be explored. Over the past 30 years or so, a revolution of sorts has been taking place in the delivery of services by the American law enforcement industry. The phrase "community policing" is now a common element of the language of policing. One cannot discuss contemporary issues in policing without devoting a good deal of time to the topic. But just what is meant by the phrase "community policing?" How does community policing fit in with rebuilding communities and reducing levels of social disorganization? Because organizational issues associated with the adoption of a community policing philosophy will come up again and again in this text (especially with respect to geographic accountability and the role of crime analysis), a good deal of attention is devoted to the topic.

The Rise of Contemporary Community Policing

Since its origination in the late 1970s and early 1980s, community policing has become a commonplace practice in both rural and urban police departments. Walker (1999) argued that community policing and problem-oriented policing (a closely related philosophy) emerged in response to a number of crises in the American policing industry. First and foremost, the turbulent era of the 1960s was a public relations nightmare for law enforcement agencies, especially in minority communities. Riots rocked many major cities, and many of the triggering events for the violent uprisings could be traced to an unpleasant exchange between a police officer and a citizen. A number of federal inquiries were conducted into the practices of the police, including the President's Crime Commission (1967), the Kerner Commission (1968), and the National Advisory Commission on Criminal Justice Standards and Goals (1973). These evaluations of the police suggested that a change from the more traditional "professional model" of law enforcement was needed to overcome the feelings of mistrust and animosity that many citizens harbored towards the police.

The **professional model of policing** was popularized by August Vollmer, who was the chief of police of the Berkley, California police department in the early 1900s. Vollmer was quite a visionary in the science of policing and a pioneer in the area of crime analysis. Prior to the professionalism era, the police had been involved in a number of social service functions, such as feeding the hungry and housing the less fortunate. Vollmer felt that the enforcement of the law should be the primary responsibility of the police, not social work. Vollmer's vision of the ideal police officer was a college-educated, crime fighting professional that would interact with citizens in an impartial, neutral manner. Discretion would be highly regulated in an organizational environment based on a para-military model (Bartollas & Hahn, 1999; Schafer, 2002).

In theory, Vollmer's ideal professional police officer did not sound bad at all. An educated, highly trained professional would apply the law without regard to race, creed, gender, or other extra legal factors. There would be no room for "alternative courses of action" or the use of discretion. Today, an officer confronted by a number of juveniles drinking beer in an abandoned house may tell the kids to pour out the beer and go home. The law requires that the officer take a certain course of action, namely to take the juveniles into custody and charge them with a number of offenses: possession of alcohol, trespassing, perhaps a curfew violation. Under the professional model, the officer would have been provided little or no individual decision-making in the application of the law. A law violation is a law violation, and the law must be enforced.

Additionally, in order for officers to maintain a professional distance from the citizenry, Vollmer advocated that patrol officers should be rotated from district to district. Since the primary responsibility of the patrol officer was impartial enforcement of the law, close personal relationships with the citizens in a beat or zone would make this task difficult. The end result of this philosophy was that officers did not know residents of the local community, nor were they encouraged to get to know them. Officers were often perceived as aloof and distant from the citizens they were assigned to protect and to serve.

In addition to the crisis of police-community relations, Walker (1999) also attributed the growth of community policing to a number of studies and reports that called the effectiveness of traditional police patrol practices into question. Throughout the 1960s and 1970s, the nation had experienced a rather dramatic increase in the level of crime, especially violent crime (Cohen & Felson, 1979). This crime wave placed even greater demands on the police to "do something" to reduce crime. The usual response to citizen demands to "do something" about crime normally results in an increase in the level of patrol activity in high crime areas.

In the mid-1970s, the results of one of the most influential pieces of police research were released which seriously questioned the effectiveness of routine police patrol activities. The results of the Kansas City Preventive Patrol Experiment (Kelling, Pate, Dieckman, & Brown,

1974) suggested that even dramatic increases in the level of routine patrol activity had little or no impact on crime. Even more interesting was the fact that the public did not perceive increases (or decreases) in the level of patrol in their local communities. Citizens did not feel any more or less safe in their neighborhood based on changes in police presence. As we shall see, fear of crime can have a crippling effect on neighborhood cohesion and the overall quality of life in communities. If increases in the level of patrol do not significantly reduce crime or levels of fear, then something else must be done. Because of the significance of the Kansas City Preventive Patrol experiment, a detailed description of this study may be found in Box 4.3.

Box 4.3. The Kansas City Preventive Patrol Experiment

"This study is a bunch of horse-pucky."

—Former Chief of Police in a mid-sized Southern police agency.

Even introductory courses in criminology include something about the Kansas City Preventive Patrol Experiment. This research study can only be described as a classic in the study of policing. Whenever crime rates increased, the standing cry from sheriffs and police chiefs was (and continues to be) to request more funds for more patrol officers on the street. Prior to the Preventive Patrol Experiment, the blind assumption by police professionals and the general public was that routine police patrols had a significant impact on the level of crime in an area. If you've got a crime problem in a neighborhood or district, simply send more officers to the area. Well, the results of the Preventive Patrol Experiment seriously called this assumption into question.

In 1971, a task force of patrol officers and supervisors within the Kansas City Police Department was faced with a number of serious crime problems, especially in its South Patrol Division. The task force members felt that if attention was focused on a few pressing issues in the South Division, then the resources available for routine patrol activities within the Division would suffer. It was during these discussions that some of the task force members began to question what impact, if any, routine patrol activities had on criminal activity in an area. The Kansas City Police Department requested and was awarded funds from the Police Foundation in order to conduct an experiment on the true impact of patrol. In addition to the effects of patrol on criminal activity, the task force and research team were also interested in measuring the effects of patrol on a number of other variables, including citizen fear, citizen behavior as a result of fear, and citizen perception of police services.

Without getting too technical, there are a number of ways of testing whether or not a change in the level of patrol activities has any impact on the level of crime, feelings of citizen security, or other variables of interest. Some of these research designs can produce results that are "better" than others. One of the reasons that this study has become such a classic is the type of research design that was selected: a **strong, quasi-experimental design**. Given the research situation, this was the strongest, "best" design that the research team could have selected.

The South Patrol division was divided into 24 beats. The research team sat down and took a look at the demographics of these 24 areas and determined that nine of the beats were unrepresentative of the rest of the city. The remaining 15 beats were then divided up into five groups containing three beats. In order to be assigned as part of one of the five groups, the three beats were matched up with each other based on a number of characteristics including crime data, number of calls for service, ethnic and racial diversity, median income, and residential stability.

The research team had three different patrol levels in mind: reactive patrol, proactive patrol, and a "control" condition which maintained the usual level of patrol activity. Within each of the five groups of three beats, one beat was assigned to the reactive condition, one to the proactive condition, and one to the control condition. This matching process, while seemingly cumbersome, was one of the strongest aspects of the study. If the research team had not assigned matched beats to the different conditions, they might have ended up with all high crime areas experiencing the reactive condition or the poorest areas receiving the proactive patrol. By matching the beats, the research team tried their best to remove any influence that pre-existing neighborhood characteristics could have had on the results.

The research team ended up with three experimental conditions with five beats assigned to each. In the reactive condition, there was no preventive patrol as is traditionally thought of. Officers did not randomly drive around in the beats, looking for suspicious activity. The only time that a patrol vehicle went into these beats was to answer a call for service, handle the call, and then leave the beat. During the times that the officer was not answering a call for service he or she was told to patrol the boundary of the reactive beat or to go to the beats assigned to the proactive condition.

In the five beats assigned to the proactive patrol condition, the level of police presence was two to three times the normal level. Additional patrol vehicles had been assigned here, and officers from the adjacent reactive beats were instructed to patrol the area as well. Finally, in the five beats assigned to the control condition, the normal level of patrol was maintained.

In order to explore the effects of patrol level on crime and citizen perceptions, the research team used a variety of techniques, including surveys, interviews, observations, and official departmental statistics. To many police practitioners and researchers, the results of the study were almost unbelievable. With a few rare exceptions, changes in the level of patrol had no impact on the level of reported crime (as measured by both official departmental statistics and interviews with citizens), arrest patterns, fear of crime, protective behaviors by citizens in response to their fear of crime, and citizen satisfaction with the police. Even response time was unaffected by changes in the level of routine preventive patrol.

In sum, the results of the Kansas City Preventive Patrol Experiment concluded that simply increasing the level of routine preventive patrol in an area had little or no impact on the level of crime, citizen attitudes, or their behavior. The dramatic findings fueled the fire for police agencies to question their underlying philosophies and re-think how police services could be more effective. This study not only increased the interest in community policing, but also enhanced interest in crime analysis and other "smart" policing tools.

Of course, it should be noted that not all police practitioners "buy into" the findings of this study. As the quote at the beginning of this section indicates, despite contrary evidence some police administrators maintain the traditional belief that the only way to win the war on crime is to send in more troops. Community policing, crime analysis, and crime mapping are nothing more than fads that have no real impact on crime. The police chief's quote was repeated to me by students enrolled in a Policy Analysis class that I was teaching. During my lecture, I had spent several hours presenting the Kansas City Preventive Patrol Experiment, discussing the strengths of the design, the findings, and its impact on the future of policing. I noticed that several of the students were laughing. When questioned, the students reported that a local police chief had covered the experiment in their Police Administration class the night before, and had summarized the results in just seven words: "This study is a bunch of horse-pucky."

Study description and results adapted from Kelling, F., Pate, T., Dieckman, D. & Brown, C. (1974). The Kansas City Preventive Patrol Experiment: A Summary Report. Washington, D.C.: Police Foundation.

"Broken Windows" and Broken Communities

A few years after the results of the Kansas City Preventive Patrol Experiment were released, a second influential thought-piece on police practices was published. To this day, James Q. Wilson and George Kelling's "Broken Windows: The Police and Neighborhood Safety" essay continues to impact many police practices. The focus of their essay was how police services have changed over the years from a personal, hands-on delivery of order-maintenance to a more impersonal crime-control orientation.

Wilson and Kelling (1982) argued that foot patrols, which had almost disappeared from use with the arrival of the automobile, provided a better means of delivering police services. Based on observations and interviews with Newark, New Jersey officers assigned to foot patrol, officers who walked their beats had greater opportunity to interact informally with members of a neighborhood than officers who drove around in a patrol vehicle. These one-on-one interactions allowed the officers to identify who belonged in a neighborhood and who did not. "Strangers" were watched closely, and the "decent folk" who were neighborhood regulars were able to work with their beat officer to develop acceptable rules for conduct. Different neighborhoods may have had very different rules for behavior, and it was up to the officer to work with the local residents to find out what rules worked best in that particular area.

The goal of the foot patrol officer was to increase the level of public order in the neighborhood that they were assigned to. Wilson and Kelling argued that crime and disorder are closely tied to each other, hence the "broken windows" analogy. If someone breaks a window and that window is left unrepaired, then in a short time all of the other windows will soon be broken. An unrepaired broken window sends the signal that "no one cares." Ultimately, this leads to the breakdown of informal community control. Wilson and Kelling (1982:31) describe the community deterioration that may result from a broken window or other physical signs of disorder:

> A stable neighborhood of families who care for their homes, mind each other's children, and confidently frown on unwanted intruders can change, in a few years or even a few months, to an inhospitable and frightening jungle. A piece of property is abandoned, weeds grow up, a window is smashed. Adults stop scolding rowdy children; the children, emboldened, become more rowdy. Families move out, unattached adults move in. Teenagers gather in front of the corner store. The merchant asks them to move; they refuse. Fights occur. Litter accumulates. People start drinking in front of the grocery; in time, an inebriate slumps to the sidewalk and is allowed to sleep it off. Pedestrians are approached by panhandlers.

> At this point it is not inevitable that serious crime will flourish or violent attacks on strangers will occur. But many residents will think that crime, especially violent crime, is on the rise, and they will modify their behavior accordingly. They will use the streets less often, and when on the streets will stay apart from their fellows moving with averted eyes, silent lips, and hurried steps. "Don't get involved." For some residents, this growing atomization will matter little, because the neighborhood is not their "home" but "the place where they live."

Once urban decay begins, it is very difficult in contemporary times to turn things around. Wilson and Kelling noted that in previous centuries, neighborhood level increases in crime and disorder had a sort of built-in correction mechanism. People could rarely leave their neighborhoods, so the residents would be forced to reclaim their turf. Now, if a neighborhood deteriorates, anyone who has the ability to leave the area will move, leaving behind the elderly, the very poor, or those whose ability to move are blocked by prejudice.

Disorder, Fear of Crime, and the Role of the Police

Disorder, crime, fear of crime, neighborhood deterioration, and social disorganization all go hand in hand. Skogan (1986; 1990) described both human forms of disorder and physical forms of disorder. Human forms of disorder may include such things as groups of teenagers hanging out on street corners, street prostitution, panhandling, public drinking, open gambling, and open drug use and sales. Physical disorder includes vandalism, graffiti, junk and trash in vacant lots, boarded up deserted homes and commercial buildings, and stripped or abandoned cars. Regardless of its form, visible signs of disorder are signals of social disorganization and a lack of informal control.

These signs of disorder also contribute to feelings of insecurity and fear of crime even if there has been no real change in the level of criminal activity in an area. Fear of crime has serious negative consequences on the quality of community life. As Skogan (1986) argued, people who are experiencing heightened levels of fear withdraw from their neighborhoods. They no longer feel comfortable walking the streets after dark, nor do they get involved when they see behavior that violates the informal social controls of the neighborhood. Fearful individuals no longer feel close personal ties to their neighborhoods, and they do not participate in community life. It is as if the problems in their neighborhoods become larger than life, and local grass roots efforts will do nothing to solve them.

Additionally, the level of fear of crime also has an impact on what Skogan called **spatial radius**. A person who is comfortable and confident in his or her neighborhood has a large territory (spatial radius) in which they feel some sense of responsibility to defend the space from suspicious activities and unsavory persons. Fear of crime reduces the spatial radius, which leaves areas without caring guardians. These untended areas then become prime targets for criminal activity and disorder.

So, what is to be done in neighborhoods that have experienced a spiral of deterioration? How can the community be turned back to the "decent folk" who live there? Herein enters the "new" responsibility of local law enforcement. At the first sign of physical or human disorder, the police need to intervene and assist local residents in shoring up their informal social control mechanisms (Wilson & Kelling, 1982). Instead of relying upon traditional crime fighting strategies, a new philosophy of policing needs to be adopted. In this new form of policing, local residents will be viewed as partners with local law enforcement in the process of identifying problems and developing solutions. This new form of policing has become known as "community policing."

Community Policing

The term "community policing" has become a buzzword used to describe a variety of programs and organizational philosophies. Trojanowiez and Bocqueroux (1990:5) defined the philosophy of community policing in the following manner:

> Community Policing is a new philosophy of policing, based on the concept that police officers and private citizens working together in creative ways can help solve contemporary community problems related to crime, fear of crime, social and physical disorder, and neighborhood decay. The philosophy is predicated on the belief that achieving these goals requires that police departments develop a new relationship with the law-abiding people in the community, allowing them a greater voice in setting local police priorities and involving them in efforts to improve the overall quality of life in their neighborhoods. It shifts the focus of police work from handling random calls to solving community problems.

Others have translated the philosophy of community policing into practical applications. Permanent assignment by both beat and shift is an essential element of community policing (Bracey, 1992; Goldstein, 1993). In order for the police to establish community partnerships with local citizens, the officers must be provided with the opportunity to develop close personal relationships with residents. One common measure of success of community policing is whether or not local residents know their locally assigned community police officer by name (Goldstein, 1987).

In addition to enhancing police-community relationships, permanent assignment also leads to the establishment of geographic responsibility and accountability (Weisel & Eck, 1994). If an officer has been assigned to a specific beat, then that officer should know what is going on in their area and be held responsible for the conditions in that area. If a rash of graffiti suddenly appears or a group of teenagers is hanging out at the local convenience store late at night, it is the duty of the locally assigned police officer to recognize that these conditions have surfaced and to work in conjunction with local residents and business owners to do something about it. Officers assigned to different areas may not have the opportunity to recognize subtle "broken windows" changes.

In order to enhance geographic responsibility, many agencies have also adopted a decentralized approach to the delivery of services. Instead of having one large, sometimes ominous, centralized command post for all police services, many police departments have turned to smaller district offices. These smaller offices may be located in strip malls, shopping malls, or freestanding buildings. Regardless of their physical design, the decentralized system provides service centers that are viewed as less intimidating and more convenient for local residents to visit. Residents can stop by the station and meet one-on-one with their locally assigned regular officer, hopefully a familiar face to them.

Another essential element of community policing is the notion that the police must become more proactive in the prevention of crime and disorder (Goldstein, 1993). Instead of just responding from call to call, police (with the assistance of the community) should attempt to identify root causes of problems in the area. Crimes are viewed as symptoms of other underlying problems in the community (Lab, 2000). An arrest may take care of a specific incident, but will do nothing to solve the larger problem. The emphasis on solving community problems has been described as "the most important element of community policing" (Lab, 2000:164). This approach, often called **problem-oriented policing (POP)**, oftentimes goes hand in hand with community policing.

Herman Goldstein, a prominent policing scholar, popularized the idea of problem-oriented policing in an essay on the improvement of police practices. Goldstein (1979) argued that police agencies had become more concerned with improving organizational aspects of policing than with the end product of their efforts, a condition he described as the "means over ends" syndrome. Staffing issues and other internal management concerns had become paramount, while community safety and quality of life issues had taken a back seat. Additionally, police agencies had become preoccupied with arrests and enforcement of the law, which Goldstein felt was simply another indication of the continued emphasis on the "means" as opposed to the "ends." Goldstein felt that the end product of policing should be re-elevated to its place of primary importance. Further, Goldstein defined the end product as dealing with community problems. In his view, community problems were the very soul of police work and the true reason for having a police force.

While Goldstein's vision of problem-oriented policing received a great deal of attention, his ideas began to have a profound impact on policing when millions of dollars were offered in incentives to agencies that adopted community policing principles (see Box 4.4 for more information).

Box 4.4. Office of Community Oriented Policing Services COPS Office

In his State of the Union Address in January 1994, former President Bill Clinton vowed to put 100,000 new police officers on the streets of America. These officers would be specially trained in the principles of community and problem-oriented policing. As part of this initiative, the Violent Crime Control and Law Enforcement Act of 1994 provided nearly $9 billion for a number of projects related to the development of community policing. In addition to the hiring of the new officers, part of this funding was designated for the creation of the Office of Community Oriented Policing Services, which is commonly called the COPS office. It was the responsibility of the COPS office to act as a clearing-house, of sorts, for agencies wishing to take advantage of the federal funds.

Since its inception in 1994, the COPS office has provided information and technical assistance to over 12,000 law enforcement agencies that have successfully applied for grants to implement various community policing strategies or hire specially trained community policing officers. In addition, the COPS office provided funding to 28 Regional Community Policing Institutes and the Community Policing Consortium.

Regional Community Policing Institutes (RCPIs). There are 28 RCPIs located throughout the United States. These Institutes provide training and technical assistance to law enforcement officers as well as community partners. Since 1997, more than 130,000 officers and community members have received training through their local RCPI.

Community Policing Consortium. Since 1995, the Consortium has provided training and technical assistance to over 50,000 law enforcement personnel and community members. The Consortium is a collaborative partnership between the International Association of Chiefs of Police (IACP), the National Organization of Black Law Enforcement Executives (NOBLE), the National Sheriff's Association, the Police Executive Research Forum (PERF), and the Police Foundation. The Community Policing Consortium is committed to the promotion of community policing and distributes a number of publications dedicated to community policing in practice, including Community Policing Exchange, Sheriff Times, and Community Links.

For more information on the Office of Community Oriented Policing Services and Regional Community Policing Institutes, see the COPS website at http://www.usdoj.gov/cops

For more information on the Community Policing Consortium, see http://www.communitypolicing.org

Community/Police Problem Solving in Action

According to the Community Policing Consortium, community policing problem solving is best defined by its parts:

- The identification of crime, disorder, fear and other neighborhood problems;

- The development of an understanding of the underlying causes that result in neighborhood problems;

- The development and implementation of long-term, innovative solutions uniquely designed to address the neighborhood-specific problems; and

- The assessment of the solution's results on the neighborhood problems.

This four-step process is commonly known in policing circles as the SARA model: Scanning, Analysis, Response, and Assessment. The SARA model will be covered in much more depth in chapter 6 when crime analysis is discussed. Suffice it to say that prior to developing solutions, problem-oriented policing involves careful analytical examination into the problems of concern. In order for the police and the community to work together to develop a solution to a problem, community residents and the police must have a clear idea of what, exactly, the problem actually is. For an example of Goldstein's principles in practice, see Box 4.5 for a description of a community policing problem solving effort in Fresno, California.

Box 4.5. The City of Fresno, California's Zone of Hope

This is one success story of a police-community problem solving effort that was originally published in the Community Policing Exchange, *one of the pub-*

lications distributed by the Community Policing Consortium. While reading this account, it should be noted that an emphasis was placed on "quality of life" community problems: Trash, graffiti, drinking in public, fear and crime, and other "broken windows" problems were all mentioned as points of concern. Due to the success of this problem solving effort, the Fresno Police Department applied for and was awarded a grant from the COPS office to expand the effort in other local communities.

FRESNO, CALIF. The Fresno Police Department's crime-reporting zone 2555 is being transformed from a zone of despair to a zone of hope. From 1995 through 1997, this half-mile-square area of residential inner city had the highest number of drug-related calls for service in the city. The traditional law enforcement techniques of drug buys, search warrants and saturation patrol were all employed, but with lackluster results. A malaise had set upon a community that suffered both high incidence of crime and fear of crime.

Zone 2555 is within the department's central district, under the leadership of Captain Tom Frost. Captain Frost's dedication to both the community and the SARA (Scanning, Analysis, Response and Assessment) model of problem solving led him to many community meetings and site visits. It was clear that the residents were interested in improving their neighborhood but needed support from their police, other public and private organizations and, perhaps most importantly, one another. The resulting police/community partnership established expectations and obligations for all involved. Establishing an atmosphere of trust, availability and communication was crucial to the relationship.

The problems identified by the community were common to most inner cities: drug use and sales, street gangs and overall issues of blight, including graffiti. The agreed-upon goal was to improve the community's quality of life through reduced incidence of crime and reduced fear of crime. A police-community partnership emerged and became known as Community Pride and Recovery, or CPR. CPR is a three-phase process consisting of community organization, multi-agency law enforcement efforts, and blight reduction through community cleanup and neighborhood revitalization.

Multi-agency law enforcement sweeps targeted violations of law and order. Enforcement was not confined to serious felonies but also included crimes of low-level social disorder, such as drinking in public and driving while unlicensed. It was imperative that communication with community members be simultaneous with enforcement operations. Enforcement efforts were conducted with the community's permission and participation, not against its will. Before long, the community was actively involved through neighborhood watch patrols that allowed them to immediately report violations and maintain ongoing communication with officers in the field. A Spanish-speaking neighborhood-watch patrol group, the first such group in Fresno, became the cornerstone of this effort and resulted in the emergence of a number of community leaders.

As crime and disorder were addressed, so too were blight and physical deterioration. Community clean-up days were facilitated by the police department and included participation from the city sanitation department, Lowell Elementary School, local businesses and residents.

Lowell Elementary School is located within zone 2555 and is a hub and key element of CPR. The school is associated with the county's neighborhood resource center (NRC), which acts as a one-stop shop for community needs ranging from health care to child care to matters of neighborhood security. The NRC has also played a major role in opening and maintaining lines of communication among the community's residents, local businesses and the police. It is through this clearinghouse of community services that local problems such as criminal activity, landlord and tenant disputes, and other concerns are identified and addressed. The NRC has also been a resource for evaluating the effectiveness of CPR. Immediate community input and feedback indicate there is reduced fear of crime and the debilitations that go with it. Children play freely in public without fear of stray bullets or injury from discarded hypodermic needles, and their parents have an improving neighborhood to pass on to their children and grandchildren.

Traditional measurements of success also give CPR high marks. Calls for police services in zone 2555 have declined from 7,457 in 1996 to 5,883 in 1998. Neighborhood-watch patrol groups have grown from zero participation to 46 active members to date. Housing vacancy rates initially increased as enforcement efforts were implemented but are now on the decline as responsible tenants replaced neighborhood troublemakers.

The strength of CPR is people and relationships, and the empowerment that emerges from partnerships. It has made possible the transformation of a zone of despair into a zone of hope.

Written by Lieutenant David Belluomini
and Officer Conrad A. Clay

Source: Community Policing Exchange, July/August 1999. The full-text version of the article as well as descriptions of other community programs may be viewed on-line at http://www.communitypolicing.org/publications

Zero Tolerance Policing

Before the end of the discussion on community policing, it should also be noted that in addition to the comparatively "warm and fuzzy" community policing approach to curb crime and disorder, another policing philosophy has also been adopted by some agencies in an attempt to address the broken windows phenomenon: **zero tolerance policing**. This form of aggressive law enforcement has been popularized by the New York City Police Department. Under zero tolerance policing, officers focus on minor criminal offenses: pubic urination, vandalism of public property, jumping the turnstiles at the subway to avoid paying the fare, and various forms of panhandling (Walker, 1999).

signed to build communities tend to fall into two general categories. First, the success or failure of these programs rests in large part on the pre-existing strength of the neighborhood. Second, many of these programs fail to address the underlying conditions that caused the community integrity to diminish.

Can a Community Be Built Where No Community Exists?

Arguably, the most serious problem facing programs designed to build communities is that the programs are least successful in the neighborhoods that need them the most (Bursik & Grasmick, 1993; Peak & Glensor, 2002). In lower income areas plagued by high levels of crime, high residential turnover, and racial heterogeneity, community programs have had the lowest levels of success. Conversely, community programs in middle class, relatively homogeneous neighborhoods where a "core" of a community already exists tend to report higher levels of success (Skogan, 1990). If there is no pre-existing sense of community or a base of local resources to initially draw upon (such as influential community leaders, churches, neighborhood alliances, or other active community centers) then any community-building effort is starting out with two strikes already against it.

Part of the problem has to do with participation in community events. Some segments of the population are more likely to get involved in their community than are others. For example, Bursik and Grasmick (1993) noted that involvement in various crime prevention and community programs is dependent upon social class, martial status, residential stability, and age. The most typical participants are middle aged, higher educated, upper to middle class, residentially stable homeowners who are married with children. Therefore, in areas with high numbers of elderly residents and/or poor, single parents renting their homes, participation is expected to be low. As many of these same characteristics go hand in hand with socially disorganized neighborhoods, the lack of success in economically challenged, residentially unstable neighborhoods should not come as a surprise.

With respect to citizen race, there have been some interesting findings. Bursik and Grasmick cited the work of Skogan (1988) who found that African American residents were more likely to participate in community crime prevention programs than were whites. Skogan argued that this was due to the limited ability of minority residents to leave their communities. While white residents had a number of options (they could choose to participate in the program, not participate, or move from the deteriorating area), African Americans were more likely to be stuck in their neighborhoods. African Americans were then left with only two choices: ignore the problem, or get involved in a program to try to do something about it.

However, participation by African Americans and other minorities may be dependent upon which organizations are backing the program. In some minority communities programs that have a number of trusted partners may have a higher probability for success than those developed solely by a local law enforcement agency. In areas with strained police-community relations, any attempt by the police to intervene in the local neighborhood may be viewed with suspicion and hostility, no matter how well intentioned the police may be. The police have not had a proud past with respect to their relations with minority citizens, and recent events involving Rodney King, Amadou Diallo, Abner Louima, and the CRASH unit of the Los Angeles Police Department have not helped to improve the image of the police in minority communities (see, generally Feagin & Feagin, 1993; Kappeler, Sluder, & Alpert, 1994).

While a detailed discussion of police-community relations in minority communities is beyond the scope of this text, the image of "Officer Friendly" is a tough sell in African American and other minority communities that have been plagued by decades of discriminatory, sometimes brutal actions of locally assigned officers. If you add an aura of resentment, suspicion, and mistrust of the police to other challenging neighborhood demographics such as high levels of crime, high residential turnover, and high levels of poverty, you may very well end up with community policing efforts that are doomed for failure.

Do Community Building Efforts Ignore the "Real" Problems?

A second problem facing community-building programs is related to the first: Do these programs address the real problems facing local residents? Is the lack of success of many of these programs due to the fact that the efforts only treat the symptoms of the true underlying problems, while the real issues are overlooked or ignored? This is a question that has haunted many community programs, including the granddaddy of them all, the Chicago Area Project.

As noted in Chapter 2, the overall impact of the Chicago Area Project in the reduction of crime and delinquency in socially disorganized areas was negligible at best. The initial programs developed by Shaw focused on social and recreational activities. While these programs did provide legitimate recreational opportunities for juveniles in the troubled areas, it has been argued that the programs did nothing to address the real problems facing residents of the inner zones. Jon Snodgrass (1976) has stated that wealthy outsiders who were using the inner city neighborhoods for their own greedy self-interests caused the social problems that existed in the inner zones. Landowners allowed their properties to deteriorate, while business owners and speculating capitalists bought up the cheaper properties and expanded their commercial enterprises into residential areas with no regard for the communities that they were destroying in the process. The poor inner city residents did not have the organizational power, political influence, or monetary resources to combat the invasion of their neighborhoods.

If Shaw and the Chicago Area Project organizers wished to address the real problems that existed in the area, then something needed to be done about the wealthy industrialists who had caused the problems in the first place. Unfortunately, Shaw was caught in a difficult predicament. The CAP was dependent upon the local businesses and wealthy speculators for donations and other acts of philanthropy. If Shaw had adopted more of a confrontational stance with the local business and landowners, then he would have jeopardized the funding and survival of the CAP.

So what were the true causes of crime, disorder, and other social problems? What caused crime and disorder to flourish in some neighborhoods but not others? Sampson and Raudenbush (1999; 2001) linked both crime and disorder to a number of structural characteristics that are specific to certain areas. The single most important factor related to the prevalence of both crime and disorder was poverty. Mixed land use, where commercial and residential areas were combined, was also found to be a strong predictor of crime and disorder. Residential instability was also noted as an important factor. If community programs do not address these real issues, then the long-term success of the program may be in jeopardy.

Sampson and his colleagues (see, for example Byrne & Sampson, 1986; Sampson, 1995; Sampson & Groves, 1989; Sampson & Raudenbush, 1999; Sampson, Raudenbush, & Earls, 1997) have been quick to point out that all is not lost in the most challenged areas. Collective efficacy has been described as a key element in the reduction of both crime and disorder. Earlier, collective efficacy was defined as cohesion, trust, and informal control mechanisms that may exist in some communities. To reduce crime and disorder in even the most impoverished communities, Sampson and his colleagues have advocated a number of policies designed to empower residents to take control of their neighborhoods. Included among their recommendations are (1) enacting policies that allow low-income residents to buy their homes or take over the management of their apartment buildings to reduce residential turnover; (2) the use of housing vouchers and other programs designed to scatter public housing residents throughout cities as opposed to concentrating the poor in centralized locations; and (3) increasing the level of services available to urban residents (Vold et al. 2002). The goal of the programs should be to increase collective efficacy, which will ultimately improve the quality of life in many urban areas.

Sampson and his colleagues have maintained that although these types of community building programs may have achieved limited success in some neighborhoods, community programs should not be completely abandoned. Even small improvements in the quality of community life may go a long way towards long-term change in urban areas.

Summary

Many practical policy recommendations have been derived from theories that focus on the role of the community in reducing crime, disorder, and other social problems. Regardless of the specifics of the program, the goal is the same: increase the level of informal social control. By enabling local residents to control the destiny of their own neighborhoods, the overall quality of life for local residents should improve. Locals will feel safe outside of their homes, neighbors will recognize outsiders, and children will be monitored and socialized by intimate handlers and other guardians who do not feel intimidated intervening when misdeeds occur. While there have been some problems with the success of these programs in the most challenging neighborhoods, programs designed to rebuild communities do show some promise in the improvement of the overall quality of life for many residents.

Chapter 5

Theory into Practice II: Altering the Physical Environment

Previously a number of practical policies derived from Shaw and McKay's concept of social disorganization and Sampson's ideas about collective efficacy were examined. These theoretical models argue that in order to reduce crime and fear of crime, the sense of community and level of informal social control must be enhanced. Neighborhoods with high levels of informal social control will have lower crime rates, fewer signs of physical and social disorder, and more adults willing to step in when something is wrong.

In this chapter, a second set of policy recommendations, primarily derived from the choice-based theories presented in Chapter 3, are discussed. Regardless of the specifics, all of the policies examined are based on the same basic assumption: a rational offender searches out a suitable target that will net the greatest reward with minimal risk of detection and apprehension. The ultimate goal of this set of policy recommendations is to somehow alter the situation to make a target less attractive for attack by a motivated, rational criminal. Some of these recommendations are rather minor, such as adding more streetlights or keeping hedges trimmed so that homeowners can see clearly out of their windows and onto the streets. Other policy suggestions are on a larger scale and involve planning models for buildings, communities, and entire cities under the driving principle of improving guardianship and reducing opportunities for criminal activities.

These choice-based policies tend to fall into three related groups: defensible space, crime prevention through environmental design, and situational crime prevention. Here they are examined in detail, beginning with a look at a few of the "classic" writings in the study of physical environment and crime.

The Beginnings:
The Works of Jane Jacobs and Oscar Newman

In 1961, Jane Jacobs' classic book "*The Death and Life of Great American Cities*" was published. Jacobs' work was written as a strong critique of the manner in which cities were being planned and rebuilt. In her words, "To build city districts that are custom made for easy crime is idiotic. Yet that is what we do (1961:31)."

Jacobs derived her arguments from observations of a number of major cities, including the Greenwich Village area of New York City where she lived. The underlying assumption upon which she built her work sounded very similar to the arguments made by Shaw and McKay in their observations of the Chicago area: Certain areas were not more susceptible to high rates of crime because a "criminal class" of people resided there. In fact, Jacobs found strong communities with high levels of informal social control in areas where the predominant residents were poor and/or racial or ethnic minorities living in lower-income housing. As she observed, "Some of the safest sidewalks in New York City, for example, at any time of the day or night, are those along which poor people or minority groups live. And some of the most dangerous are in the streets occupied by the same kinds of people (1961:31)." The problem was not with who lived there, but the characteristics of the places themselves. According to Jacobs, some areas were more crime-ridden than others because of their poor design and planning (Crowe & Zahm, 1994; DeLeon-Granados, 1999; Jacobs, 1961).

Based on her observations, Jacobs offered a number of practical suggestions to urban planners that could reduce the level of crime and disorder and improve the overall quality of life for urban residents. For example, Jacobs discussed the importance of a well-designed sidewalk system in urban areas. To be a "successful" sidewalk, first the pathway should provide a clear boundary between what is public space where one would expect to see strangers and what is private space where strangers should be noticed and monitored. Second, buildings along the sidewalk should be oriented in such a manner as to encourage the "natural proprietors" of the area to keep their "eyes upon the street." Third, the sidewalk should have a good level of continuous use. More people using the sidewalk at various hours of the day and night lead to greater surveillance of the area. Further, the greater level of activity on the sidewalks encourages people to look out of their window and observe the passers-by. As an added benefit, a well-used sidewalk can enhance what Jacobs called the "normal, casual manpower for child rearing." Any adult—strangers, residents, the owner of the corner store and other natural proprietors—who happens to be walking by can easily monitor and correct inappropriate behavior of children playing on the safe, exciting city street.

Jacobs felt that the physical design of an urban area would have an impact on the behavior of local residents—whether they interacted with each other, whether they were able to recognize who belonged and who did not, and whether they intervened to maintain the peace and serenity of their neighborhood. Furthermore, the cohesive behavior of the local residents would in turn have an impact on the behavior of potential offenders. If a rational offender perceived a strong sense of community, apprehension and detection would be more likely since local residents would be more likely to notice their presence and step in if they attempted to commit a crime (Taylor & Gottfredson, 1986).

While Jacobs' work was influential, a book released a few years later by Oscar Newman had worldwide impact. Newman built on the notion that given the proper environmental design, residents would alter their behavior to defend their homes and neighborhoods from the intrusion of criminals (Murray, 1995; Newman, 1971). While Jacobs focused on broader city planning and urban design issues, Newman was an architect and tended to be more narrowly focused on the design of buildings.

Oscar Newman's Defensible Space

Newman's book was released in 1971 during an era of rapidly increasing levels of crime. The crime wave was a very serious concern for police practitioners, academics, and the general public. Additionally, after the turbulent decade of the 1960s, there were questions raised about the effectiveness of the police to control crime and criminals, especially in our nation's inner cities. Newman stressed the important role of informal community control in the task of crime reduction. In Newman's words (1971:204):

> Within the present atmosphere of pervasive crime and ineffectual authority, the only effective measure for assuring a safe living environment is community control. We are advocating a program for the restructuring of residential developments in our cities to facilitate their control by the people who inhabit them. We see this as the only long-term measure of consequence in the battle for the maintenance of a sane urban society. Short-term measures involving flights to suburbia or additional police manpower and equipment are only palliatives.

Newman's theory was based on the idea that many buildings (especially high rise public housing buildings) had been poorly designed. Many of these buildings were enormous and impersonal, making it difficult for residents to recognize who belonged and who did not. In addition to their sheer size, the buildings had too many unsupervised entry doors that made it very easy for a motivated offender to access the living space of the residents and escape unrecognized (Clarke, 1995). Newman felt that the design of the physical environment needed to be changed in order to engender feelings of ownership and encourage the level of guardianship by the legitimate users. In order to encourage the local residents to take ownership of their neighborhood and defend it, his **defensible space** theory had four elements: territoriality, natural surveillance, image, and milieu.

Newman defined the concept of **territoriality** as "The capacity of the physical environment to create perceived zones of territorial influence (1971:50)." His idea was based on the fact that human beings are territorial animals who will defend an area they define as their own. Places need to be designed to enhance the perception of territoriality and ownership not only for the homeowner or apartment dweller, but also for the motivated offender. If a rational offender feels a strong sense of proprietary ownership, then they may select a less guarded target.

Newman provided a number of practical design suggestions that he felt would increase this sense of territoriality. A properly designed environment needed to provide visual cues or boundaries that would indicate where a personal territory began and ended. These boundaries between public and private space could be real or symbolic. "Real" barriers included such things as high walls and fences or locked gates and doors. "Symbolic" barriers would include such things as an open gateway, changes in the lighting or in the texture of the walkway, a short distance of steps, or the use of shrubs or other plants. According to Newman, both real and symbolic barriers served the same purpose: "To inform that one is passing from a space which is public where one's presence is not questioned through a barrier to a space which is private and where one's presence requires justification (1972:63)."

Newman felt that **natural surveillance** was essential. A building or housing project with good surveillance opportunities will reduce feelings of fear and uneasiness for the residents. The entire building will project a sense of safety to both residents and potential offenders. Because their movements may be easily seen and detected by the local residents, motivated offenders may seek out a less guarded target.

In order to enhance natural surveillance, Newman argued that buildings should be oriented in such a manner that the residents could easily see the outside street. Lobby areas should be designed so that activities occurring inside the building may easily be seen from the street. As an example, Newman described a poorly designed lobby area at the entrance of a Bronx, New York housing project. In order to get the to elevators, residents had to make two turns. This design forced the residents to enter the building with no idea what (or who) was waiting at the end of the second turn. Additionally, once a resident made it to the elevators, if a problem did occur their location was out of sight and sound of people passing by on the street and as well as the residents who were inside of their apartments. Newman argued that fire escapes, windows, floor plans, and roof landings could all be altered to enhance the ability of residents to monitor the activities of both friends and strangers and thereby reduce the opportunities for crimes to occur.

Image refers to the "message" that the building sends out about itself. Newman felt that in the United States, high-rise, publicly supported housing projects had been designed to be very visually distinctive from the urban landscape. Newman argued that if you stood on the street looking at two housing buildings, one a low income housing building and the other an upper middle income housing building, you could easily distinguish which was the low income housing project because of the use of cheaper finishes on the facades, the lack of outdoor balconies, and other cues sending out a stigmatizing message about the project and its residents. Newman felt that the design of lower income housing projects emitted a negative image that made the residents easy targets for crime. To reduce crime, lower income housing projects should be designed in such a manner that they better fit in with the surrounding buildings.

Milieu refers to the placement of housing projects in areas that are considered to be safe places. In the spirit of Jacobs, Newman felt that housing projects built in commercial and industrial areas with large numbers of people coming and going were generally viewed as being safe due to the large number of "eyes on the streets." However, Newman added that one must be careful to evaluate the nature of the commercial activity, the hours of operation, the intended users of the businesses, and whether or not the users of the business identified with the local residents. Not all commercial enterprises would automatically enhance the safety of local residents. While pool halls, schools, or hangouts for bored teens may increase foot traffic in an area, these commercial establishments may also increase the level of criminal activity in the neighboring homes.

Will Defensible Space Be Defended?

Within just a few years, Newman's defensible space theory enjoyed worldwide excitement, especially in Great Britain (Poyner, 1983). In the United States, interest was fueled by a multi-million dollar project funded through the Law Enforcement Assistance Administration to implement design modifications suggested by defensible space theory (Murray, 1995). The Department of Housing and Urban Development (HUD) similarly provided funding to renovate public housing projects (Merry, 1981). All around the globe, urban planners, architects, and law enforcement agencies turned to defensible space as the answer to the growing crime problem. While the implementation of Newman's concepts of territoriality, natural surveillance, image and milieu may seem like common-sense approaches to fight the war on crime, the question remains: Does it work? The answer depends on whom you ask.

While some studies that have tested the effectiveness of defensible space applications have enjoyed positive results with respect to the reduction of fear of crime and actual crime levels, other studies have reported either short-term reductions or a negligible impact at best. For example, Newman and Franck (1980) reported that residents who lived in buildings with defensible space features such as limited access, better surveillance opportunities, and not as many floors were more likely to report lower levels of victimization and reduced levels of fear. Other studies have found some evidence to support greater social interaction among the residents, but little or no consistent reduction in the level of crime (Fowler & Mangione, 1982).

When practical aspects of defensible space theory were implemented, in many cases the more important element of Newman's theory was lost in the translation. It is relatively easy to add shrubs to demarcate private space, add lighting to enhance natural surveillance, or repaint a building to reduce its stigmatizing appearance. However, if these simple physical alterations are the only steps taken, then the effectiveness of defensible space theory may be questionable at best. What is lost is an understanding of the underlying social processes at work in buildings or communities where defensible space theory is applied (Merry, 1981). The pre-existing social fiber (or lack thereof) can ultimately "make or break" any changes in the physical environment.

Recall that Newman's central thesis was that the physical design of buildings has an effect on the behavior of its residents. If a building was properly designed with defensible space in mind, the physical environment would enhance social cohesion and increase the level of informal social control. This heightened level of informal social control would then reduce crime (Murray, 1995; Newman, 1972). Unfortunately, when defensible space concepts have been implemented, this very important intermediate step between changes in the physical environment and its effect on crime rates has been skipped.

In what has become somewhat of a "classic" critique, Sally Merry tested the effectiveness of defensible space theory in a small, inner city, low-income housing project she called Dover Square. In terms of physical design, Dover Square followed many of the suggestions of defensible space. The buildings were small in size. The placement of the windows made it easy for the residents to survey their territory, and access to private space was limited with appropriate real and symbolic barriers. Despite the "good" design that was found in most of the areas of the housing project, crime was high and the residents were fearful. Defensible spaces were not being defended like they were supposed to be. Merry set out to find out why.

Merry found that modifications in the physical environment were not enough to reduce crime. The fragmented social organization of the residents of Dover Square seemed to override the strengths of defensible space theory. Even though turnover was relatively low in the project (which would seem to lead to strong social cohesion), the residents were sharply divided along racial and ethnic lines. This lack of community seemed to undermine the positive impact of the design of the project. In her words,

> Spaces may be defensible but not defended if the social apparatus for effective defense is lacking. Residents will not look out well-positioned windows if there is nothing to see. Even if buildings are low, entrances and public spaces clearly linked to particular apart-

ments, residents will not respond to crimes if they feel that the space belongs to another ethnic group, if they believe that the police will come too late or they will incur retribution for calling them, or if they are unable to distinguish a potential criminal from the neighbor's dinner guest (Merry, 1981:419).

As a result of Merry's critique, a second generation of defensible space theory began to evolve (Taylor, Gottfredson, & Brower, 1980; Taylor & Harrell, 1996). In this new and improved model, greater emphasis was placed on the pre-existing social and cultural setting in which the design modifications were made. Researchers needed to carefully consider how the physical alterations to the environment would encourage social interaction and greater use of communal space. These neighborly interactions would lead to heightened levels of resident-based informal social control. It is important to bear in mind that if all sense of community has collapsed, changes in the physical environment may have little or no impact on the level of crime or resident fear (Merry, 1981; Murray, 1995).

Despite the limited success of defensible space modifications in some settings, Newman's ideas continue to have great impact. While Newman's primary focus was on the design of buildings, others have applied his ideas to a variety of settings including schools, commercial strip centers, and entire residential communities (Clarke, 1992; Poyner, 1983).

Crime Prevention through Environmental Design

Newman's basic ideas were used in the development of **crime prevention through environmental design (CPTED)**, a popular prevention technique that is praised by many law enforcement agencies and city planners. The first use of this phrase is usually credited to C. Ray Jeffrey who used it as the title for a book (1971). In this work, Jeffrey argued that the current crime control policies being used were ineffective. According to Jeffrey, the predominant method of crime control involved what he called "indirect measures" that were used after a crime had occurred. These indirect measures included such things as various forms of rehabilitation and vocational training, arrest, court proceedings, prison sentences, probation, and parole. Instead of the current practice of addressing criminal acts "after the fact," Jeffrey felt that the best way to reduce crime was to initiate direct controls over environmental conditions prior to the commission of an offense. According to Jeffrey, "Placing a man on probation or giving him remedial education will not prevent him from breaking the window and stealing jewelry; placing a steel bar over a window will prevent the theft of jewelry from that window (1971:20)." Jeffrey argued that through the use of environmental engineering, the number of crimes could be reduced.

Jeffrey's concept of CPTED was usually viewed as incorporating a more diverse set of techniques than were advocated by Newman's defensible space theory. This was especially true with respect to places where territoriality may seem less natural than the protection of one's personal residence, such as the workplace or school (Clarke, 1992). The strategies used by CPTED closely dovetail with the ideas developed by Newman.

The Strategies of CPTED

According to Crowe (2000), there are three interrelated strategies associated with CPTED: access control, surveillance, and territorial reinforcement. **Access control** refers to limiting the opportunities for a motivated offender to come into contact with a potential target. If a potential target is perceived as being hard to get to, then an offender may feel that any attempts to gain access to the target would involve greater risk of detection and apprehension. Since the offender is assumed to be rational, the offender may move on to a different target that is viewed as an easier hit. Access control strategies are sometimes referred to as **target hardening** (Lab, 2000).

Access control strategies usually fall into three categories: organized, mechanical, and natural. An example of organized access control includes guards posted at the entrances to gated communities. Mechanical access control is best defined by the use of devices designed to limit entry to only legitimate users, such as locks, key-pad entry systems, or swiping identification cards prior to access. Natural access control refers to what Crowe calls "spatial definition." This is a rather broad category that would include the relationships between space type — such as whether a space is public, semi-public, or private; commercial or residential — and traffic or pedestrian flow patterns in and around the space. In a well-designed space with good natural access control, it should be unnatural for people to easily wander into areas where they do not belong. Limiting the number of entrances or exits may enhance natural access in buildings. In communities, natural access may involve using fewer through streets as access routes and, instead, relying on more cul-de-sacs and dead end streets to limit traffic flow.

Closely related to access control is **surveillance**. Space should be designed in such a manner that potential offenders may be easily observed. It is assumed that a rational offender would not select targets that are easily monitored by residents, business owners, or other legitimate users of the space. Surveillance is also broken down into the same three categories: organized (including such things as routine patrols by police or private security officers), mechanical (strategic placement of street lights or surveillance cameras), and natural (windows and lobbies that enhance the monitoring of the outside streets; carefully placed park benches; landscaping that is designed with surveillance in mind, such as low hedges or well trimmed trees).

Territorial reinforcement has to do with how the physical environment impacts feelings of ownership of a space. A well-designed space enhances feelings of proprietary ownership by the legitimate users while at the same time sending out a message to potential offenders that the space they are entering is off limits to outsiders. According to Crowe, territorial reinforcement is closely linked to natural access control and natural surveillance. Traditionally, CPTED projects primarily used mechanical and organized strategies to reduce opportunities for crime. It is relatively easy (though expensive) to add more locks, alarm systems, lights, or a security guard or two. However, primary reliance upon mechanical and organized strategies does not encourage territorial reinforcement. In order to build feelings of ownership, the natural elements of the environment must be considered. When natural access control and natural surveillance are taken into account, legitimate users will be more likely to get involved in the protection of their turf. Strangers will be monitored and suspicious behaviors will be reported to the police. The effectiveness of even the best security systems will not operate to its greatest potential if the primary users do not share a real sense of ownership and truly care about their residence, workplace, or community.

CPTED in Practice

CPTED strategies have been applied in a variety of settings, including schools, parking garages, parks and recreation areas, and entire residential and commercial developments as well as individual homes and businesses. The physical changes implemented as part of an overall crime prevention strategy are limited only by the imagination of the police agency, planning office, business owner, or resident. Some changes may be relatively minor, such as moving the desk of a receptionist to a more centralized location where he or she may better monitor the lobby area, or planting prickly bushes to cut off pathways for escape used by burglars. Other modifications may be more extensive in nature and involve planning and design considerations for entire cities (see, for example, Wekerle & Whitzman, 1995). In some areas, such as Tempe, Arizona, Sarasota, Florida, or Alexandria, Virginia, police officers carefully trained in CPTED techniques regularly review blueprints of all newly proposed structures and building renovation plans to ensure that crime prevention strategies have not been overlooked. In the case of Tempe, Arizona, planners are required by city ordinance to have blueprints approved by the police prior to the issuance of a building permit (Bureau of Justice Assistance, 1997; Davis, 1998; Plaster & Carter, 1993). As the popularity of CPTED grows, more and more police agencies are becoming involved in urban planning issues (Deleon-Gradanos, 1999).

Many CPTED projects have been initiated in conjunction with community policing efforts. According to the National Institute of Justice (2000), CPTED projects and community policing complement each other. Both community policing and CPTED begin with a careful analysis of problems that occur in a specific geographic location. Based on the specifics of that particular location, various crime prevention strategies may be adopted. Because each CPTED solution is tailor-made to fit a specific location, no two CPTED projects are exactly the same (Crowe, 2000; National Institute of Justice, 2000). The following section will highlight some successful CPTED projects that have been conducted in collaboration with community policing efforts.

Spotlight on Practice

Rebuilding Genesis Park, Charlotte, North Carolina

Encompassing a relatively small area of only eight square blocks, an inner-city neighborhood known as Genesis Park had become one of the worst areas in the city of Charlotte, North Carolina some time ago. Violent crime and open-air drug markets, especially heroin sales, were common occurrences in this area. Yards were overgrown and the homes that had not been vacated were in need of repairs.

In order to improve the quality of life for the urban residents, the Charlotte-Mecklenburg Housing Partnership (CMP) and the Charlotte Police Department initiated a number of environmental changes. First, the poor neighborhood conditions were addressed. Vacant homes being used as centers for drug sales were closed down. Dilapidated, rental, duplexes were converted into single-family residences, and low-income families were provided special financing opportunities to purchase these newly renovated properties.

Second, in order to gain better control of the area, traffic barriers were put in place to restrict free vehicle movement. As a result, a more complex street pattern was created. No longer could potential drug customers easily come and go in the targeted area. To add even more confusion to outsiders entering the area, street names were officially changed. After one year of implementing these and other changes (including a greater emphasis on community policing), crime rates dropped dramatically in the Genesis Park area (Feins, Epstein, & Widom, 1997).

Fresno, California's Child Custody Program

The city of Fresno, California Police Department was experiencing a number of problems related to the transfer of custody of minor children from one parent to another for their scheduled visitation outings. In a single 12-month period, the department had responded to over 2,000 calls for service related to child custody violations and requests for assistance with child custody transfers. To make the matter even more frustrating for the officers, very few cases were ultimately prosecuted by the State Attorney's Office.

As part of their response to this problem, a centralized facility for child custody transfers was designed using CPTED principles. The Child Custody Program (CCP), which is housed in this carefully designed facility, fosters a safe environment for peaceful custody exchanges. In order to reduce the opportunities for unpleasant and potentially violent confrontations between parents or other child guardians, each parent is assigned a separate building entrance for the transfer. At no time do the parents come into contact with each other. Additionally, private security guards are on hand to assist in surveillance of the facility. By implementing simple and common sense CPTED design techniques, the CCP boasts that the police have never been summoned to the facility to resolve a child custody transfer issue (National Institute of Justice, 2000).

Taking Back an Intersection

A single intersection in Vancouver, Canada's Grandview Woodland community was identified as being especially problematic for the Vancouver Police Department. The agency's 911 system was bombarded with complaints related to "quality of life issues," such as aggressive panhandling, public intoxication, graffiti, litter, and frequent attacks by "squeegee people," individuals who wash car windows at traffic lights, often uninvited, for a fee.

As part of a larger community policing project, criminology students from Simon Fraser University, under the direction of Patricia Brantingham, attempted to identify and implement CPTED strategies that could ultimately improve the poor conditions that existed at the intersection. First, the students observed that a bench located on the northeast corner of the intersection was a common location for disputes between intoxicated people. Behind the bench were a number of newspaper vending boxes that provided a convenient hiding spot for liquor bottles and squeegees. The bench and the newspaper boxes were located adjacent to an automatic teller machine (ATM), and the police were frequently called out to the location by fearful legitimate users. Once the bench was removed and the newspaper boxes relocated nearer to the curb, 911 calls for service dropped dramatically.

Local businesses got involved as well. A branch of the Royal Bank was located on the southwest corner of the intersection. Alcoves, built into the structure of the buildings, had become a popular place for panhandlers to rest and squeegee people to hide the tools of their trade. The Bank made a number of design modifications to the alcoves to make them less attractive to unwanted users. A slanted structure was installed in the alcoves that made it impossible for the panhandlers to sit down. A glass window was installed near the entrance of the bank, which effectively eliminated a convenient hiding place for squeegee storage. Landscaping was also modified to enhance surveillance and reduce cover. Additionally, the Vancity Credit Union, which was located on the northwest corner of the intersection, took steps to eliminate a hiding space for squeegee people awaiting the next red light. By adding a gate to an alcove that housed an ATM, access to this hiding area and makeshift shelter was reduced. These relatively easy design modifications resulted in fewer calls for service to the area and greater feelings of safety by the legitimate users of the area (National Institute of Justice, 2000).

The Bottom Line: Does CPTED Work?

As is the case with many "bottom line" questions, the answer depends on whom you ask. If you posed this question to Timothy Crowe, former director of the National Crime Prevention Institute and author of many articles and several books on the topic, you would get a resounding "yes." Crowe, who provides training workshops to law enforcement agencies and serves as a consultant for CPTED techniques, has noted rather dramatic success stories in a variety of settings, including the following (Crowe, 2000:9,10):

- Convenience stores have used CPTED to increase sales and reduce losses from theft of up to 50% and from robberies of 65%.

- Malls in Sacramento and Knoxville have reduced incidents by 24% and noncrime calls to police by another 14% using CPTED parking management concepts; the largest mall in the world located in West Edmonton, Alberta, Canada, has used CPTED concepts with well documented success...

- Neighborhoods in Ft. Lauderdale, Tallahassee, Bridgeport, Knoxville, Jacksonville, Dayton, North Miami Beach, Calgary, Toronto, and many others have produced dramatic reduction in drug sales, burglaries and general crime by 15–100%.

- Schools using CPTED throughout the world are reducing construction costs, lowering conduct and crime violations, and improving achievement and matriculation levels.

- Design research on office environments has determined that the lack of territorial identity in the office space contributes to lower morale, less productivity, and greater tolerance of dishonesty among fellow workers.

Other researchers have been less enthusiastic about the impact of CPTED techniques (Clarke, 1992; Lab, 2000; Taylor & Harrell, 1996). For every study that has reported reduced levels of crime and lower levels of fear after CPTED techniques were introduced, one may uncover another study reporting little or no impact. Without getting too in-depth on the subtle nuances of policy evaluation techniques, the problem has to do with how CPTED techniques are implemented and their effectiveness measured.

For example, my father owned a pizza shop for many years. After being robbed several times, he installed a number of CPTED design modifications, which included adding more lighting both inside and out, raising the front counter height by several feet (to prevent potential robbers from jumping over the counter), removing posters and decals from the front windows to enhance surveillance of the parking area, and adding various access control devices such as automatic locking doors and a buzzer system for limiting entrance into the business. After implementing these various CPTED techniques, he did not have another robbery occur at the business. So, what worked? Was it the lighting, the counter height, the locks, the improved surveillance ability, or some combination? Or was something else responsible for the reduction in robberies? It is impossible to tell for sure.

Oftentimes, when CPTED techniques are employed, it is not just a single modification that is made. This makes it difficult to isolate the impact of each modification alone. When multiple techniques are used, it is impossible to zero in on which technique had an impact. Also, one cannot be sure whether it was the CPTED techniques that were responsible for the reduction in robberies or other factors at work. It is always possible that the police had increased patrols in the area or the local economy had improved and more jobs were available.

Additionally, it should also be noted that CPTED techniques are more than just adding a lock and measuring whether or not this physical change had an impact on the number of burglaries. The effectiveness of the design change rests on territorial reinforcement—have the modifications caused the proprietary owners to take control of the area? As noted by Lab (2000), if the changes to the physical environment do not bring out the desired changes in the behaviors of the residents, storeowners, and other legitimate users of the space, then the design change may appear to be a failure.

Situational Crime Prevention

The third and final group of techniques designed to reduce criminal opportunities is referred to as situational crime prevention. These strategies may involve various techniques to reduce the opportunity for crimes to occur, including physical changes to the environment and/or target hardening techniques. Situational crime prevention may also involve the use of broader strategies than those used in defensible space or CPTED. For example, consider the crime of motorcycle theft. By enacting laws requiring the use of helmets, motorcycle thefts may be reduced since it would be difficult for a potential thief to drive off unnoticed (Mayhew, Clarke, & Elliot, 1989). When was the last time you received an obscene phone call from a stranger? The availability and use of caller identification service has significantly reduced the number of such phone calls (Clarke, 1992). While the techniques that fall under the situational crime prevention umbrella may be a bit broader than what has been examined so far in the discussions of defensible space and CPTED, the criminal opportunities that these crime prevention strategies are designed to reduce are bit more narrow — as the name implies, situational crime prevention techniques are designed to reduce very specific criminal opportunities that arise in a particular situation.

What is situational crime prevention? According to Ronald Clarke, a criminologist who has written extensively on this topic, situational crime prevention is defined in the following manner:

> Situational crime prevention can be characterized as comprising measures (1) directed at highly specific forms of crime (2) that involve the management, design, or manipulation of the immediate environment in as systematic and permanent a way as possible (3) so as to reduce the opportunities for crime and increase the risks as perceived by a wide range of offenders (Clarke, 1983:225)

In a nutshell, situational crime prevention techniques are designed to reduce the opportunity for criminal acts by either (a) increasing the amount of effort a motivated offender must exert (b) increasing the level of risk of apprehension and detection or (c) reducing the potential reward. As noted by Murray (1995), situational crime prevention is not as concerned with the relationship between design changes and the impact on community life, such as increased social interaction, greater feelings of territoriality, and enhanced levels of informal social control. While these factors are important to the success of defensible space and CPTED strategies, they play a less important role in situational crime prevention. In this realm, the real cause of crime is opportunity — if you want to reduce crime, reduce the opportunities for crimes to occur.

Opportunity As a Cause of Crime

How does one go about reducing opportunities for crime? First, it might help to understand how crime and opportunity are linked. Felson and Clarke (1998:v, vi) have outlined the following principles of opportunity and crime:

Opportunities play a role in causing all crime. While it has been argued that situational crime prevention places too much emphasis on property crimes that occur in public places (Crawford, 1998), Felson and Clarke maintain that opportunity causes all crimes—violent crimes, property crimes, white-collar crimes, and "victimless" crimes, like drug sales and prostitution. Even the occurrence of suicide has been linked to opportunity (Clarke & Mayhew, 1988).

Crime opportunities are highly specific. Consider for the moment the crime of burglary. Instead of all burglaries being lumped together, opportunities must be evaluated for very specific types of burglaries. The motives, risks, rewards, and techniques for residential burglary must be analyzed separately from commercial burglary. Even if only residential burglaries are considered, subcategories must also be considered with respect to the target type (such as single-family homes, apartment dwellings, duplexes, etc.) point of entry (windows versus doors, front or rear) or even time of day (daytime versus nighttime). Since each offense is different, opportunity reduction strategies must be tailored to fit each specific offense.

Crime opportunities are concentrated in time and space. Crime is not randomly distributed in time and location. Certain locations and times are more dangerous than others. In the next chapter, "hot spots" and "burning times" are explored in greater depth. For now, suffice it to say that certain locations and certain times provide more opportunities for crimes to occur than other times and locations.

Crime opportunities depend on everyday movements of activity. Chapter 3 includes a discussion of routine activities theory, which argues that motivated offenders, suitable targets, and the lack of capable guardians converge in time and place as we conduct the business of our everyday lives. As we go to work, attend class, or partake in late night activities in our various activity nodes, our presence in these areas and our movements between them may provide opportunities for motivated offenders to come into contact with us.

One crime produces opportunities for another. A criminal may set out to commit one crime, but may end up committing many other offenses because of the other opportunities that arise. Felson and Clarke provide the example of a burglary. Once a burglar has entered a home, additional opportunities to commit crimes may develop. If the offender stumbles across a gun and chooses to take it, the offender has now committed armed residential burglary. If the homeowner suddenly returns to the residence, the burglary is now presented with the opportunity to commit a robbery, battery, or rape. The commission of the burglary may also lead to other opportunities, such as dealing in stolen goods.

Some products offer more tempting crime opportunities. Felson and Clarke argue that there are four characteristics that determine whether or not a target will be attacked: **Value, Inertia, Visibility, and Access (VIVA).** Some products are valued more than others, even though they may cost the same. For example, certain brands of tennis shoes, or compact disks by popular artists are more valued than other products of comparable price. Inertia refers to the weight of the item, which has to do with how easily the product can be transported. Visibility refers to the amount of exposure the target has to potential offenders. Access has to do with how easy the product is to get to. Items placed near open windows have easy access, while items carefully secured in a monitored showcase have less access. Therefore, certain products offer greater opportunities of theft than others, such as laptop computers or portable compact disk players.

Social and technological changes produce new crime opportunities. Felson and Clarke argue that mass-produced consumer goods pass through four stages: Innovation, Growth, Mass Market, and Saturation. New products are introduced during the innovation stage. For example, when home computers first came out, there was a very limited market. They were user hostile, expensive, and limited in their use. At the innovation stage, few home computers were stolen since not many people wanted them anyway. At the growth stage, thefts began to increase. During the growth stage, home computers became easier to use and less expensive. More and more people wanted home computers, which drove up demand. At the mass market stage, home computers became commonplace. Demand was high and many home computers were sold. The demand also fueled the theft of home computers, which was widespread. Finally, at the saturation stage, the price of had dropped and most people who wanted to purchase the product have done so. Stealing a home computer now offers little potential reward, and thefts have declined. As technological innovations occur, the cycle starts again providing new opportunities for crimes to occur. Laptop computers, CD players, hand-held calculators, and airbags all follow the same cycle, providing different opportunities for theft at the various stages of market saturation.

Crime can be prevented by reducing opportunities. Felson and Clarke state that this assumption guides several crime prevention strategies, including defensible space, CPTED, problem-oriented policing, and situational crime prevention, which they argue is the best developed of the various strategies.

The 16 Opportunity Reduction Techniques of Situational Crime Prevention

Clarke and his colleagues (Clarke, 1983, 1992, 1995, 1997; Clarke & Homel, 1997; Clarke & Mayhew, 1980; Felson & Clarke, 1998; Newman, Clarke, & Shoham, 1997) continue to develop and expand on the notion of situational crime prevention. In his earlier writings, Clarke attempted to develop a classification scheme or typology that categorized twelve specific crime prevention strategies under three headings. These headings were based on rational choice theory: increasing the effort; increasing the risks; and reducing the rewards. The idea behind the development of such a classification scheme was to provide a framework for the ever-expanding number of situational crime prevention strategies. As argued by Lab (2000), without such an organizational framework, various techniques may be employed without any rationale or understanding of why the strategy should be effective.

In Clarke's original model, a great deal of emphasis was placed on modifications of the physical environment. However, as the popularity of situational crime prevention grew, researchers expanded the scope to include a greater emphasis on the social and psychological elements of committing crimes (Lab, 2000; Newman, Clarke, & Shoham, 1997). The most recent typology has been modified from twelve techniques to sixteen. In the new classification scheme, the headings have been modified to *perceived* effort, *perceived* risk, and *anticipated* rewards. While this change may not seem major, it does reflect a greater emphasis on the psychological impact of environmental changes (Lab, 2000). In theory, seemingly minor alterations may result in great changes in the perception of effort, risk, and/or reward. Additionally, in the new typology, a fourth category has been added which is titled "Remove excuses for crime." The "new and improved" typology, which includes examples of each technique, is presented in Box 5.1.

Box 5.1. Sixteen Opportunity Reducing Techniques of Situation Crime Prevention

Increase the perceived effort of crime

1. Harden targets:	Steering column locks, anti-robbery screens
2. Control access to targets:	Entry phones, electronic access to garages
3. Deflect offenders from targets:	Bus stop location, street closings, segregation of rival fans
4. Control crime facilitators:	Photos on credit cards, plastic beer glasses in pubs

Increase the perceived risks of crime

5. Screen entrances and exits:	Electronic merchandise tags, baggage screening
6. Formal surveillance:	Red light and speed cameras, security guards
7. Surveillance by employees:	Park attendants, CCTV on double deck buses
8. Natural surveillance:	Street lighting, defensible space architecture

Reduce the anticipated rewards of crime

9. Remove targets:	Phonecards, removable car radios, women's refuges
10. Identify property:	Vehicle licensing, property marking, car parts marking
11. Reduce temptation:	Rapid repair of vandalism, off-street parking
12. Deny benefits:	Ink merchandise tags, PIN for car radios, graffiti cleaning

Remove excuses for crime

13. Set rules:	Hotel registration, customs declaration, codes of conduct
14. Alert conscience:	Roadside speedometers, "idiots drink-and-drive" signs
15. Control disinhibitors:	Drinking age laws, car ignition breathalyzer, V-chip in TV
16. Assist compliance:	Litter bins, public lavatories, easy library check-out

Source: Felson, M. & Clarke, R. (1998). Opportunity makes the thief: Practical theory for crime prevention. London, UK: Home Office.

As you can see, situational crime prevention includes many of the same strategies employed by defensible space and CPTED. We have already discussed many of these techniques including target hardening, various forms of surveillance, and access control.

The newest category, removing excuses for crime, includes strategies that make it more difficult for the offender to dismiss his or her involvement in criminal activity due to lack of knowledge of the violation, laziness, or other justifications. The setting of rules provides clear-cut definitions of what is and what is not acceptable behavior. People may be reminded of the rules (and possibly their violation of the rules) through the various "conscience alerts." Department stores often post signs reminding shoppers that read "Shoplifting is a crime." Some of these signs also include penalties for such violations of the law. These signs remind customers of the rules and hopefully make a rational person think twice before taking items from the store.

Controlling disinhibitors refers to limiting access to alcohol, violent television, or other things that might free a person from their regular rational law-abiding state. By controlling disinihibitors, justifications for criminal activities may be removed (such as, "I was drunk and didn't know what I was doing"). Finally, strategies, included in the category of assisting compliance, make it easier to follow the law. For example, at a poorly planned outdoor event with few trash cans and even fewer restroom facilities, a good deal of littering and public urination may occur (especially if there was heavy alcohol consumption at the event!).

Situational Crime Prevention in Practice

Situational crime prevention techniques have been applied in a seemingly endless variety of settings, including schools, jails, convenience stores, shopping malls, parking garages, public housing complexes, and even amusement parks (see Box 5.2 for an examination of Disney World's use of situational crime prevention techniques). Due to the successful implementation of various techniques in a number of different settings, situational crime prevention has been described as an area of promise in reducing crime (Barnes, 1995; Murray, 1995; Weisburd, 1997).

Box 5.2. Situational Crime Prevention in Disney World

In what has become an oft-reprinted manuscript, Clifford D. Shearing and Phillip C. Stenning provide a guided tour of Disney World, which the authors describe as 'an exemplar of modern private corporate policing.' The strategies of crowd control, crime prevention, and discipline are built into the design of the park, with messages of safety and desired pathways of movement constantly being reinforced. The authors describe a typical visit:

> The fun begins the moment the visitor enters Disney World. As one arrives by car one is greeted by a series of smiling young people who, with the aid of clearly visible road markings, direct one to one's parking spot, remind one to lock one's car and to remember its location and then direct one to await the rubber-wheeled train that will convey visitors away from the parking lot. At the boarding location one is directed to stand safely behind guardrails and to board the train in an orderly fashion. While climbing on board one is reminded to remember the name of the parking area and the row number in which one is parked. Once on the train one is encouraged to protect oneself from injury by keeping one's body within the bounds of the carriage and to do the same for children in one's care... (1992:250).

The authors point out that Disney World's success at handling huge crowds of people rests on its methods of anticipating problems and taking the necessary steps to prevent such incidents from occurring. Opportunities for rule violation and disruptive behavior are minimized by the constant messages from the staff directing the movement of the crowds. Physical barriers, such as fountains, flower gardens, and safety rails are used to limit the pathways that one would take. Surveillance is maximized by the roving Disney staff who, in addition to their various other duties, keep an ever-vigilant eye out for signs of disorder, stepping in immediately to politely (but firmly) request compliance. Those who choose to violate the rules are asked to leave the park.

Source: Shearing, C.D. & Stenning, P.C. (1992). From the panopticon to Disney World: The development of discipline. In R. Clarke (ed.) Situational crime prevention: Successful case studies (pp. 249–255). New York: Harrow and Heston.

Successful applications of situational crime prevention techniques begin with a careful analysis of the specific crime problem. While issues related to crime analysis are discussed in later chapters, the specific context of the selected crime must be carefully examined. What is happening? Where is it happening? When? How? Why? What situation seems to be giving rise to the problem? Once full understanding of the situation surrounding the criminal event is reached, one can move on to consider various methods of limiting opportunities for the crime to occur. Once a technique has been implemented, the impact of the change(s) must be carefully monitored. If the technique has demonstrated success, the strategy may be tried in similar situations (Maxfield, 2001).

As an example, a municipal police officer was quite proud of a recent reduction in the number of automobile thefts that had occurred in the city in recent months. About six months prior to this proclamation, the number of auto thefts had been climbing quite dramatically and his agency was under a good deal of pressure to get results. A number of officers had researched recent reports of auto thefts to see if there was any sort of pattern to the crimes. What the officers found was quite interesting: In the majority of the car thefts, the owner of the vehicle had left the keys in the ignition. Over the past ten years or so the city had been experiencing dramatic growth and was changing from more of a rural town to a booming urban area. It is quite common for people in small towns to leave their doors and windows unlocked and their keys in their cars, a practice unheard of in larger metropolitan cities. After their careful analysis of the situational conditions that contributed to the stealing of cars, the agency implemented an educational campaign designed to increase awareness. Billboards and public service messages broadcasted on television and radio stations reminded drivers to remove their keys when exiting their vehicles. Within a few months, the number of auto thefts had declined.

This example illustrates one of the important considerations of situational crime prevention: the technique used will vary with the particular circumstances of a specific type of crime. The educational campaign employed by this agency might not work in other settings. Further, the billboards and other reminders may no longer be as effective a few years (or even a few months) later. While motivated offenders may no longer be able to easily open the door and drive off using the keys, the car may still be stolen through the use of other techniques that require a greater amount of effort, such as hotwiring. In situational crime prevention each solution is tailor made to fit the specific crime problem as it occurs in a single location at a precise moment in time.

Box 5.3. Situational Crime Prevention on the Metro

The subway system running through the Washington D.C. area is one of the safest systems in the country. Crime on the Metro is much lower than similar public mass transit systems in Boston, Chicago, and Atlanta. The relative safety of the Metro is attributed to the various situational crime prevention strategies that have been employed on the train. The opportunity reduction strategies include the following:

- Long, winding corridors and hidden corners were avoided in the design in order to reduce potential hiding places for offenders
- Farecards may be purchased in any dollar amount at the vending machines, which reduces the amount of time that a passenger would have to fumble through his or her wallet searching out the correct currency to use
- The exterior and interior surfaces are designed to be resistant to vandalism and graffiti.

- There are no restrooms or lockers available to the general public, which reduces places for offenders to loiter.
- There are no fast food restaurants, which serves to reduce the opportunity for litter as well as the potential for robbery or pick-pocketing of hungry, distracted customers.
- The area is under intense surveillance by staff, custodial workers, and closed-circuit televisions.

Adapted from La Vigne, N. (1997, November). Visibility and vigilance: Metro's situational approach to preventing subway crime. Washington, D.C.: National Institute of Justice.

Summary

Three related sets of policy recommendations that have been derived from choice-based theories have been examined. Defensible space, CPTED, and situational crime prevention all rest on the assumption of a motivated rational offender. Proponents of these strategies argue that crime may be reduced through modifications that reduce the opportunity for a rational offender to commit a crime. Through the use of these various techniques a target may become less attractive to a motivated offender either by increasing the perceived risk of apprehension, increasing the perceived amount of effort, or reducing the anticipated rewards. These modifications may include changes in the physical environment; technological advancements (such as caller ID) or other strategies that will make an offender think twice before committing a crime.

Critiques and Concerns

While this family of crime prevention strategies has received a great deal of excited interest from some, others have voiced strong concerns over wide-spread implementation of these techniques. While these issues will be explored in greater detail in the final chapter, it is important to briefly mention these critiques.

The most common critique of crime prevention strategies concerns the issue of **displacement**. In general, this argument claims that the various techniques explored in this chapter really have nothing to do with preventing crimes from happening—the crime simply moves. There are a number of different kinds of displacement and the most common forms are summarized in Box 5.4. While proponents of crime prevention strategies must often defend their methods against charges of displacement, in actuality there is no empirical evidence that complete displacement has ever occurred. In the cases where some displacement has occurred, overall the crime level has been reduced (Barnes, 1995; Eck, 1993).

Box 5.4. Displacement Types	
Displacement Type	Example
Temporal	Crime is moved to a different hour of the day or day of the week that is perceived to be less risky
Target	Crime is moved from a well-protected target to a more vulnerable one
Spatial	Offenders move from one location to another that is perceived to be a safer location
Tactical	Offenders change their methods of committing a crime to overcome the design modification
Perpetrator	As one offender becomes deterred from crime (either through their own choice or through arrest) another offender step in
Type of Crime	Offenders deterred from one form of crime will now select an entirely new form of crime

Source: Adapted from Felson & Clarke (1998) and Barnes (1995)

There have also been a number of critiques raised on ethical grounds. It has been argued that the ability to implement crime prevention strategies is related to social class. Those with the resources to do so may turn their homes into fortresses. Poorer individuals cannot afford to move into gated communities and install expensive alarm systems. If you combine this argument with the notion of displacement, essentially the concern is that crime gets moved from the well-protected targets of the affluent to more vulnerable targets of the poor.

There have been other ethical and ideological charges against the various forms of crime prevention discussed in this chapter. For example, it has been argued that intensive video surveillance infringes on individual rights and personal freedoms. Others have charged that implementation of target hardening strategies and other tactics divert attention from the root causes of crime. Instead of investing in crime prevention strategies, we should be investing in social prevention — improving education, job training, and delinquency prevention programs (Felson & Clarke, 1997).

Since many of these same critiques could be leveled against other techniques explored in this text (crackdowns, directed patrol, even some community policing efforts), the final chapter will include a more detailed discussion of these issues. For now, suffice it to say that not everyone is enamored by the success of the techniques presented in this chapter.

Chapter 6

The Analysis of Crime

Thus far the examination of space, time, and crime has included an exploration of a number of theoretical explanations that have attempted to address why crime, disorder, and other social ills seem to be concentrated in certain geographic locations. Practical policies that have grown from these theoretical frameworks have also been studied. In this next section, the examination of a variety of tools available to law enforcement, private security agencies, local communities, government agencies, and other interested parties who are concerned with the study of patterns of crime and disorder is included.

What Is Crime Analysis?

In its most rudimentary form, the term "crime analysis" has been applied to a patrol-oriented tool used by police agencies to identify patterns of criminal activity and to assist in a more rational deployment of patrol officers (Peterson, 1998). Through a careful analysis of police reports, calls for service, and other available data, police agencies may use crime analysis to concentrate their efforts where they are needed the most. While this is still an important aspect of crime analysis, there are many uses beyond this limited application.

Crime analysis is a broad term that is used to describe a number of different methods associated with the systematic examination of crime and crime-related data. According to Rachel Boba, Director of the Police Foundation's Crime Mapping Laboratory, crime analysis is defined as:

> The qualitative and quantitative study of crime and law enforcement information in combination with socio-demographic and spatial factors to apprehend criminals, prevent crime, reduce disorder, and evaluate organizational procedures (Boba, 2001).

This is a rather complicated definition, so the various components will be considered. First, crime analysis may use a variety of data sources in order to gain knowledge about a particular situation. **Qualitative data** is usually conceived of as non-numerical information. Qualitative studies include such things as a systematic observation of a problem location or neighborhood; careful examination of in-depth interviews with local residents, offenders, or victims; or a content analysis of various informational documents, such as property or real estate records or the narrative descriptions within arrest reports. On the other hand, **quantitative studies** usually involve number crunching of numerical data. For example, a crime analyst working in a police agency may calculate a range of times (such as 2:00 a.m. to 4:00 a.m.) in which a particular robber is likely to hit the next target or predict how many new officers will be needed given an increase in the population.

Depending on the specific situation or task, a crime analyst may use one or both types of data. It is important to remember that regardless of the data type, the crime analyst must carefully follow the rules associated with research methodology and statistical analysis. This is not "voodoo science," but a deliberate scientific examination of data carefully gathered, following the rules of social science research.

Boba's definition also includes a reference to socio-demographic and spatial factors. According to Boba, socio-demographic factors include descriptions of individuals and groups, such as gender, race, income, age, and education level. On the individual level, these factors may assist law enforcement officers in the identification and apprehension of a specific suspect, such as "Be on the look out for a white male, age 27, with blonde hair and green eyes." On the group level, crime analysts may use socio-demographic information to try to explain why one neighborhood has a higher number of calls for service than another area. For example, census data may be used to compare the median income, proportion of renters, and race and ethnicity characteristics of several different neighborhoods. This information may then be used to examine for correlations or relationships between the number and type of calls for police services. Spatial factors are important in the understanding of why certain locations seem to be more crime-ridden than others. Spatial factors include the location of a crime as well as other important considerations, such as street network patterns, zoning regulations, and locations of schools, liquor stores, or other places of interest.

Boba's definition ends with the four goals of crime analysis: apprehending criminals, preventing crime, reducing disorder, and evaluating organizational procedures. These goals are obviously centered on crime analysis in a law enforcement agency. While a great deal of this discussion will center on the use of crime analysis for police purposes, it is important to remember that members of the law enforcement community are not the only consumers of such information. Place managers, real estate speculators, academics, and program evaluations all make use of crime data and analysis for various purposes.

Historical Development of Crime Analysis

The information-gathering process associated with crime analysis may be traced back to ancient Chinese cultures and to Biblical times. According to Peterson (1998), historical references to the gathering, analysis, application, and use of information, especially during times of war, may be found dating back thousands of years. Crime analysis was also used during the feudal period of England. There is evidence that during this period "analysts" examined available data to specifically identify possible suspects and patterns of crime (Gottlieb, Arenberg & Singh, 1998).

In the United States, crime analysis as tool for law enforcement has had a much shorter history. August Vollmer was Chief of Police in Berkeley, California, from 1905-1932. Vollmer was highly influential in his quest to professionalize policing. He advocated the hiring of college graduates to serve as police officers and was the first to establish college-level courses in police science at the University of California in 1916 (Walker & Katz, 2002).

As part of his professionalization agenda, Vollmer advocated a number of practices designed to make policing more effective and efficient. While the English had been using a systematic technique called modus operandi (MO) analysis to classify known offenders, Vollmer is credited with introducing this technique to the United States. In MO analysis, the peculiar aspects of an offender's actions in committing the crime are recorded. For example, a burglar may enter homes through sliding glass doors located in the rear of the home. Once inside, this particular burglar may ransack the home, taking televisions, stereos, and other electronic equipment but leaving behind valuable jewelry. If this same MO is found in a number of different crime scenes, one can reasonably assume that the same person is committing these crimes. Through the use of MO analysis, police agencies may carefully examine other characteristics of crimes committed by this same offender in order to more efficiently identify and apprehend the suspect (Gottlieb et al., 1998; Haley, Todd & Stallo, 1998).

In addition to the introduction of MO analyses, Vollmer is also credited with the development of more scientific patrol management procedures, such as examining calls for service in order to perform analyses based on "beats" or predetermined geographic zones. Vollmer used pin maps to identify the specific locations of crimes and/or calls for service. Through a visual examination of where the pins were clustered in the city, Vollmer was better able to deploy policing resources to the beats or locations where the crime and calls were concentrated (Gottlieb et al., 1998). Vollmer was quite a visionary for his time, and his ideas of police management continue to impact contemporary law enforcement practices. Because of his influence, he has been called "the father of American police professionalism" (Walker & Katz, 2002:33).

One of Vollmer's former students, Orlando W. Wilson, greatly expanded Vollmer's vision of policing as a modern professional science. Wilson held a number of influential positions both in police agencies and in academia, serving as chief in Wichita, Kansas, superintendent of the Chicago Police Department, and as dean of the University of California School of Criminology. Wilson wrote two widely read textbooks on police management principles, including *Police Administration* (1950). This textbook became known as the "bible" of police management, and although new contributors have been added, the text is still popular and influential in contemporary times (Cox, 1996; Walker & Katz, 2002).

Wilson contributed a number of revolutionary ideas to law enforcement. To enhance efficiency, Wilson developed an assignment allocation formula that provided an optimal number of patrol officers based on the level of criminal activity and calls for service in a specific area. Additionally, Wilson advocated the use of crime analysis, which he felt was an essential police function. In the second edition of his text, which was released in 1963, Wilson envisioned a crime analysis unit whose members would systematically review crime reports on a daily basis. From these reports, the crime analysts would categorize information on the location, time, MO, and other important factors in order to assist in the identification of crime patterns and/or offenders (Gottlieb, et al., 1998; Walker & Katz, 2002).

The Growth of "Smart" Policing

The 1960s were a revolutionary time for the country and law enforcement. Police agencies were increasingly under attack for their heavy-handed tactics, especially among minority citizens. Riots rocked major cities where oftentimes the root cause was a real or perceived act of police misconduct that had involved a minority citizen. Crime rates were on the rise. A number of reports were released that criticized the police, calling for better hiring practices, improved training, more education, and greater professionalism (National Advisory Commission on Civil Disorders, 1968; President's Commission on Law Enforcement and Administration of Justice, 1967).

As a result of the intense interest in improving police practices, the Federal Government provided a great deal of money to fund policing-oriented research and to offer educational opportunities for police officers. The Law Enforcement Assistance Administration (LEAA) and the Police Foundation were born out of this era. The LEAA provided a billion dollars a year to improve the effectiveness of criminal justice agencies. Both the LEAA and the Police Foundation provided funding for research designed to study and improve police practices. Some of the research that was conducted during these times dramatically changed the way law enforcement services were provided (Swanson, Territo, & Taylor, 1998).

The Kansas City Preventive Patrol Experiment, which was funded by the Police Foundation, raised serious questions about the effectiveness of routine, random patrol on crime (Kelling, Page, Dieckman, & Brown, 1974). A study conducted by the RAND Corporation questioned the effectiveness of police investigations, reporting that many detective units were highly unproductive (Greenwood, 1975). The importance of faster response times, long heralded as being the key to effectively identify and arrest suspects, was also challenged by research findings (Department of Justice, 1978). As a result of these and other studies, police chiefs were under a great deal of pressure to alter their practices. The economy was also experiencing a downturn. No longer could police chiefs and sheriffs count on additional funds for the hiring of more police officers. Instead, administrators were forced to make better use of the resources that they already had. The need for more reliable and accurate information that could be used to assist law enforcement grew dramatically, as did interest in crime analysis.

In the mid-1970s, Robert O. Heck, a senior program specialist for the LEAA, developed the Patrol Emphasis Program (PEP). The goal of

PEP was to provide a plan for police agencies to use crime analysis to assist in the management of calls for service and to enhance the quality of criminal investigations. The PEP plan did enjoy some success, and Heck expanded on these ideas to develop the Integrated Criminal Apprehension Program, or ICAP (Gottlieb, et al. 1998). The importance of crime analysis was stressed once again in ICAP, especially in the identification of habitual offenders. The general assumption was that a small number of career criminals was responsible for a large number of offenses. This small group of offenders would, in all likelihood, have numerous recorded contacts with the police either through arrest reports, field interview reports, or other documents. Heck felt that if police agencies could somehow easily retrieve and categorize information that they already had within their grasp, the investigative process could be greatly improved. One of the changes recommended by ICAP was to improve the quality of record keeping allowing for easier access to needed information.

Unfortunately, the popularity and utility of crime analysis in everyday operations was hampered by the available technology. Even with improved record keeping, the use of computers to retrieve needed information was extremely limited. For example, if a detective was looking for the name of a white male suspect with brown hair and brown eyes who had a tattoo of Mighty Mouse on his left shoulder, the information could not be readily accessed. In many agencies, important information was kept on note cards or paper reports that had to be searched by hand. In modern times, the task of finding a name, address, and other information on an individual based on a physical description would take a few seconds, assuming that the data had been entered into a computerized database.

During the 1970s, software applications were very complicated. Trained experts were needed to make modifications to Fortran-based programs that were housed on a mainframe system (Peterson, 1998). As a result of the "user-hostile" systems as well as the expense, few agencies used computers for analysis. In 1980, a survey was conducted to investigate the level and sophistication of computer use by larger police agencies. A total of 122 agencies (out of 150 contacted) responded to the survey. The results revealed that only 12 of the 122 agencies that responded to the survey were using their computer systems for crime analysis related tasks (Tafoya, 1998). It was still a few more years before computer equipment and software applications had evolved to the point that many larger agencies could purchase and actually use the new tools (Peterson, 1998).

Contemporary Crime Analysis: The Building of a Profession

Interest in the analysis of crime continued to grow throughout the 1980s. More and more agencies began to develop crime analysis units, often with little or no idea of what, exactly, a crime analyst is supposed to do. In many cases, a person designated as a "crime analyst" received minimal (if any) training on analysis techniques. It was not unheard of for injured patrol officers to be assigned to the crime analysis unit before returning to full duty on the streets (a practice that continues today in some agencies, which we will discuss later).

In response to the demand for training and standards, a number of organizations were created in order to enhance professionalism in the field. In 1980, The International Association of Law Enforcement Intelligence Analysts (IALEA) was created. **Intelligence analysis** is a special type of crime analysis. The use of this term usually refers to the analysis of data to solve major crimes or to assist in the investigation of organized criminal activity. The goal of the IALEA organization was to develop professional standards for the growing field of intelligence analysis. Currently, the organization has members from around the globe and continues to provide training, career development, and technology awareness (Peterson, 1998). For more information, see Box 6.1.

Box 6.1. The International Association of Law Enforcement Intelligence Analysis

IALEA, which was formed in 1980, continues to provide services to law enforcement agencies interested in improving the skills of their analysts. According to the IALEA website:

> The purpose of IALEIA is to advance high standards of professionalism in law enforcement intelligence analysis at the Local, State/Provincial, National and International levels. Its aim is to enhance general understanding of the role of intelligence analysis, encourage the recognition of intelligence analysis as a professional endeavor, develop International qualification and competence standards, reinforce professional concepts, devise training standards and curricula, furnish advisory and related services on intelligence analysis matters, conduct analytic-related research studies and provide the ability to disseminate information regarding analytical techniques and methods.

IALEIA welcomes student members. For a nominal fee, you can join the organization to learn more about intelligence analysis, job opportunities, and training materials. For more information, please go to their website at http://www.ialeia.org

In 1989, the Society of Certified Criminal Analysts (SCCA) was created to complement the goals of IALEA. This organization has developed standards and testing for the professional certification of crime analysts. Individuals who have attained certification as a crime analyst are held in high regard by their peers, and some agencies require certification for advancement. As of 2001, nearly 200 analysts have met the standards of this organization and are working as certified crime analysts. In order to become a certified criminal analyst, applicants must meet a number of criteria including the successful completion of a number of training courses, documented experience as a crime analyst, and the passing of an exam (for more information, see their website at http://www.ialeia.org/scca).

Box 6.2. The Society of Certified Criminal Analysts

The goal of this organization is to promote standards and professionalism to crime analysts working in a variety of settings. The organization promotes its mission through the development of standards in education, training, and continued professional development.

The organization has two certification levels: regular and lifetime. In order to attain a regular certificate, a crime analysts must meet the following criteria:

1. Minimum 24-hours of training from an approved source on various crime analysis techniques.
2. A minimum of an Associate's Degree or the equivalent credits (generally 60), or five years of documented experience in a related criminal justice position.
3. Passing composite grade on SCCA examination.
4. Working, or having worked for at least three years as an analyst, analyst supervisor or analyst manager for law enforcement, private security or the military.
5. Membership in International Association of Law Enforcement Intelligence Analysts (IALEIA) and/or the Australian Institute of Professional Intelligence Officers (AIPIO).

Source: Adapted from the SCCA website at http://www.ialeia.org/scca

---

The International Association of Crime Analysts (IACA) was formed in 1990. The purpose of this organization is to encourage communication between crime analysts so that they may learn from each other and improve their skills. The IACA maintains a "members only" list serve for the sharing of information and ideas. Students may join the organization and are then able to view employment opportunities, announcements of training courses, as well as to get a feel for the sorts of every day issues confronting crime analysts. This organization has several hundred members. Each year the organization holds an annual conference and offers many training and networking opportunities. Additionally, venders are on-hand to alert members to newly available technology and provide demonstrations.

Box 6.3. So You Want to Be a Crime Analyst?

As I tell my students, crime analysis is a great field to consider. The position can be very challenging and rewarding. Oftentimes, students wish to work in a law-enforcement related position but are put off by the odd working hours as well as the dangers associated with patrol. Crime analysis offers the best of all worlds. One can work on the identification and apprehension of criminals from the comfort of your air-conditioned office. Additionally, depending on the individual agency, crime analyst positions may be filled by non-sworn personnel. For those wishing to pursue a career as a crime analyst, the International Association of Crime Analysts offers a number of suggestions.

First, while there are few existing standards for employment and training, a degree in criminology/criminal justice, political science, or geographic information systems may give an edge. When looking for an elective course, the IACA suggests the following areas:

- Criminology/Criminal Theory
- Geographic Information Systems (GIS)/Crime Mapping
- Criminal Justice/Social Science Research Methods & Statistics
- Improving your writing capabilities (creative and otherwise)
- The relationship between geographic and environmental factors and crime
- Police Science & Strategy
- Police Administration
- Desktop Publishing, Spreadsheet, and Database applications (especially Excel, Access, and similar applications)

Second, the options available to you locally should be explored. Some colleges and universities offer certification programs in crime analysis (especially in California). Sign up for an internship with the crime analysis unit. Call your local Regional Community Policing Institute to see if there are any training courses you can take. There are also a number of private companies, such as the Alpha Group Center for Crime and Intelligence Analysis Training, which provide courses in crime and intelligence analysis at various locations throughout the country. Also, be aware that an in-depth background check will be required of applicants for crime analyst positions. This is true even for non-sworn personnel.

Sample Job Description/Position Announcement

The IACA provides a number of position announcements on its website. The following was contributed by the Cambridge, Massachusetts Police Department:

Crime Analyst III

A professional civilian position involving the collection, management, and analysis of crime, calls for service, and other data to find crime trends, patterns, series, sprees, hot spots, and other crime problems. The analyst disseminates this information to the department (through bulletins and reports) and assists, if necessary, in the process of developing strategies to address identified problems.

Duties and Responsibilities

Analysis and dissemination of crime data

- Receive, sort, and review reports of crimes and arrests submitted by officers, supplemental reports submitted by investigators, calls for service, and data from other agencies. Code and classify incidents.
- Prepare detailed analysis of crime patterns and trends identified through daily review.
- Prepare weekly analysis of five ""target crimes,"" describing current status of the crimes and noting recent activity and developments.
- Maintain daily email briefing for command staff members and superior officers, updating them on serious crime and crime patterns.
- Work with the Crime Analysis Intern to create and publish daily bulletin and review of serious crime incidents, current patterns, and other police information.
- Co-write Quarterly and Annual Crime Reports for the department and community.
- Identify potential offenders involved in crime patterns by searching crime and arrest histories.

Special Tasks

- Prepare pin maps and thematic maps of crime, police routes, and other police information in MapInfo.
- Work with analysts from nearby jurisdictions to identify cross-jurisdictional crime patterns.
- Provide information on neighborhood safety to residents or prospective residents.
- Prepare neighborhood analyses for community presentations.
- Maintain crime analysis section of police department World Wide Web page.
- Prepare monthly statistical reports on total crime, arrests, and selected calls for service.

Source: The International Association of Crime Analysts web page at http://www.iaca.net

The "Haves" versus the "Have-Nots"

Crime analysis is a rapidly evolving field with a great deal of potential. While some agencies have enthusiastically embraced crime analysis, others seem to purposely resist the introduction of this new crime-fighting tool, dismissing it as a "fad" that is nothing more than formalized common sense. It is truly fascinating to see the great disparity in the funding, support, and respect given to different crime analysis units, some within the same jurisdiction. In Box 4, Haley et al. (1998) describe three stages of evolution of crime analysis units. While some agencies are outstanding examples of sophisticated units, others agencies do not have the capabilities (or perhaps the interest) to provide even the most rudimentary crime analysis.

Box 6.4. Stages of Development of Crime Analysis Units

I. Informal

- Based on an officer's memory and past experience
- Hampered by officer's limited duty time and interest and large volume of crime
- Subjective, biased, and out of date
- Time consuming
- Limited MO storage, analysis, and ability to recognize patterns
- Uncoordinated and ineffective communications

II. Formal Crime Analysis: Basic Operations

- Staffed by one or two people
- Normal business hour operations
- Analyzes three or four crime categories
- Manual filing and storage with limited cross-referencing
- Lacks crime prediction and known offender/MO analysis
- Limited visual geographical analysis, usually pin maps

III. Formal Crime Analysis: Advanced Operations

- Rapid correlations among offenses involving expanded numbers of crime categories
- Names of suspects provided for operational units
- Computer storage database with rapid searching criteria
- Large staff with a twenty-four hour operation
- Crime reports reviewed for quality before entered into database

- Complex storage of known offender information, including descriptions, vehicles, and MOs

Source: K. Haley, J. Todd, & M. Stallo (1998). Crime analysis and the struggle for legitimacy. Presented at the annual meeting of the Academy of Criminal Justice Sciences in Albuquerque, New Mexico, March 10-14, 1998.

As amazing as it might sound, it has been estimated that as many as one-third of law enforcement agencies still do not have computers (Pilant, 1999). Even when the agencies do have computers, there are no guarantees that the technology is being used efficiently. I worked with one agency that had no access to the Internet or email. At this same agency, I was told to never ask for the same information twice, since there would be no correspondence between the data. While attending a training session for crime analysis in the summer months of 2000, I met one crime analyst who was not provided with a desktop computer of her own and an agency statistician who had never taken a course in statistics. While there are still some crime analysts who have only a high school education (that may have been earned many, many years ago), other agencies have employed individuals with doctorate degrees in statistics to crunch their numbers.

Types of Crime Analysis

What does a crime analyst have to do with the our broader discussion of space, time, and crime? Crime analysts are asked to perform a variety of different tasks, not all of which are directly related to our immediate concerns. For example, one form of crime analysis is called **administrative crime analysis.** This type of crime analysis involves the provision of crime data to administrators, city council members, and citizens. The crime analyst may be asked to prepare a report for the city council on the feasibility and potential impact of a juvenile curfew ordinance; provide crime data for the preparation of grants; or maintain a crime analysis website for local citizens to access (Boba, 2001; Gottlieb et al. 1998).

We have also previously mentioned intelligence analysis, which is a specialized type of crime analysis. Intelligence analysis involves the study of "organized" criminal networks. Movies often portray a crime family or other criminal network in the form of a pyramid, with the kingpin or don at the top, followed by a layer of lieutenants, then a layer of lower-level people. This is an example of intelligence analysis.

Intelligence analysts may use such tools as telephone toll analyses (to monitor who is connected to whom), financial or tax analyses, or various methods to study family or business relationships. In light of the September 11th attacks on the World Trade Center and the Pentagon, intelligence analysis has been used to monitor terrorist networks both domestically and abroad (Boba, 2001).

Criminal investigative analysis is often associated with the investigation of serial murders and is often known as "profiling." While this type of analysis was made wildly popular by the movie "Silence of the Lambs," in actuality analysts at the local level rarely perform this function. Since serial murderers rarely respect jurisdictional lines, this type of analysis is normally conducted by federal law enforcement agencies. A victim may be picked up in one state, murdered in another, and the body recovered elsewhere (Boba, 2001; Gottlieb et al. 1998).

Of greater interest to our discussion of space, time, and crime are **tactical crime analysis** and **strategic crime analysis**. Tactical crime analysis is focused on more immediate concerns. On a daily basis, the analyst reviews available crime data gathered from arrest reports, field interview reports (FIRs), calls for service, trespass warnings and other available information to identify how, when, and where criminal activity has occurred. After reviewing this information, the analyst attempts to identify a potential **crime pattern** or **crime series**. Gottlieb et al. define a crime pattern as "the occurrence of similar offenses in a defined geographic area, either a single reporting district, a beat, or an entire jurisdiction (1998:17, 18)." In a crime pattern, there is no evidence that the same person or persons committed the crimes. Conversely, a crime series is a type of crime pattern where there is evidence to believe that the crimes were committed by the same person or persons.[1] Tactical crime analysis also involves the identification of "hot spots" and "burning times," issues discussed at length in the next section.

While tactical crime analysis is primarily used to make more informed decisions regarding the deployment of policing resources, strategic crime analysis is more focused on long-term issues (Velasco & Boba, 2000). An easy way to keep the definitions of strategic versus tactical

---

1. At this point, it is important to mention that definitions of "crime patterns" and "crime series" may vary between agencies. Some agencies will flip the definitions of these terms, while others will assign completely different definitions to the terms. Please bear in mind that crime analysis is an emerging profession with no standardized vocabulary.

crime analysis separate is to focus on the timeliness of the information used. Tactical crime analysis uses data that have been collected over the past several days, while strategic crime analysis uses information that has been collected over a much longer period of time, normally a year or more (Canter, 2000). According to Boba (2001:13) strategic crime analysis is "the study of crime and law enforcement information integrated with socio-demographic and spatial factors to determine long term 'patterns' of activity, to assist in problem solving, as well as to research and evaluate responses and procedures." Along with crime data, the analyst also considers neighborhood characteristics such as the race, education level, family structure, and income level of local residents.

Space, Time, and Crime Analysis: Hot Spots & Burning Times

The analysis of hot spots has been described as the new "catchphrase" of research on crime (Swartz, 2000). The study of hot spots is, well, hot. Brantingham and Brantingham (1999) argue that the study of hot spots has evolved into "one of the most important contributions of environmental criminology both to contemporary criminological research and to criminal justice practice" (1999:7). The Brantinghams define a hot spot as the concentration or cluster of crimes in space. Hot spots are usually differentiated from high crime areas. Hot spots are small geographic locations, such as an intersection or even a single address, while a high crime area is geographically larger than a hot spot (Farrell & Sousa, 2001). Burning times are defined as "temporal clusters of crimes at specific, repeated moments in some temporal cycle" (Brantingham & Brantingham, 1999:8).

It is important to recognize a few points regarding high crime areas, hot spots, and burning times. First, not every target (individuals, homes, or businesses) in a high crime area will experience crime. No matter how large or small the area, some locations will have a higher number of crimes than others (Block & Block, 1995; Eck & Weisburd, 1995). Second, a hot spot may not be hot all of the time—you need to consider both the location and time of day. For example, there is a relatively small entertainment district in the Tampa area known as Ybor City. Without fail, when the bars close on Friday and Saturday nights at 3:00 a.m., the number of assaults, acts of vandalism, and incidents of driving under the influence predictably increase. However, during the day, the area reports far few criminal events when the streets are filled with business people and a few tourists looking for a quick bite for lunch.

Targeting Hot Spots: Directed Patrols

Lawrence Sherman and his colleagues have done a great deal of research on hot spots and the distribution of crime in urban areas (see, for example, Sherman, 1995; Sherman, Gartin, & Buerger, 1989; Sherman, Schmidt, & Velke, 1992; Sherman, Shaw, & Rogan, 1995; Sherman & Weisburd, 1995). In one study, Sherman et al. (1989) conducted an analysis of the calls for service to the police in the city of Minneapolis. The researchers found that half of the 323,000 calls could be traced to only 3 percent of the addresses in the city. The concentration was even greater if one only considered predatory crimes such as robbery, auto theft, and criminal sex acts. A single address accounted for 810 calls for police service over a one-year period. Conversely, no calls for service were received from 60 percent of the addresses in the city. If police efforts could be concentrated to target these "repeat customers," both the crime rate and the workload of the police could significantly be reduced.

Sherman, Shaw, and Rogan (1995) tested the impact of concentrated police efforts in a hot spot area. In beat 144 located in Kansas City, the homicide rate was nearly 20 times greater than the national average. Additionally, there were 14 rapes, 72 armed robberies, and 222 aggravated assaults in this single, relatively small beat. Drive-by shootings were also common in this relatively small area. In this particular study, a technique called **directed patrol** was used to target gun crimes in hot spot locations within beat 144 during the burning times of 7 p.m. to 1 a.m., seven days a week.

In contrast to random patrol, directed patrol provides officers with specific instructions on who or what they should be focusing their attention on. Some agencies employ directed patrol plans for the officers to use in their uncommitted time (when they are not responding to a call, for example) while other agencies free officers from responding to 911 calls, making directed patrol activities their sole responsibility. In the Kansas City study, additional officers assigned to the hot spot areas did not answer calls for service, but were expected to focus exclusively on gun detection and gun seizures. Sherman and his colleagues found that the directed patrol efforts were successful. Significant reductions were found in the number of gun-related crimes, including homicides and drive-by shootings. Additionally, citizens living in the target area reported lower levels of fear, greater neighborhood satisfaction, and lower perceptions of social and physical disorder. The researchers concluded that directed patrol efforts targeted at hot spots was a cost-effective means of fighting gun-related crime. Successful directed patrol efforts have also been noted in targeting drug markets (Weisburd and Mazerolle, 2000); high crime taverns (Sherman et al., 1992), arson (Martin, Barnes, & Britt, 1998), residential burglary (Reno, 1998) and even serial rapists (LeBeau, 1992).

It is the responsibility of the crime analyst to gather the daily reports of criminal activity, identify potential hot spots, burning times, or other patterns that may exist, and assist in the development of directed patrol plans to resolve the crime problem. For a discussion of this process, see the description of a typical day in the life of a tactical crime analyst, written by Christopher Bruce, at the end of this chapter.

Strategic Crime Analysis: The Next Step

As phrased by Bruce (2000:10), tactical crime analysis is described as "where the action is," "urgent *and* important," and "dealing with the immediate, the critical, the here and now." When you read Bruce's daily journal, you get a feel for the almost frenzied flurry of activity surrounding the efforts in quickly gathering, analyzing, and disseminating timely information to the troops. When working in the tactical dimension, crime analysts are under great pressure to quickly identify patterns, series, and hot spots for activity. The strategic analysis of crime is a more reflective process. For example, in an analysis of the calls for service data, the tactical analysts may identify a specific neighborhood as having a higher than normal level of requests for police services. However, the analysts may not have the time (or all of the necessary information) to develop a long-term solution to this problem. One of the important elements of strategic analysis is to use the tactical data to identify problems and develop innovative solutions to these problems. Strategic crime analysis is an essential component of problem-oriented policing.

Wolves and Ducks and Dens: Oh My!

The most important conclusion of this book is that crime is not evenly distributed among persons, places, or times. It has been argued that 10 percent of the offenders committing the most crimes are responsible for about 50 percent of all crimes; 10 percent of the most victimized people are involved in about 40 percent of all crimes; and that 10 percent of the locations with the most crime are responsible for about 60 percent of all crime (Eck, 2001; Sacco & Kennedy; 2002).

Tactical crime analysts may determine that a neighborhood has a high level of criminal activities. However, one cannot be sure whether or not the high rate of crime is due to a high concentration of motivated offenders (which Eck, 2001 calls ravenous wolves), a rather small number of victims who are repeatedly targeted (sitting ducks), or a few hot spot locations where a large number of crimes occur (a den of iniquity). How effectively a police agency responds to a troubled area will depend on careful analysis of the data. Does the agency have a wolf problem, a duck problem, a den problem, or some combination of the three?

Additionally, the police may not have access to all of the necessary information to accurately diagnose the problem. It is important to keep in mind that even the best crime analysis is based on the data that police have access to. If citizens do not call the police to inform them of a crime problem, then there are no reports of the incident. If there are no reports, then crime analysts do not have the input to identify possible patterns of criminal activity. While a police officer may possess a good deal of familiarity with his or her beat, the quality and quantity of this information cannot compare to the intimate knowledge held by a local resident. In order to correctly identify problematic conditions and develop successful plans to address these problems, police need to tap into the informal database of the local community.

Strategic Crime Analysis and Community Policing Problem Solving Efforts

In chapter 4, the underlying concepts of community policing and problem oriented policing were discussed at length. Under a community policing philosophy, local law abiding residents are viewed as partners in the safeguarding of their neighborhood. Police cannot successfully reduce crime and improve the quality of life in a neighborhood without the cooperation and input of the people who live there.

Crime analysis has been described as the most important element of the problem solving process (Bynum, 2001). Gotleib et al. (1998) assert that it is "incomprehensible" to believe that problem solving community policing programs can be successful without the input of crime analysis. Problem solving policing assumes that patterns and trends in community problems may be detected. "Community problems" may involve criminal activity or quality of life issues, or some combination of both. Correct identification of patterns and trends will lead the police and the community to understand why these conditions exist and ultimately develop methods to resolve the problems (Bynum, 2001).

The SARA Model: Analysis in Action

The SARA model is the most commonly used course of action in the process of problem solving. This four-step model involves scanning, analysis, response, and assessment (Eck & Spellman, 1987).

Scanning is the first step in the problem solving process. During this phase, the actual problem is identified through a preliminary review of available information. Data from a variety of sources are considered, such as calls for service, reports of criminal incidents, perceptions of patrol officers assigned to the area, and citizen input. At this stage the goal is to try to move beyond the rather simple conceptualization of singular incidents. Instead, scanning involves standing back and trying to see "the big picture." For example, a patrol officer may move from one call for service to another, viewing each call as a singular, isolated incident. The purpose of the scanning phase is to move beyond this level and identify clusters or groups of similar, related, or recurring problems (Boba, 2001). Once the clusters or groups have been identified, the agency must prioritize these problems for consideration and select which issues will be addressed.

The **analysis** phase involves careful consideration of a variety of data sources in order to answer the questions of what, where, when, how, and why the problem has developed. While police agencies have demonstrated success in the identification of problems, proficiency during the analysis stage has proven to be more challenging (Bynum,

2001). One of the problems is that agency personnel may *assume* they already know what the "true" nature and cause of the problem is. As a result, an agency may feel that an exhaustive analysis of the problem is a waste of time (Boba, 2001). However, data collected during the analysis stage can provide information that the agency may not have considered important or relevant.

During the analysis stage it is important to solicit input from as many sources as possible. Full knowledge of an area's problems cannot be gained from a single source (Block, 1998). For example, a patrol officer working in a specific geographic area may have a different view than an officer assigned to a gang or narcotics unit working in the same zone. A local resident may offer additional information, as can the owner of a neighborhood business. Community social service workers may also provide relevant input. This becomes even more important when one considers the element of time: The manager of a local bank may have a much different perspective than the owner of a convenience store that is open 24 hours a day.

During the **response** phase, the police agency solicits input from local residents, business owners, various community groups, schools, churches, and other interested partners to develop innovative solutions to the problem (Gotlieb, et al., 1998). If a neighborhood problem involves a large number of juveniles hanging around on local street corners with nothing to do, the agency would be wise to include representatives from this group in the development of possible solution. If an agency requests input from a number of different sources, then the agency will (hopefully) end up with a larger number of possible solutions from which to choose the best course of action. Some of the action plans will not be feasible due to financial or legal constraints. Once the police and their new partners have agreed on the best course of action, the plan should be implemented.

Finally, the **assessment** phase involves an evaluation of the effectiveness of the chosen response. The assessment phase allows the agency to determine whether or not the action plan worked as planned. In some cases, the assessment may show that the initial problem was misidentified during the scanning phase, or that more detailed analysis was needed. As an example of the SARA process in action, I will walk you through an experience I had with the City of Pensacola, Florida Police Department.

Box 6.5. The SARA Problem Solving Model

SUMMARY OF SCANNING STEPS

    Step 1

- Laundry list of potential problems.

    Step 2

- Problems identified.

    Step 3

- Problems prioritized.

    Step 4

- State the specific problem.
- List examples of where the problem occurs.
- Which setting is causing the most difficulty?

Review and Preparation for Analysis

    Hypothesis

- From what you already know, what do you think is causing the problem?
- General goal statement.
- How will data be gathered and reported?
- When will data collection begin?

SUMMARY OF ANALYSIS STEPS

    Step 1

- What conditions or events precede the problem?
- What conditions or events accompany the problem?
- What are the problem's consequences?
- What harms result from the problem?

    Step 2

- How often does the problem occur?
- How long has this been a problem?
- What is the duration of each occurrence of the problem?
- Now that the data has been collected, should you continue with analysis or return to scanning and restate the problem?

    Hypothesis

- What are your conclusions about why the problem occurs?

    Step 3

- Define a tentative goal.
- Identify resources that may be of assistance in solving the problem.

- What procedures, policies or rules have been established to address the problem?

SUMMARY OF RESPONSE STEPS

Step 1

- Brainstorm possible interventions.

Step 2

- Consider feasibility and choose among alternatives.
- What needs to be done before the plan is implemented?
- Who will be responsible for preliminary actions?

Step 3

- Outline the plan and who might be responsible for each part.
- Will this plan accomplish all or part of the goal?
- State the specific goals this plan will accomplish.
- What are some ways data might be collected?

Step 4

- Realistically, what are the most likely problems with implementing the plan?
- What are some possible procedures to follow when the plan is not working or when it is not being implemented correctly?

Implement the plan.

SUMMARY OF ASSESSMENT STEPS

Step 1

- Was the plan implemented?
- What was the goal as specified in response?
- Was the goal attained?
- How do you know if the goal was attained?

Step 2

- What is likely to happen if the plan is removed?
- What is likely to happen if the plan remains in place?
- Identify new strategies to increase the effectiveness of the plan.
- How can the plan be monitored in the future?

Step 3

- Post-implementation planning
- Plan modification
- Follow-up assessment

The SARA Process: One Agency's Experience

A few years ago I was asked by the Pensacola Police Department to assist them with a Community Oriented Policing Services (COPS) grant. As per the requirements of the grant, the agency used the SARA model to identify a community problem, perform careful analysis, develop innovative solutions to the problem, and assess their efforts.

Prior to the application for the funds, agency personnel set up the scanning phase in order to identify the problem that would be targeted by the grant funds. Based on a preliminary evaluation of the data available to the PPD, a relatively small lower income area known as the East King Tract was selected as the targeted neighborhood. The area had recently experienced an increase in the number of calls for service, and local residents were repeatedly calling in complaints to the police regarding the open sales of drugs. The PPD was also aware of a number of law abiding elderly residents who resided in the area for a number of years and had previously been active in a local Neighborhood Crime Watch Program. Conditions in the neighborhood had deteriorated to the point where the Crime Watch members were so afraid of being victimized that they no longer held meetings. More and more renters moved into the area and a number of run-down uninhabited homes were being used as crack houses. A number of vacant lots were overgrown with weeds and strewn with garbage. It was not uncommon to see inoperable vehicles parked in driveways and on unkempt lawns without a current license plate. Based on the preliminary scanning meetings with community leaders, neighborhood watch organizers, patrol officers, supervisory personnel, elected officials, and local business owners, the grant was written to develop innovative strategies to curb the open drug sales and to improve the quality of life for residents in the neighborhood.

During the analysis phase, the PPD tried to gather information about problems in the East King Tract from a variety of sources. The agency analyzed its own internal sources of data, looking back at calls for service, field interview reports, arrest records, and crime reports for the past

12 months. Additionally, specialized units in the PPD were asked for their input. The agency also turned to external sources for information. A telephone survey of local residents was conducted in order to solicit their opinions regarding the conditions in their neighborhood and possible suggestions for improvement. Meetings were scheduled with local residents to discuss possible solutions to the problems. Community outreach workers at the local recreation center were contacted as well. Based on the data collected during the analysis phase, it was determined that what had appeared to be two separate problems—drug dealing and the deteriorating physical appearance of the neighborhood—were actually part of the same problem. Drug dealers were hiding their cache of drugs in the overgrown vacant lots and the abandoned vehicles. If these convenient hiding places could be eliminated, then the drug dealers would (hopefully) stop selling drugs in the neighborhood.

The initial response phase involved a virtual frenzy of activity. Agency personnel videotaped the area, carefully noting the locations of unsightly vacant lots, abandoned houses, and dilapidated cars. Officers went door-to-door, alerting residents to the agency's efforts and asking for their help. The PPD also contacted the Codes Enforcement Department and the Litter and Sanitation Department, asking for their assistance. Owners of rental properties, who often resided out of state, were alerted to problems with their properties and provided with a number of options to assist the police in correcting them, such as allowing the police to issue trespass warnings to unauthorized individuals loitering on the properties. Dozens of vehicles were towed from the area, and several abandoned houses were scheduled to be condemned. A major clean-up effort was scheduled, with representatives from the PPD, various community groups, local church members, volunteers from the University, and local elected officials all chipping in to help remove more than 13 tons of trash from this neighborhood. The physical appearance of the neighborhood greatly improved.

The PPD also conducted a number of undercover drug sweeps in the area, targeting local street dealers. Local residents were encouraged to contact the PPD when they witnessed drug activity and were provided with the pager numbers of the crime analysts to alert the unit when, where, and how such activities were taking place. The crime analysts kept a careful record of each call, and quickly fed the information back to the patrol officers and specialized units responsible for the area.

Several months later, an assessment of the PPD's efforts was conducted. While drug related arrests and calls for service were down, unfortunately the deteriorated conditions of the neighborhood had returned. Much to the distress of the PPD, many of the vacant lots were again strewn with garbage. The agency had felt that they had successfully repaired this "broken window," but obviously there was still a problem, and an unsightly one at that. Residents were frustrated with the police, and felt that the neighborhood looked worse now than when the grant had begun. The agency personnel were quite discouraged and scheduled a second clean up. Once again local residents and volunteers from a variety of community programs worked to pick up the lots, throwing out several tons of trash, abandoned sofas, and even a discarded toilet. The agency personnel recognized that these clean-ups provided a temporary solution. A long-term solution to this problem was needed.

The agency personnel then went back to the drawing board, or in SARA terms, returned to the analysis phase. Why did the level of trash return so quickly? Where had they gone wrong? It was brought to the attention of the PPD that local residents could be seen dumping their trash in the vacant lots in the wee hours of the morning. Additionally, local residents also reported that people would "steal" water from their neighbors, filling up gallon jugs with water from a garden house. Based on the information provided by the local residents, the PPD began to do a little homework.

The PPD contacted several county records offices and was able to determine that a sizeable number of residents living in the East King Tract had no regular trash removal service. In this particular area, residents could choose from a number of different trash removal companies and were independently responsible for contracting and paying for these services. The East King Tract was a lower income community and many of the residents simply could not afford to pay for such services. Since these residents had no way to legally dispose of their trash, they would simply wait until late at night and dump the trash in the vacant lots. The PPD also determined that several homes did not have their water activated, thereby necessitating the theft of water from other sources. Thus, the PPD set out to identify charitable organizations or other funding sources to provide trash service and water to those families who could not afford to pay for such amenities.

The experience I gained by working with the PPD on this project was truly invaluable. I was able to observe crime analysts perform tactical crime analysis as they prepared timely reports for the patrol officers and narcotics unit based on daily internal crime data and the input of the concerned citizens. I was also able to watch as a strategic crime analysis function unfolded. The East King Tract problem solving effort was an informative exercise in how a law enforcement agency uses various sources of input to detect long-term patterns of activity, develop responses to these patterns, assess the effectiveness of the response, and modify the response as needed.

I also saw how input from the crime analysts contributed to the quality of data that was collected by the line officers. For example, a call for service is initially classified based on the information provided by the complaining citizens. This initial classification may be different from the actual situation. Often, residents would phone in complaints about drug dealers hanging out on the corner. When the officer responded, the "perpetrators" (1) may have left the area; (2) may have turned out to be completely innocent teenagers who were bored and had nothing better to do, or (3) were actually drug dealers who fled the scene once they saw the patrol car approaching. Unfortunately, for the crime analysts, all three of these situations were closed out with no report written. In fact, prior to the intensive scrutiny given to the data generated by the patrol officers as part of the East King Tract problem solving effort, the majority of calls for service were disposed of with no final report completed by the patrol officers. The crime analysis unit was able to convince the supervisors that follow-up data from the patrol officers was invaluable, and the agency modified its report writing policies to assist in the data collection efforts.

Summary

The analysis of crime data has become an important tool for many law enforcement agencies in their efforts to reduce crime and improve the quality of life for community residents. Crime analysis can provide answers to such questions as who, what, where, when, and how criminal acts and other problematic conditions have occurred. In this chapter, the various types of crime analysis have been discussed with a focus on tactical and strategic crime analysis. In the next chapter, crime mapping will be introduced, one of the specialized tools available to the crime analyst.

Spotlight on Practice I

Tactical Crime Analysis
Musings from the Cambridge Police Department*
Christopher Bruce

Tactical crime analysis is the meat and drink of a crime analyst's life. It is fast-paced and exciting, dealing with the immediate, the critical, the here and now. It's dirty, grueling, arms-in-the-mud work that has to be done every day. There is no rest for tactical crime analysts, no breaks. Strategic crime analysts can stay in their ivory towers, dithering with their inferential statistics and long-term trends, afraid to get their hands dirty. They can work on the new redistricting plan for next year; we'll be identifying, analyzing, and putting an end to that robbery pattern that's happening right now. Tactical crime analysis is where the action is—which is why it's also called "action-oriented analysis."

Both urgent and important, tactical crime analysis is the crime analyst's A-1 priority. When it's effective, it's done first—before you answer your e-mail, before you make those phone calls, before your morning break. No time to mull over coffee: Read! Analyze! Disseminate!

Such, anyway, is the philosophy of the Cambridge Police Department's Crime Analysis Unit, which is proud of its fierce dedication to this process. Consequently, we've developed a number of procedures and policies to help us optimize this vital job.

The Day Begins with the Reports

We have written a document called The Ten Commandments of Crime Analysis. Commandment #2 is: "Thou shalt read thy agency's crime reports every day." This means reading the physical copy of the written report, not the RMS or CAD Entry. There's just something about poring over those actual carbon copies, with a blue pen and a caffeinated drink close at hand, that embeds the crime in your mind— so that when you come across a related incident, you're likely to identify a pattern instantly. Plus, it avoids the timeliness, accuracy, and other data quality problems inherent in many records management systems.

Calls for service are important, too—and many of them don't result in written reports, at least in our department. Thus, while one analyst

* Source: Bruce, C. (Spring, 2000). *Crime Mapping News*, 2, 10–12. Reprinted with permission.

works his way through the pile of crime reports, the other reviews the non-crime entries in the CAD system.

The analyst with the reports cross-checks each one against the crime analysis database for any related incidents. The nature by which each report is checked varies from report to report. For a regular housebreak, for instance, the analyst may look for all housebreaks in the same neighborhood for the past month. A housebreak with a peculiar M.O. may warrant a check of all housebreaks, going back several months, for a similar M.O. If the report lists a suspect or an arrested person, the name will be checked for any previous reports. In this manner, we try to catch any pattern, series, or hot spot within two or three incidents.

A Database for Crime Analysts

The Cambridge Police Department's quest to procure a "new" records management system — now in its tenth year — is a comedy of errors that we won't bore you with here. But it has indirectly benefited the Crime Analysis Unit because, faced with no adequate commercial system, we were forced to design our own — and, of course, we designed it to be of optimal use to crime analysis.

As masters of this system — created in Microsoft Access — we assumed data entry responsibility for crime incidents, hiring a full-time data entry clerk for this task. A lot of units might balk at the idea of taking on Records Unit responsibilities like this, but we feel that the confidence we can feel in the accuracy and timeliness of the information outweighs the six to eight hours a week we have to spend on it.

One field in particular makes this database unique: the "analysis" field. It allows the analyst to enter his or her own notes and thoughts about a crime and the likelihood that it's connected to a pattern. A note on a housebreak might read, for example, "Two blocks away from break yesterday, but significant differences; probably no pattern." Or: "One of two breaks in this building this date. Such incidents unusual for this building on such a high floor — maybe inside job?"

The "analysis" field for an acquaintance house burglary reviews the history of the parties involved: "Suspect and victim go way back. Suspect used to live in the building, and had some kind of relationship with VI, producing several assault reports. Since suspect moved out some time in 1999, she has tried to break into victim's apartment twice."

Of course, a large number of reports simply read, "No history on suspect," or "No patterns in the area." Overall, this system makes it

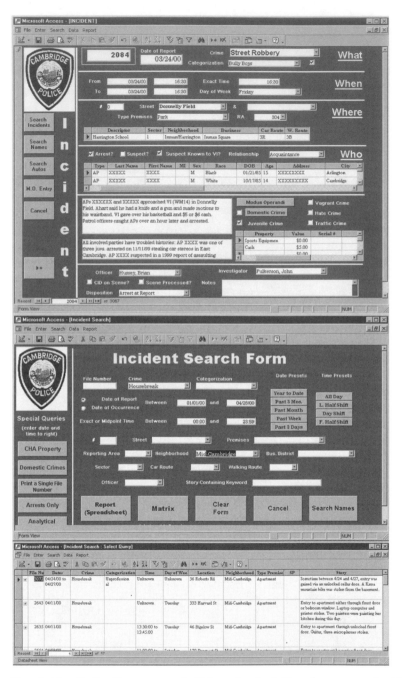

The Cambridge Police Department's Crime Analysis Database entry, incident search, and incident search result screens. This is a Microsoft Access database developed by the Crime Analysis Unit over the course of several years.

easy to keep track of patterns, and to provide investigators a way to look up a quick analysis on their assigned cases.

Mapping

Because our jurisdiction is geographically small (6.2 square miles), and because both analysts have been working here for many years, we rarely use crime mapping to help identify crime patterns—we can usually assess geographic proximity just by looking at the addresses.

Once a pattern is found, of course, mapping helps us analyze it and provides a visual aid for the written analysis published in the Daily Crime Bulletin.

(Just in case we've missed something in our daily review of crime reports, however, we map and review each of our five "target crimes"— street robberies, housebreaks, larcenies from motor vehicles, auto theft, and commercial breaks—once per week. Occasionally, we catch a pattern during this review process that we originally missed. An example of one of these reviews appears below.)

Geography being one of two ways that potential crime patterns are initially identified (the other is modus operandi), many agencies do map crimes on a daily basis to find patterns. These agencies need to be aware that a cluster of crimes does not necessarily signify a pattern of crimes. The map is never the end product, and any apparent cluster needs to be analyzed more thoroughly before the existence of a pattern can be ascertained. Geographic coincidences occur far more often than one might expect, so that four housebreaks that occur over the course of a week within two blocks of each other may be obviously and entirely unrelated (e.g., one is a professional job, another amateur, the third between warring acquaintances, and the fourth a landlord/tenant matter).

Tactical crime mapping, like tactical crime analysis, can be a down and dirty process. The annals of etiquette in crime mapping go out the window: when you're trying to quickly find or display a crime pattern, elements like scale bars, legends, layout windows, tables imported from your RMS, and other frilly GIS features take more time than they're worth. It's a thirty second process: CTRL-F a dozen locations on the street layer, choose a symbol, zoom in, and maybe drop some text, circles, lines or arrows on the cosmetic layer to highlight certain features. Then copy the entire mess to the clipboard and paste it into your word processing application. Sure, it's only a few degrees removed from

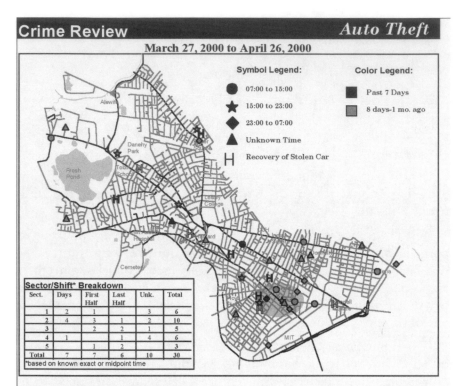

Crime Review   *Auto Theft*

March 27, 2000 to April 26, 2000

Symbol Legend:

- ● 07:00 to 15:00
- ★ 15:00 to 23:00
- ◆ 23:00 to 07:00
- ▲ Unknown Time
- H Recovery of Stolen Car

Color Legend:

- ■ Past 7 Days
- ▨ 8 days–1 mo. ago

Sector/Shift* Breakdown

Sect.	Days	First Half	Last Half	Unk.	Total
1	2	1		3	6
2	4	3	1	2	10
3		2	2	1	5
4	1		1	4	6
5		1	2		3
Total	7	7	6	10	30

*based on known exact or midpoint time

There were 30 auto thefts reported in Cambridge in the past month, a **19% decrease** from the 37 reported during the same period of 1999. This is the first monthly decrease this year.

Central Square has emerged as the prime hot spot for auto theft, particularly the area around **Lafayette Square** (Sector 2, Route 4R, Walking Routes 4A and 4B). These have been primarily **Hondas** and **Toyotas**. Times of day have varied. Six of the cars stolen in this area have since been recovered, all of them in the north shore communities of Lynn, Revere, and Chelsea. Chelsea Police, while making the most recent recovery of a 1998 Honda Accord stolen from Washington Street, chased two white males in their 20s, both over six feet tall. Neither was caught. The most recent three thefts have been off of **Main Street**.

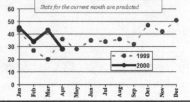

Above: A Target Crime Review for auto theft. Each of five target crimes is reviewed once per week in the Daily Crime Bulletin.

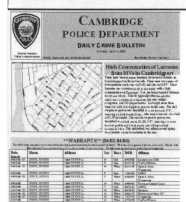

Left: The Daily Crime Bulletin.

paper maps and push pins, but it gets the job done fast. (Incidentally, for this type of "down and dirty" crime mapping, we find MapInfo to be a more user-friendly, adaptable application than ArcView, though we own and use both applications.)

Dissemination

Since the Crime Analysis Unit's inception more than 20 years ago, the primary means of dissemination of crime and pattern information has been the Daily Crime Bulletin. In the early days, we used a typewriter and a drafting table; now we use Microsoft Word. Among other things, the Bulletin contains:

- a review of all target crimes since the previous bulletin
- an analysis of any current crime patterns and trends
- a comprehensive review of that day's target crime
- a list of recently issued warrants
- abstracts of articles from various newspapers
- interdepartmental memoranda and notices

Creating a four-page bulletin for your department every day can be a grueling, repetitive process. This is why we recommend interns. We employ a full-time and a part-time intern from Northeastern University to edit and publish the Daily Crime Bulletin.

More recently, we've availed ourselves of technology to put this information out faster. A daily e-mail goes out to all command staff members and superior officers as soon as we've finished going through the crime reports for the day. This e-mail serves as a pre-Bulletin: a way to get pattern information out in a timelier manner.

The next step, of course, is live, interactive information via an intranet, currently under development. This may serve to replace the paper Bulletin entirely, once it's accessible from the MDT's in the cruisers.

The End of the Day

By two o'clock, the Bulletin is done, and we have moved into the stage of the tactical crime analysis process — strategy development — that we no longer directly control. The Crime Analysis Unit can now focus on other projects, including the occasional strategic crime analysis.

But tactical crime analysis is like garbage collection: there's always more waiting for you the next day; and if you don't do anything about it, it gets out of control real fast. Our nights are filled with tortuous dreams of the insidiousness occurring in our jurisdictions while we sleep; our mornings brim with nervous anticipation until we hold a new, fresh stack of poorly-written, illegible, coffee-stained reports once again.

Chapter 7

The Mapping of Crime

Chapter 6 introduced the importance of crime analysis for fighting crime, identifying high crime areas and problem locations, and developing responses to improve the quality of life in these problem areas. In this chapter, a specialized tool used by many crime analysts called crime mapping will be explored.

The Growth of Computerized Crime Mapping: From Push Pins to PCs

While the use of crime mapping in the form of pin maps has been traced back to the early 1900s, computerized crime mapping through the use of powerful geographic information systems (GIS) is becoming more and more popular. In the early 1900s, August Vollmer advocated the use of more scientific methods in police practices, including the use of pin maps to identify the locations of criminal activity. There is evidence that the New York City Police Department was using manual pin maps as early as 1900 (Harries, 1999). In contemporary times, chances are many police agencies still use pin maps displayed prominently in their briefing rooms. Different color push pins may be used to depict the location of different categories of crime, time of occurrence, or beat. The pin map might include incidents that had occurred over the past 24 hours, week, month, or other meaningful units of time. Pin maps might include crimes for an entire jurisdiction, or may be based on small units, such as beats or reporting districts. While some agencies still use pin maps to assist in the identification of crime patterns, there are a number of drawbacks to their use.

A crime analyst in a small agency who has painstakingly created a pin map for his or her agency's jurisdiction, carefully color-coding criminal offenses that have occurred over the past month may run into a problem on the first day of the new month. A picture of the previous month's map could be taken to "store" the data; pins could be continually added (perhaps in different shades?) to the old map; or the pins could be removed all together. As one can imagine, pin maps are difficult to continually update with new information. Once the pins are removed, it is difficult to keep track of previous crime patterns that may continue into the new month. Month to month comparisons of crime data are difficult to make, if not impossible. One cannot "ask' the map to store information, nor can the pins be easily manipulated (Boba, 2001; Harries, 1999).

Additionally, pin maps can become quite large and cumbersome. For example, the jurisdiction of Baltimore County covers 610 square miles. In order for a pin map of the entire area to be viewed, 12 different maps have to be joined together. The final map takes up 70 square feet of wall space (Canter, 1997, cited in Harries, 1999).

Overcoming the Obstacles

Much of the same can be said for the integration of GIS technology in law enforcement as was true for the discussion of the technological impediments that challenged the growth of crime analysis. Early software programs were slow and user-hostile, and hardware systems were cost prohibitive. The first computer-generated maps of crime were made during the 1960s and 1970s. In 1967, the St. Louis, Missouri Police Department used computer generated maps to depict the frequencies of larcenies from automobiles (Weisburd & McEwen, 1998). Despite the appeal of automatic crime mapping, the technological challenges were great and only a few agencies incorporated mapping technology into their operations.

Interest in crime mapping was fueled in the late 1980s, when the National Institute of Justice established a program called the Drug Market Analysis Program. This program provided federal grants to establish partnerships between law enforcement agencies and academic researchers. The goal of the partnerships was to use innovative analytic methods to identify and track drug markets. Five awards were made, marking some of the first crime mapping projects funded by the federal government. The success and publicity surrounding these projects resulted in great interest among law enforcement and researchers alike in the use of GIS as a new tool to explore crime patterns and trends (LaVigne & Groff, 2001).

In the 1990s, even more federal funding was provided to allow law enforcement agencies to purchase crime mapping hardware and software. The Community Oriented Policing Services (COPS) Office provided funds to agencies to enhance and improve their community policing activities through the use of the new technology. Agencies could apply for grants from the Making Officer Redeployment Effective (MORE) program, which had a budget of one billion dollars. Additionally, since 1995 the COPS Office has provided funding for the Police Foundation's Crime Mapping Laboratory, which provides technical assistance and advice for agencies wishing to incorporate crime mapping technologies into their operations (Boba, 2001). The National Institute of Justice continues to actively encourage the use of crime mapping by offering grants, fellowships, and other forms of assistance to agencies wishing to adopt the new technology.

Box 7.1. Information Clearinghouses for Crime Mapping Issues

The Crime Mapping Laboratory of the Police Foundation offers a number of services to agencies interested in crime mapping technology. Laboratory personnel will provide training, technical support, and consultation services to law enforcement personnel, especially to those agencies that have received COPS funding to purchase crime mapping technology to enhance their community policing efforts. Additionally, the Crime Mapping Laboratory publishes a regular newsletter, the *Crime Mapping News*, which provides a wealth of information on training opportunities, upcoming conferences, successful stories from the field, web site reviews, and information on new software and crime mapping analysis techniques. For more information, please check out their web site at: http://www.policefoundation.org and follow the links to the Crime Mapping Laboratory.

The National Institute of Justice Mapping and Analysis for Public Safety (MAPS) Office was established in 1997. Formerly known as the Crime Mapping Research Center, the goal of MAPS is to promote the use of GIS technology for applications in criminal justice research and practice. MAPS offers grant opportunities, conferences, and acts as a clearinghouse for GIS information. MAPS also maintains the Crime Mapping Listserv, which students are welcome to join. The Listserv members provide useful tips on the use of GIS, answer "how-to" questions and keep the members informed of training opportunities, conferences, and other useful events. For more information or to join the Crime Mapping Listserv, see their website at http://www.ojp.usdoj.gov/nij/maps/

Today, the use of crime mapping is still in its infancy. A 1997 survey of 2,004 law enforcement agencies conducted by the Crime Mapping Research Center found that while most agencies (73 per cent) use some form of crime analysis, only 261 (13 per cent) use computerized crime mapping. While that may not sound like a great number of agencies, interest in the new technology is growing. Most of the agencies indicated that they were familiar with crime mapping, and another 20 per cent of the responding agencies noted that they planned on acquiring a computerized crime mapping system within the next year, which would imply that an additional 400 agencies are in the planning phase to begin crime mapping in the near future (Mamalian & Lavigne, 1999).

The survey also found that the size of the agency had a great impact on whether or not an agency used crime mapping. While crime mapping was used by 36 per cent of the agencies employing 100 or more officers, only 3 per cent of agencies employing less than 100 officers used the technology (Mamalian & LaVigne, 1999). When many picture a police department, huge agencies such as the New York Police Department or the Los Angeles Police Department may come to mind. These agencies are the exception, not the rule. While there are about 40 police departments in the U.S. that employ 1,000 or more sworn officers, there are 20 times as many agencies that boast a force of a single individual! The typical police department employs few officers. About half of the police departments in the U.S. employ fewer than 10 sworn officers, and nearly 80 per cent have less than 25 sworn officers (Walker & Katz, 2002).

Given that fact that most agencies are small, it is difficult to budget funds and personnel to devote their time to such "luxuries" as crime mapping. However, as the cost of the hardware and software continues to drop and the programs become more and more efficient and user-friendly, it is anticipated that more agencies will adopt computerized crime mapping.

Uses of Crime Mapping

Just what is computerized crime mapping, and how can agencies use this tool? In its most basic function, computerized crime mapping allows agencies to create high-tech pin maps. Crimes, calls for service, arrests, or other incidents may be plotted on a digitized map of a reporting district, beat, neighborhood, or entire jurisdiction. However, because the information is stored in a computerized database, the "pins" can be easily saved from month to month. The "pins" can also be manipulated to display specific incidents for the previous shift, day, week, month, or year. As a result, visual detection of crime patterns may be easier than with a traditional pin map (LaVigne & Groff, 2001). According to the previously mentioned 1997 survey, the use of computerized pin maps was the most common application of crime mapping technology (Mamalian & LaVigne, 1999). This type of mapping is sometimes referred to as **descriptive mapping**.

Box 7.2. How Are Computerized Pin Maps Created?

In order for a computerized pin map to be generated, the location of a crime incident must be **geocoded,** or assigned an **x** and **y** coordinate, so that it may be placed on a map. In the course of their duties, police officers regularly collect data that include an address: location of the call for service, arrest, field interview report, or accident. One of the primary jobs of the geographic information system (GIS) is to convert these addresses to an **x** and **y** coordinate, usually in latitude and longitude decimal degrees, and identify its correct location on a map. In practice, this can be a very painful process. There is an existing street file database that acts as a base for the GIS. An agency may purchase street file databases, borrow the databases from other city offices (such as the planning office or fire department) or download them for free from the U.S. Census Bureau. In better GIS systems, the street file database may be pre-loaded on the system (ESRI, 1999). Regardless of the source, the street file database may or may not be accurate, especially in areas where new subdivisions (and thus new streets and addresses) are being built in large numbers.

So, when the street address for a homicide is entered into the GIS, the address is compared against the existing street file database. Sometimes you will get a successful "hit," but oftentimes, the search may result in a miss. Misses must be manually re-entered into the system. Sometimes, a "miss" may not be able to be corrected, especially if essential information is left out (such as "boulevard" or "street"). Additionally, in some areas, it is all too common for multiple streets to have the same name. This ambiguity makes it difficult (and sometimes impossible) to correctly identify which street is the "right" one.

As a consumer of map information, it is important to recognize that many cases may be missing from the map because geo-coding issues were not able to be resolved. Harries (1999) notes that maps may be produced with a successful hit rate as low as 25 per cent—which means that 75 per cent of the addresses have been lost. While there is no "industry standard" as far as a minimum hit rate for distribution of maps, Harries suggests that hit rates of 60 per cent or less are unacceptable and may lead to incorrect conclusions. Additionally, it is important to let the consumer know how many cases were 'lost' in the geocoding process. While most consumers may not understand the impact, Harries (1999:99) suggests a footnote that reads "X per cent of cases were omitted due to technical problems, but the police department considers the pattern shown to be representative of the total cases under consideration" to clarify the issue.

For more information, see the following sources:

K. Clarke (2001) Getting started with geographic information systems. Upper Saddle River: Prentice Hall.

K. Harries (1999) Mapping crime: Principle and practice. Washington, D.C.: National Institute of Justice.

In addition to automated pin mapping, computerized crime mapping also allows agencies to compare their in-house crime data against various community-level characteristics. External data bases, such as census data, property assessment data, city planning data, parks and school data, utilities data, and even digital images and photographs can become part of the agency's database, allowing the analyst to consider spatial relationships between crime problems and various demographic characteristics (Boba, 2001; Mamalian & LaVigne, 1999). This powerful analysis tool requires a bit more technical and statistical expertise and as a result, only about half of the police agencies that employ crime mapping reported using these advanced features (Mamalian & LaVigne, 1999). This more advanced type of mapping is one form of **analytical mapping**.

Descriptive Mapping: Computerized Pin Maps and More

As previously noted, the use of computer generated pin maps is by far the most popular and most rudimentary use of crime mapping technology. According to the 1997 survey of law enforcement agencies conducted by the Crime Mapping Research Center (now known as MAPS), among the agencies that actually used a crime mapping or a GIS program, the most commonly used mapping application was automated pin maps. While agencies that use their system solely to create pin maps are barely scratching the surface of the potential of their crime mapping system, this basic application is still a very useful, flexible, and somewhat powerful tool.

In practice, law enforcement agencies can use descriptive mapping in a variety of ways. The article on tactical crime analysis written by Christopher Bruce in Chapter 6 described the use of descriptive mapping by the Cambridge, Massachusetts Police Department. One of the primary advantages of using computerized crime mapping techniques is that the maps can be easily printed and distributed to all concerned parties—patrol officers, detectives, and community crime watch groups. Instead of having to discern and memorize the information presented on a wall pin map, computerized crime maps can focus the reader's attention on very specific pieces of information, such as a rash of residential burglaries that have occurred in a specific area over the past several days.

Police agencies can also use descriptive mapping to assist in criminal investigations. For example, the Hillsborough County, Florida Sheriff's Department uses one form of descriptive mapping to assist in the identification and apprehension of auto theft suspects. Both the location of the theft and the vehicle recovery site are mapped. The identification of theft sites allows the agency to visually locate possible hot spots for auto theft, an important piece of information that is then passed along to patrol deputies assigned to the area. The plotting of recovery sites is also very useful. Based on careful analysis of its auto theft problem, the crime analysts from the HCSO are able to determine that in many cases, juveniles are stealing cars in order to get transportation to go home. By comparing the recovery locations for the stolen cars to the home addresses of known auto thieves, the HCSO has been successful in narrowing down the list of potential suspects.

Other agencies regularly use crime mapping to display the home addresses of sexual predators living within their jurisdiction. After the brutal rape and murder of 7-year-old Megan Kanka in 1994, President Clinton signed Megan's Law into effect. Megan's Law requires that all sex offenders convicted of crimes against children be registered and their personal information be made available in a publicly accessible database (for more information, see http://www.klaaskids.org). Police

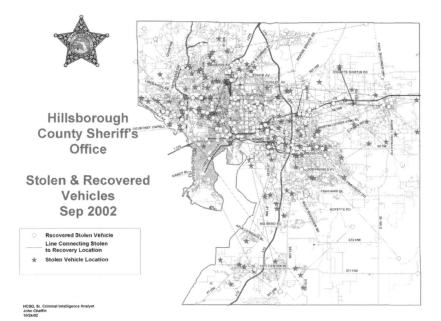

Hillsborough County Sheriff's Office

Stolen & Recovered Vehicles Sep 2002

○ Recovered Stolen Vehicle
— Line Connecting Stolen to Recovery Location
★ Stolen Vehicle Location

HCSO, Sr. Criminal Intelligence Analyst
John Chaffin
10/24/02

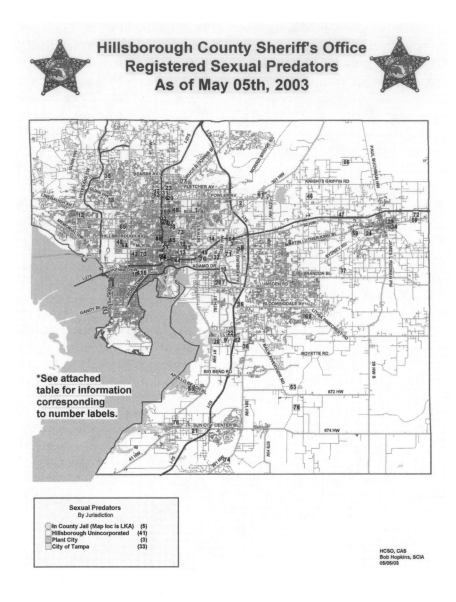

agencies may then use this information to assist in their criminal investigations.

Law enforcement agencies can also use descriptive computerized pin maps to visually demonstrate the effectiveness of an intervention strategy. For example, if an agency has been concentrating its efforts on street level drug dealing in a specific neighborhood, the agency can create a map that displays the number of drug related calls for service before and after their intervention (McEwen & Taxman, 1995). This visual depiction can be quite useful (and dramatic), especially when interacting with community members and local government officials. No special training or lengthy explanations are needed to decipher the movement of the data points.

The usefulness of descriptive mapping does have its limits. While computerized crime mapping can be useful in allowing agency personnel to detect patterns and trends in the data points, there is still a great deal of subjective interpretation (McEwen & Taxman, 1995). What one person identifies as an important pattern in the data points may be completely dismissed by another.

This subjectivity can be especially problematic in the identification of hot spots. The vast majority of agencies that use crime mapping technology (86 per cent) have indicated that hot spots of criminal activity were identified by visual inspection (Mamalian & LaVigne, 1999). As discussed in the previous chapter, understanding and controlling a hot spot can be very effective in reducing the overall level of crime in a jurisdiction. Before attempting to address a hot spot, one has to know exactly where it is located. Identifying a hot spot simply through visual inspection can lead to errors.

There are a number of different analytical methods for identifying a hot spot. In one relatively basic technique, called **repeat address mapping,** only those address that meet a pre-set minimum criteria (called a **minimum plotting density**) are shown on a map. For example, an agency may wish to identify the worst of the worst crime locations in the city. In an analysis of data provided from the New York City Police Department, researchers mapped addresses in the Bronx that had four or more crimes occur over a 13-month period. By using this criterion, the researchers limited the number of mapped addresses to less than 7 per cent of all locations and were able to account for nearly a quarter of all of the crimes that had occurred. The researchers could then concentrate on what was happening at this relatively small number of locations that caused them to be hot spots for crime (Eck, Gersh & Taylor, 2000).

Other types of analyses exist for identifying hot spots. In one type of analysis, called **kernel smoothing,** the individual data points depicting crime locations are "smoothed out" to create an image that shows the areas with the highest density or concentration of crime. Another type of analysis uses what are called **standard deviation ellipses.** A free computer program called STAC—Spatial and Temporal Analysis of Crime—is available to law enforcement agencies and other interested parties from the Illinois Criminal Justice Information Authority. This program (as well as other programs on the market) will automatically analyze individual geo-coded addresses and identify clusters. The location and size of the hot spots are clearly identified by an ellipse that is drawn around the areas with the highest concentration of criminal activity (Rich, 1999).

A detailed discussion of these techniques requires more statistical expertise and is really beyond the scope of this text (see, for example, the Crime Mapping Research Center, 1998; Langworthy & Jefferis, 2000; or McLafferty, Williamson & McGuire, 2000 for more information on these and other techniques). Oftentimes these techniques can be quite confusing for practitioners to employ, and researchers disagree on which method is the best (LaVigne & Groff, 2001). Part of the problem is that since crime mapping is still in its infancy, even the most basic spatial analysis techniques are beyond the comfort level of many law enforcement personnel. Hence, at this point in time, the use of descriptive mapping is much more popular than analytical mapping, which requires more advanced skills.

Analytical Mapping: Beyond the Individual Crime Incident Locations

Analytical mapping is a bit more complex than descriptive mapping. While descriptive mapping focuses on the visual presentation individual data points, analytical mapping displays the results of data analysis. Data points are analyzed and the results of the analysis are then mapped. Analytical mapping allows for better understanding of the trends and patterns of criminal events than does descriptive mapping (McEwen & Taxman, 1995).

Analyzing Domestic Violence in Baltimore

The Baltimore County, Maryland Police Department used analytical mapping techniques to gain a better understanding of the county's spouse abuse problem. The agency wanted to know the addresses and areas that experienced a high number of spousal abuse calls. Additionally, the agency wanted to locate areas of under-reporting; that is, where incidents of spousal abuse may be taking place but were not reported to the police.

Using the agency database, it was relatively easy to identify the locations with high volumes of calls related to spousal abuse. However, the identification of under-reporting areas was a bit more complex. The agency added social and demographic information broken down by census tracts to its database that already included the locations of spousal abuse incidents. The goal was to develop a mathematical equation where the number of spousal abuse calls could be predicted based on the area's demographic characteristics. This equation, called a multiple regression model, represented the best fitting model for all of the data values. The agency then compared the actual number of spouse abuse calls with the number of calls expected using the regression model. In some of the areas, the number of spousal abuse cases that was predicted using the model was much higher than the actual number of cases. This provided evidence of under reporting.

Through their detailed analysis of the combined databases, the agency was able to identify five possible areas where victims were not reporting cases of spousal abuse. These areas were highlighted on a map of the entire county, thereby easily allowing consumers of this information (social service providers, domestic violence counselors) to see the areas that were possibly in need of victim assistance (for a more detailed and statistically advanced discussion of this project, see Cantor, 1990, 1998; McEwen & Taxman, 1995). These maps, therefore, provided the results of the analysis as opposed to a more rudimentary pin map display of where the spousal abuse calls had taken place.

Geographic Profiling: Hunting Serial Criminals

Geographic profiling is an advanced form of analytical crime mapping. Drawing heavily on crime pattern theory, routine activities theory, and other environmental criminology principles, geographic profiling assists in the investigation of criminal activities by identifying the most likely location where a serial criminal lives. In this type of analysis, information concerning the location of a number of crimes in a series is carefully examined. The goal is to create a map that displays the most probable location of the home or workplace of a serial offender (Rich, 1999; Rossmo, 1995).

Dr. Kim Rossmo, a detective in the Vancouver, Canada Police Department, developed geographic profiling in the early 1990s. Dr. Rossmo studied criminology at Simon Fraser University in Vancouver under the tutelage of Patricia and Paul Brantingham, noted environmental criminologists. Rossmo, now the Director of Research for the Police Foundation, has been instrumental in training detectives in the strategies of hunting serial offenders based on geographic indicators. His work led to the development of a software program called RIGEL Profiler. Geographic profilers in the United States, Canada, and Europe use this program to identify the most likely home address of serial offenders (Laverty & MacLaren, 2002).

According to routine activities theory, crime tends to cluster in areas where motivated offenders come into contact with suitable targets. The Brantingham's notions concerning crime pattern theory added the concepts of activity spaces and awareness spaces. An offender's activity space consists of the areas he or she regularly travels to and between: work, school, home, or recreational areas. Awareness spaces are usually much larger, and may include locations in the city where one rarely visits. Both activity spaces and awareness spaces together form a cognitive map of the city or area in which one lives.

According to Rossmo, within the regularly traveled activity space there is one point that can be described as the most important place in one's spatial life (1995:223). For the majority of people, their home is the most important anchor point in their activity space. For criminals, it would follow that their crimes would be centered near their home addresses following a **distance-decay function**. That is, the further you get away from the regular activity space of an offender, the less likely that person is to engage in predatory criminal activity. Suitable targets will be hunted close — but not too close — to the home or spatial anchor point. An offender may avoid locations that are too close to the home so as to avoid detection by neighbors who may recognize him or her as the perpetrator (Rossmo, 1995; 2000). Using this theoretical basis, Rossmo and his colleagues developed a criminal geographic targeting (CGT) model. This model analyzes the geographic coordinates of criminal events that are part of a series in order to produce an image that depicts the likelihood that an offender resides within a specific hunting area. Consider the following case:

> In October 1995 two teenage girls in the municipality of Abbotsford British Columbia, were attacked on the street at night by a man with a baseball bat. One victim was murdered and dumped in the Vedder Canal, some 20 miles away; the other was left for dead, but she somehow managed to survive and make her way to a nearby hospital. A few days later, the Abbotsford Killer began a series of bizarre actions starting with several taunting 911 telephone calls. He then stole and defaced the murder victim's gravestone and dumped it in the parking lot of a local radio station. Finally, he threw a note wrapped around a wrench through a house window;

in the note, he admitted to other sexual assaults. These actions provided 13 different sites for the geographic profile. He was eventually caught through a local-based strategy initiated by the Abbotsford Police Department. His residence was in the top 7.7% of the geoprofile (Rossmo, 2000:215).

The easiest way to imagine how the program works is to use the example of a burglar who has broken into eight different businesses around his home. The best guess of where the burglar lived would be to find the exact center point of the eight known crime locations, a sort of spatial average or mean. Of course, the development of a real geographic profile that identifies the home of a serial offender is much more complex. Rossmo (2000:213) lists a number of factors that are of particular importance when building a profile. These factors include the location and time of the crime, the type of offender (single versus multiple offenders), street layout patterns, bus stops and other public transportation hubs, zoning and land use, and the demographic characteristics of various neighborhoods — that is, a white serial rapist may not venture into Hispanic neighborhoods to search out a potential victim, etc. To make the situation even more complex, an offender may very well have multiple spatial anchor points, such as the home and the workplace.

If crime mapping is in its infancy, then geographic profiling is at the embryo stage. This is an area of great excitement, and is truly at the cutting edge of analytic crime mapping technology. As of 1999, only three police agencies, all in Canada, employed full time geographic profilers (Rich, 1999). More and more criminal investigators, however, are being trained in geographic profiling techniques. While initially these techniques were reserved for more serious serial murder, rape, arson, robbery or terrorism cases, the techniques may also be used in identifying the home address of serial burglars, auto thieves, and credit card fraud offenders (Laverty & MacLaren, 2002). For more information on geographic profiling, visit the website for Environmental Criminology Research Inc. at http://ecricanada.com.

Crime Mapping for Police Operations: The COMPSTAT Model

Arguably, one of the most exciting trends in law enforcement circles today is the incorporation of the COMPSTAT model for managing patrol operations. Depending on which source you look at, COMPSTAT either stands for "Compare Stats" (Silverman, 1999) or "Computer-Driven Crime Statistics" (McDonald, 2002). No matter the source of the acronym, the central meaning is the same: police decision-making should be driven by timely, accurate data. The program began in New York City and, based on their widely publicized success, has quickly expanded across the country to an ever-growing number of municipal and county law enforcement agencies.

When Commissioner William Bratton assumed his duties as the new head of the New York City Police Department (NYPD) in 1994, one of his first policies was to hold weekly meetings with a commanding officer from each of the City's eight bureaus. The goal of these meetings was to discuss the current levels of crime in each area. Quite to Bratton's surprise, the bureau representatives did not have a clue as to what their current crime statistics were. It was not uncommon for the data to have a time lag of three to six months. Bratton set out to change this trend, demanding that accurate and timely crime statistics be gathered and distributed. Precinct commanders were held accountable if data from their zone were in error. The importance of geographic accountability cannot be stressed enough in the COMPSTAT model. Instead of being confined to the comfort of their offices, patrol commanders and higher level supervisory personnel were now required to be intimately familiar with the inner workings of a their zone, as much as the patrol officers assigned to the area. A clear message was sent to the 31,000 sworn officers that a new era had arrived — the COMPSTAT era (Silverman, 1999).

The Principles of COMPSTAT

As described by McDonald (2002), the COMPSTAT model is based on five principles: (1) specific objectives; (2) timely and accurate intelligence; (3) effective strategies and tactics; (4) rapid deployment of personnel and resources; and (5) relentless follow-up and assessment. In this next section we will spend some time discussing each of these principles, especially as they relate to the use of crime statistics, crime mapping, and geographic accountability.

Specific Objectives: Defining Priorities

When he took office in 1994, Bratton defined a number of specific objectives that needed to be addressed. By clearly identifying these areas of emphasis, Bratton sent out a message to his patrol officers and command staff stating which problems were important and worthy of attention and effort, and which were not. Bratton's objectives included reducing the number of crime incidents in a variety of categories, including youth violence and delinquency, domestic violence, and auto-related crime. Additionally, the availability of guns, street level drug dealing, and public disorder crimes were also elevated to primary importance. Once the specific objectives or areas of importance were identified, the NYPD set out to address these problem areas.

Accurate and Timely Intelligence

The central component of COMPSTAT is the scientific analysis and use of quality, timely crime data. The data are drawn from a variety of sources, including both internally and externally generated information. Internal data include such things as calls for service, arrests, field interview reports, and crime reports. External data can come from a variety of sources, including information that is gathered from other law enforcement or correctional agencies, interviews with arrestees, or even tips from private security firms. The underlying assumption is that without accurate data, the police cannot develop an effective response.

The NYPD relies heavily on the use of crime mapping technology to identify crime patterns and hot spots of criminal activity. In fact, the ability to utilize crime mapping is viewed as an essential component for any agency wishing to adopt a COMPSTAT model (McDonald, 2002). Brightly colored maps that display locations of criminal acts are projected on a large overhead screen in weekly COMPSTAT meetings, providing an important (and dramatic) visual tool for fighting crime.

Once a pattern or hot spot has been identified, the heat is on patrol commanders to do something to address the problem(s). Responsibility for crime in one's assigned area is a key component to the success of COMPSTAT. If a hot spot is identified, the commander is challenged to explain why the hot spot developed and to provide a clearly articulated tactical plan for dealing with the hot spot.

Effective Tactics

One of the more interesting components of the COMPSTAT model is that effective tactics are developed based on a geographic area, not a specific specialized unit or shift. All units assigned to an area, including narcotics, gang units, community policing, crime prevention, and major crimes are expected to work together to assist the patrol division in developing and implementing effective crime fighting strategies. This spirit of cooperation within and between the units is a dramatic change from the way traditional law enforcement is often carried out. Even in relatively small agencies, a robbery detective may not know the patrol officers working in the area. He or she may not be familiar with other detectives assigned to property crimes or other violent crimes, even though they may be looking for the same criminal working in the same area. Additionally, many times these specialized units work in competition with each other for case clearances and resources, which may further erode cooperation. COMPSTAT is designed to alter the independent nature of the various specialized units in order to get them organized around fighting crime in a specific geographic location.

In order for this strategy to be successful, the lines between divisions become blurred. If a lieutenant or patrol commander feels that the problems in his area could be reduced if the narcotics unit conducted an undercover sting operation in a hot spot location, then he should have the authority and influence to get the needed assistance. Under traditional policing strategies, the lieutenant may not be made aware of the undercover operations of the narcotics unit, even if the narcotics officers were working in the lieutenant's own zone. In some cases, this sort of tactical information is provided on a need-to-know basis only. In traditional law enforcement the unit of analysis is the specialized unit, not the geographic area. Under COMPSTAT, all specialized units work together to develop innovative strategies to reduce crime in their assigned area.

In addition to the emphasis on specialized units, in many cases traditional policing has been focused on shifts. The day commander is aware of all crimes that occurred during his or her assigned time. However, the day commander may not be aware of crimes that occurred outside of the time window of responsibility (like the night or afternoon shift). Geographic accountability makes patrol commanders responsible for reviewing all crime reports that occur within their assigned zone, regardless of the time of occurrence. This is very important in the identification of patterns and trends of criminal activity—criminals do not confine their activities to coincide with a patrol commander's shift.

A Note on Strategies within COMPSTAT

The goal of COMPSTAT is not simply to move crime into someone else's backyard, but to solve the crime problem. For this reason, the

COMPSTAT management system of patrol operations dovetails well with the community policing philosophy. The goal is to reduce crime within a specific geographic region, calling in whatever resources necessary to develop strategies in order to achieve the goal. In fact, many elements of the principles of COMPSTAT do not sound that much different from the SARA model of community policing (Scanning, Analysis, Response, Assessment).

It should be noted that in some circles, COMPSTAT has become synonymous with zero tolerance policing, though this is not always the case. **Zero tolerance policing** is an aggressive form of law enforcement that emphasizes the "broken windows" philosophy. By focusing attention on relatively minor offenses, the quality of life for area residents will be improved and ultimately, major crimes will be reduced (Walker & Katz, 2002). The reason that COMPSTAT and zero tolerance policing are tied together is that the NYPD adopted both strategies at the same time, leading the media to conclude that the approaches were the same (McDonald, 2002). Within a COMPSTAT model, an agency can adopt any number of strategies to reduce the level of crime in a geographic area. An agency may adopt zero tolerance policing as part of its COMPSTAT model, or may decide that a community policing strategy would be best (or even some combination of the two).

Rapid Deployment of Personnel and Resources

Once a plan of action has been developed, it is essential that the strategy be implemented as soon as possible. Once again, the key to this component is coordination of various specialty units along with patrol operations in order to achieve a common goal. One of the important points of COMPSTAT is accountability. Once a problem has been identified and a strategy is developed, it is the responsibility of a command supervisor to ensure that the appropriate steps are taken. If not, that individual may be humiliated, reassigned, or demoted due to their lack of attention to the COMPSTAT process.

Relentless Follow-up and Assessment

Once a strategy has been implemented, the COMPSTAT process does not mark the end of an investigation. In fact, it is really only the beginning of the process of relentless follow-up and assessment. Though *"relentless"* is a very powerful word it truly captures the spirit of COMPSTAT. As phrased by McDonald (2002:21), "The term *relentless* is an emotionally charged adjective that encapsulates several forces—determinism, doggedness, urgency, energy, and single-mindedness. These are all forces that improve performance by virtue of the fact that relentless or consistent follow-up increases alertness, productivity, and attention to detail."

Once again, the responsibility falls on the patrol commanders to discuss the success or failure of their intervention strategy. If a tactical plan has proved to be successful in one particular area, then a similar strategy may be used in similar areas to address comparable problems. If the assessment shows that a strategy was not effective, it is the responsibility of the patrol commander to explain why the strategy failed and to develop new alternatives. As an additional source of pressure, these new alternatives need to be developed in a timely manner for presentation and discussion at the next COMPSTAT weekly meeting.

The Future of COMPSTAT

The COMPSTAT model has been given a great deal of credit as a contributing factor in the dramatic reduction in crime rates in New York City. As a result of the positive publicity, larger agencies across the country are jumping on the COMPSTAT bandwagon. Many agencies have already replicated the system or plan to do so in the future. Agencies that have already adopted the COMPSTAT model include Boston, Massachusetts Police Department; New Orleans, Louisiana Police Department; Washington, D.C.; Los Angeles, California Police Department; Maryland State Police; as well as Sheriff's Departments in Broward County and Sarasota County, Florida. McDonald (2002) noted that as many as two-thirds of police chiefs in major cities plan on adopting a similar system in the very near future. It should follow that as agencies adopt a data-driven management tool, greater emphasis will be placed on the importance of crime analysis and crime mapping technology.

Summary

Crime mapping allows interested parties to clearly identify the exact location for criminal offenses, monitor the effectiveness of crime intervention strategies, and assist in the deployment and management of police operations. More advanced crime mapping techniques allow researchers and agency personnel to move beyond the identification of individual crime locations to a deeper analysis of crime trends and patterns. Interest in crime mapping appears to be growing, as more and more agencies express interest in adopting the new technology.

Spotlight on Practice II

Tactical Crime Analysis and Geographic Information Systems:
Concepts and Examples*
Mary Velasco and Rachel Boba, Ph.D.
Crime Mapping Laboratory, Police Foundation

Introduction

The purpose of this article is to lay a foundation for law enforcement practitioners and researchers to develop a common understanding of tactical crime analysis and the role of geographic information systems (GIS). Having observed that people in the field use the same terms in many different contexts, we feel that clarifying concepts is a necessary step to improving communication among us. It is our hope that this article will encourage a dialogue, not only about the ideas themselves, but also about how they are used in everyday crime analysis.

The aim of crime analysis in the context of law enforcement is to provide information that will inform and assist crime control activity. Generally speaking, it is the development of information of use for crime prevention and detection activities. Crime analysis can also be used to inform policy and decision makers about the actual or anticipated impact of interventions, policies, or operational procedures. In this article, we concentrate upon "tactical crime analysis," one of the three types of crime analysis as identified by Steven Gottlieb in his book "Crime Analysis: From First Report to Final Arrest" (1994).

In the most general sense, tactical crime analysis is the study of reported crime, calls for service, and other related information in order to inform short-term operational crime control activities and problem solving. The emphasis upon informing short-term operational activities typically means that data from immediately preceding days, weeks, or months are most useful. All of this information is analyzed by *modus operandi* characteristics, spatial and/or temporal factors, as well as offender, victim, or other target characteristics. The use of GIS is an essential component of tactical crime analysis, as spatial characteristics are key factors to linking criminal activity and identifying relationships.

---

* Mary Velasco is a research associate in and Rachel Boba, Ph.D. is Director of the Police Foundation's Crime Mapping Laboratory. This article was reprinted with permission from the *Crime Mapping News*, (Summer, 2000) pp. 1–4, Washington DC: Police Foundation.

The goal of this article is to outline general tactical crime analysis concepts as well as provide specific examples of how mapping can be used in tactical crime analysis. These examples do not represent all that is possible in tactical crime analysis mapping, but give the reader a place to start.

Tactical Crime Analysis Approach

The first section defines the overarching concepts of pattern and trend, then defines particular types of patterns and trends that the analyst may seek to identify. Our definitions of pattern and trend are simple and based on dictionary definitions: A *pattern* is an arrangement or order discernible in any crime-related phenomena. A *trend* is a specific type of pattern that has or assumes a general direction or tendency. In practice, a trend often has a time component and is represented as an increase or a decrease in a given phenomenon over time.

Patterns and trends are important to the crime analyst since they represent a framework to begin identifying relationships. For practical purposes however, more specific categories of analysis are useful, and some of these are outlined below. These categories and the following examples are not meant to be comprehensive, but are designed to serve as general guidelines for analyzing criminal activity when conducting tactical crime analysis in a police department. Even though these categories of activity apply to other law enforcement information such as calls for service and accidents, this discussion focuses on and draws examples from the context of reported crime.

Series

While the term "series" is widely used in research, law enforcement, and everyday life, this discussion focuses on a specific use of the term. Thus, a series is a run of similar crimes committed by the same individual(s) against one or various victims or targets. For example, a suspect in a white sedan is approaching young females as they walk home from school and threatening them with a handgun while ordering them to enter his vehicle or an elderly gentleman is repeatedly burgled by the same local youths. These types of activity are notable against various victims or a single victim.

Spree

A spree is characterized by the high frequency of criminal activity, to the extent that it appears almost continuous. It involves the same offender(s) and usually occurs over a short time period, although this could be a few hours, a few days or a longer period depending upon the circumstances. For example, the driver's side window is broken and property is stolen from several vehicles parked along the same residential street overnight. Even though there is no suspect information, this activity is categorized as a spree due to the similarities in MO and the proximity in time and location. These similarities suggest that the incidents were committed by the same individual.

Hot Spot

In the context of tactical crime analysis, a hotspot is a specific location or small area where an unusual amount of criminal activity occurs that is committed by one or more offenders. For example, over several months, two armed robberies of pedestrians and seven burglaries occur at an apartment community that is usually crime-free. For tactical crime analysis, this area is a hotspot because it represents a notable amount of activity at one location. It should be noted that hotspots can overlap with the other types of activity.

Hot Dot

While this term has been coined previously to refer only to "the victim who repeatedly suffers crime" (Pease and Laycock, 1996), we have included the offender in the definition as well. We define a hot dot as an individual associated with an unusual amount of criminal activity, either as an offender or a victim For example, over the course of two months, the same individual has been arrested for assault, theft, and criminal trespass and has also been the subject of several field contacts by police. This individual is categorized as a hot dot because of the notable amount of police activity.

Hot Product

A hot product is a specific type of property that is the target in the same or different types of crime. This term was coined by Clarke (1999), who defines hot products as "those consumer items that are most attractive to thieves." For example, during a six-month time span, twenty tailgates are stolen from trucks of various makes and models throughout the city. This activity is notable because the same type of property has been taken.

Hot Target

We propose the term "hot target" to refer to particular types of targets that are frequently victimized but which are not included in the definition of hot spot (small areas), hot dot (persons), or hot product (goods). For example, ten incidents of vandalism of churches across a city, a dozen burglaries of sports shops across the city, or a number of crimes against public transit commuters might make any of them "hot targets," particular if there is no indication that the crimes are committed by the same offender(s).

Tactical Crime Analysis Mapping

GIS is an integral part of both the analytical and presentation phases of tactical crime analysis. Tactical crime analysis mapping is not a refined process, and each analyst has his or her own methods for mapping criminal and other types of activity. Where police officers and crime analysts previously used pins and wall maps to geographically analyze and display data, many individuals now have the power of sophisticated GIS tools at their fingertips. GIS is not just the process whereby a computer program is used to place electronic pins on static electronic maps; it is a tool with many capabilities for analyzing and interacting with the data.

Pin maps are one of the simplest methods for analyzing and presenting tactical crime pattern data. However, crime data combined with other types of geographically related data such as field contacts, schools, bus stops, or liquor stores allow for a multi-layered analysis. Additionally, using graduated symbols and colors to analyze incidents by frequency of address, date of occurrence, time between hits, or property taken are other useful methods of tactical crime analysis mapping. Lastly, aerial maps are useful for analyzing and illustrating criminal activity, as this type of map allows analysts to assess the environmental characteristics of a location, including lighting, access, and natural surveillance.

The following are three basic examples of tactical crime analysis mapping to illustrate this discussion.

Example 1:
Analysis of Residential Burglary

One of the most prevalent methods for locating related property crimes is simply to map a group of incidents and look for geographic clusters of activity. A first step in analyzing residential burglary patterns and trends, as with many types of property crime, is mapping the incidents and analyzing clusters of burglaries to determine if a geographic pattern exists. Once a cluster of incidents is identified, it is possible to drill down further into the data to analyze the specific characteristics of each incident, such as point of entry (e.g. door, window), method of entry (e.g. door kick, window break), and/or property taken. The following map depicts one month of residential burglary data: the circle indicates a cluster of activity that may require a more detailed analysis.

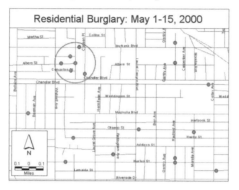

In some jurisdictions, geographic parcel data are available to use for analysis. These data consist of a geographic layer that outlines each parcel of land. Parcels are particularly helpful in mapping residential areas because they allow users to identify geographic features such as alleys, cul-de-sacs, and the specific location of an address on the street (e.g. two houses from the intersection). The following map is an example of a parcel map.

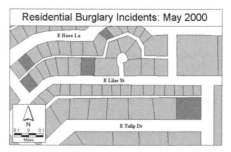

Example 2:
Analysis of Auto Theft and Recovery Locations

One way of identifying auto theft patterns is to map both the auto theft and recovery locations of particular vehicles. The following map depicts one week of auto theft and recovery data in one part of a city. The group of incidents in the Northeast corner of the map represents the recovery hot spot. By drawing a line between the theft and recovery of a particular vehicle (the line does not indicate the travel pattern), one can see which incidents may be related and which may not be. Closer examination of the *modus operandi*, time of day, day of week, and/or type of vehicle may show a stronger connection such as a series or spree.

Example 3:
Identifying Investigative Leads for a Sexual Assault

Tactical crime analysis also assist short-term problem solving by identifying investigative leads. For instance, to develop a pool of potential leads for a recent sexual assault, one may begin by mapping all registered sex offenders that live in the area of the incident. One can then assess the candidates based on other characteristics, such as physical description, previous offenses, and travel patterns in order to determine similarities to the crime in question. For areas with a high number of registered sex offenders, this process my need to be completed before the map is created to limit the number of candidates. In other words, this is an iterative process in that with every inclusion or exclusion of information, relationships are reexamined. The following map depicts a sexual assault incident and all registered sex offenders that reside within a one-mile radius.

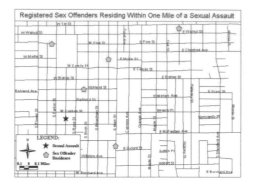

Summary

The intention of this article is to contribute to the ongoing conversation relating to terminology, methods, and techniques of tactical crime analysis and the role of GIS. By outlining some concepts used in tactical crime analysis, we hope that we have aided the development of a common language that practitioners and researchers will use to discuss and debate these ideas.

References

Clarke, R.V. (1999). *Hot products: Understanding, anticipating, and reducing demand for stolen goods*. Police Research Series, Paper 112. Policing and Reducing Crime Unit. London: Home Office.

Gottlieb, S., A. Sheldon, and R. Singh (1994). *Crime analysis: From first report to final arrest*. Monclair CA: Alpha Publishing.

Pease, K. and G. Laycock (1996). *Revictimization: Reducing the heat on hot victims*. Washington DC: National Institute of Justice.

Chapter 8

Some "Radical" Closing Thoughts

The journey through space, time, and crime is almost complete. This text began with several families of theories that have been used to try to explain the geographic concentration of crimes in certain places and spaces, namely Positivism and Classical criminology. It then examined a number of policy recommendations that were derived from these families of theories. Finally, it introduced crime analysis and crime mapping, tools that are used by law enforcement agencies and other interested parties to identify patterns and locations of criminal activities. Today, the study of space, time, and crime is generating a great deal of excitement and energy among law enforcement practitioners and researchers alike. There has been a virtual explosion of interest in these topics over the past several decades. However, it must be noted that not all of this interest has been positive.

Not all researchers share the same level of enthusiasm regarding the study of crime and space. In fact, some are downright critical of the topics explored in this text. In order to understand the criticisms that have been made, the theory behind the negative reactions must be explored. Specifically, the ideas of **radical criminology**, a third family of criminological theory that is closely associated with the writings of Karl Marx, needs to be discussed.

Radical Criminology

Theoretical Assumptions

A number of different but related theoretical perspectives are contained under what I will define as "radical criminology." These various viewpoints on the nature of the law, crime, and society are known by a number of different names—conflict theory, critical criminology, Marxism, feminist theory, postmodern criminology, to name a few. While each of the subgroups has their own distinct arguments, all share a few common threads. The similarities between these various perspectives and then the important differences between a few of the subgroups, specifically conflict criminology and Marxist criminology, will be examined.

First, radical criminologists maintain that inequality of power is at the very root of the crime problem in the United States. While the various radical theorists may debate over who actually holds the ultimate power and why, one cannot escape the issues of power, domination, and control in the radical perspective. Radical criminologists force attention on disadvantaged, less powerful groups in our society such as the poor and/or members of racial and ethnic minority groups. Second, since inequality of power causes crime, the only way to reduce crime is to change the existing power structures. Hence, this family of theories is "radical"—crime and other social problems will be reduced only through the advancement of political initiatives that involve real and lasting changes in our social structure (Bohm, 1997; Curran & Renzetti, 2001; Vold, Bernard, & Snipes, 2002).

Conflict criminology begins with the assumption that society is comprised of a number of different groups, all of which are vying for control and power. These various groups have competing ideas of what is right and what is wrong, hold different values, and push their own individual political agendas that are designed to further the self-interests of the particular group. The group that is in power has the ability to control the actions of the state, which includes directing the content of the laws as well as the behavior and functions of the court system and the police. Less powerful groups in society are more likely to have the "normal," everyday expected behaviors of their group defined as criminal. Less powerful group members are thus more likely to find themselves caught up in the formal processing of the criminal justice system (Vold et al., 2002).

To help illustrate this point, consider the beliefs of Christian Scientists. Growing up in Detroit, my neighbors were members of this religious group and I was often invited to attend church functions with the family. Since my parents were happy to get me out of the house, I attended a number of these events and became somewhat familiar with their beliefs. One of these excursions involved a trip to Cedar Point, an amusement part in Ohio. "Jungle Larry," who hosted the wild animal shows and was a Christian Scientist himself, met with our group of about 30 kids and chaperones. Jungle Larry told us a story about how he had been seriously injured by a lion while he was on safari. Jungle Larry had been mauled by the animal, and was left to die in the wilderness with several broken bones and open gaping wounds. But there he was—fully healed and back at Cedar Point. In keeping with the beliefs of his religion, it was the power of prayer (and prayer only) that ultimately healed Jungle Larry.

You see, Christian Scientists do not endorse the use of what most folks in our society would deem "normal" medical practices. It is this aspect of their beliefs that lands Christian Scientists in the news occasionally. From time to time, you may hear cases in which parents have been brought up on criminal charges of neglect for not seeking medical attention for their sick children. Instead of injecting their child with insulin to counteract the effects of diabetes for example, a Christian Scientist parent may follow what is normal, expected behavior for their group—they pray for their child. Indeed, seeking out medical treatment would violate the beliefs of the group and would be viewed as an act of deviance among Christian Scientists. Since a minority of individuals in our society holds these beliefs, the group does not have a great deal of power and influence. Therefore, what is considered to be normal behavior for the group of Christian Scientists has been defined by more powerful groups in society as "wrong" and "criminal."

Think about how different our society would be if Christian Scientists held power and were able to have their beliefs, values, and norms translated into law. Blood transfusions, organ transplants, the use of prescription drugs, and other medical practices would be outlawed. We would see news reports of parents brought up on criminal charges for seeking black market chemotherapy therapy treatments for their seriously ill child. Society at large would scratch their heads and wonder how parents could subject a child to such horrible, seemingly abusive treatments. It is very important to keep in mind that for conflict theorists, what is "right" and what is "wrong" is completely relative—it is the definitions of the group in power that get translated into what is and is not acceptable behavior for society. As phrased by Chambliss and Seidman (1971:473–474), "the higher a group's political and economic position, the greater is the probability that its views will be reflect in the laws." The definitions of the more powerful groups ultimately become the law of the land—even though these definitions are no better or worse than the definitions held by less powerful groups.

Conflict Criminology and the Control of Public Space

Principles of conflict criminology have been used to analyze the enactment and enforcement of laws designed to control the activities of less powerful groups in society, especially in public spaces. Jeff Ferrell (2001) adopted a conflict stance in his analysis of laws and police practices designed to control the behavior of African Americans, Hispanics, and other less powerful groups as they conduct the everyday business of their lives in public areas. According to Ferrell, public space is a battleground for the control of less powerful groups in society. The presence of racial and ethnic minorities, the poor, and other groups defined as threats to the safety and status of public spaces must be closely monitored and regulated. To illustrate his point, Ferrell describes several case studies involving laws designed to control the behavior of minority group members in public spaces, specifically street cruising and hip hop graffiti.

Controlling Street Cruising

Street cruising is a popular, positive cultural event in Hispanic and Mexican-American communities. Younger men and women take great pains to customize their cars with brightly painted murals that symbolize their cultural heritage. Many of these vehicles are also converted into "lowriders." The proud car owners and their passengers cruise around the city streets in what has been described as a positive, constructive alternative to gang membership, an important source of shared cultural pride, and an integral step in the building of a public ethnic identity.

Unfortunately, not all share the same level of enthusiasm for the street cruisers. Neighborhood activists in a number of cities brought pressure against City Councils and their local police, demanding that something be done to eliminate cruising. Instead of describing the activity as a celebration of ethnic heritage, a Phoenix newspaper described street cruising as "a slow-moving parade of noise, litter, vandalism and violence" (Konig, 1997:B1, cited in Ferrell, 2002).

Since the street cruisers are members of a less powerful group in society, their activities have been defined as improper and illegal. The more powerful community activists have been successful in their mission to remove the cruisers from public space, drawing on the power of the legal system. Popular cruising areas have been blocked with barricades, curfews have been enacted, traffic fines have been increased, and laws that regulated the volume of car stereos have been enforced. Hundreds of arrests have been made in the newly designated "no cruising" zones. Ferrell (2002:60) closes this case study with the following observations of the impact of the anti-street cruising campaign in Denver, Colorado: "In the years following the erasure of cruising from the streets of north Denver, the neighborhoods there have continued to see skyrocketing housing prices, a steady influx of middle class Anglo homeowners eager to live near Denver's revitalized downtown, and thus the steady flushing out of north Denver's largely working class, Hispanic population from these newly upscale areas." By controlling the behavior of the largely Hispanic street cruisers, wealthier whites were able to drive the "less desirable" element from their newly claimed territory.

Outlawing Hip Hop Graffiti

While Ferrell described street cruising as an important source of cultural identity and pride in Hispanic communities, hip hop graffiti provides a similar avenue for African Americans to display their ethnic character and individuality. Graffiti writers display their works in a variety of locations: subways, trains, and exterior walls of buildings. While graffiti art or "tagging" is sometimes confused with gang-related graffiti, it should be noted that hip hop graffiti developed as an alternative to gang membership and conflict.

Unfortunately for the hip hop graffiti writers, their particular form of artistic presentation has been defined as one of the early, very negative signs of a community spiraling out of control. Following the "broken windows" philosophy, cities have aggressively targeted any evidence of graffiti, removing the paintings as soon as they are discovered. In what has become described as a racialized panic over hip hop graffiti, an all out war has been launched in many cities to apprehend the writers. Harsher penalties have been enacted and enhanced enforcement methods have been employed, including citizen surveillance teams, infrared video cameras, night vision goggles, and helicopter patrols. What is defined by the writers and members of the hip hop culture as a positive activity that expresses their cultural identity has been effectively criminalized by the larger society. Since the writers and their supporters are a subordinate group in society, their views do not carry any weight. The more powerful groups in society define the actions of the writers as "bad", and ultimately the apprehended writers find themselves caught up in the criminal justice system.

Of course, it must be pointed out that not all graffiti is labeled as bad. Once again, "bad" is a relative term. In the city of Tampa, Florida, a team of "graffiti busters" aggressively targets any signs of graffiti, removing the murals, tags, and other painted messages within 24 to 48 hours of their discovery. However, the graffiti busters have been ordered to leave one form of graffiti alone. Visiting college crew teams regularly come to the Tampa area for rowing practice along the Hillsborough River. These team members—many of them from Ivy League schools— paint their school emblems on sea walls in the downtown area (Morgan, 2002). These "tags" of the wealthy and powerful are viewed as perfectly acceptable and not really graffiti at all. In fact, the spray painted college emblems have been described as part of the city heritage and tradition; the emblems of the less powerful are defined as criminal. If you stand back and view this objectively, is there really any difference between the two forms of graffiti—other than who has painted it?

Who's Got the Power?
Conflict versus Marxist Perspectives

Central to the arguments of conflict criminology is the issue of power. Some groups will have the power to influence our political and legal systems, while most groups will not. Members of less powerful groups are really at the mercy of the powerful groups, as these more powerful groups have the ability to advance and promote their values and norms through the legal system. In effect, crime is directly caused by relative powerlessness (Bohm, 1997). Crime results when the actions of a subordinate group violate the values and norms of another group that has control of the law and the legal system (Akers, 1994). While conflict criminology does focus our attention on how the law and the police may be used against subordinate groups in society, a few important points are missing. Where does the power come from? How did one group rise to power over all others? Conflict criminology does not directly address the questions of where the power came from or how the power structure evolved (Vold, et al. 2002). Conversely, these questions are central to the assumptions of Marxist criminology, another radical perspective.

While conflict criminology dodges the issue of how power became so unequally distributed, Marxist criminology addresses this point head on. Marxist criminology focuses on class-based struggles between the rich and the poor and is premised on the works of Karl Marx. The writings of Karl Marx were greatly impacted by the Industrial Revolution, which had literally turned the world upside down. The manners, customs, and traditions that had been in place for a thousand years had changed, suddenly and dramatically. Marx set out to analyze what had happened, why the changes had take place, and to predict what changes would follow. His theories are very complex, drawing on history, economics, political science, and other disciplines. Since Marx did not directly address the issue of crime at any length, different criminologists have developed very different interpretations of what Marx really meant in his writings. The result is a number of related but competing theories that fall under the umbrella of Marxist criminology (Bohm, 1997; Taylor, Walton & Young, 1973; Vold, et al. 2002).

Marx argued that power was concentrated in the hands of a relatively small group of ruling elites. While conflict criminology rested on the idea of a number of competing groups in society struggling for power, Marx saw a single power-elite that had control of the real power in society—social power, political power, and economic power were all concentrated in the hands of the elite. This ruling elite had evolved through the workings of the capitalist system. Capitalism is a highly competitive economic system in which only the strongest survive. Though the competitive process, the **bourgeoisie** class (owners of the means of production, like factories, businesses, etc.) becomes smaller and smaller. Less successful businesses fail, and the former business owners fall into the much larger **proletariat** class. The proletariat is comprised of large numbers of oppressed, working class people whose only choice for survival is to sell their labor to the bourgeoisie. While the proletariat is virtually powerless, the power of the bourgeoisie is derived from their monopoly ownership of the means of production.

According to Marx, this small ruling elite not only controls the economic system, but the political system as well. This implies that the bourgeoisie is able to control the laws, the police, and the entire criminal justice system to further their own interests. The capitalist class holds all real power. Their primary goal is to maintain their position of dominance in society at the expense of the proletariat. Following this argument, we would expect to find members of the proletariat over-represented in all stages of the criminal justice system, including official police contacts, arrests, prosecution, and incarceration. Since the rich and the powerful control the criminal justice system, crimes that are more likely to be committed by the poor are defined as more serious, elicit greater fear, receive greater levels of attention by the police (the social control agents of the state), and carry harsher penalties than crimes committed by the affluent.

To help illustrate this point, consider the crime of robbery. Robbery has been defined as a very serious crime of personal violence. The FBI has deemed this crime as one of the Part I Index crimes, which would imply that the vast majority of police agencies pay careful attention to the number of robberies occurring in their jurisdiction. After all, the total number of robberies appears on the front page of the local newspaper and is often used as an indicator of public safety. Back when I used to own a carry out pizza shop, the threat of an armed robber entering the business was always very real. The fear associated with a stranger entering my shop, threatening my crew (and me, of course!) with violence, and taking the hard earned cash was very unsettling.

Objectively speaking, what is robbery? Someone wants or needs more of something (usually money), so they take it from someone else. Who commits robbery? A typical offender is poor, young, male, and disproportionately African American (Miethe & McCorkle, 2001; Wright & Decker, 1997). Why are robberies committed? In a qualitative study of active robbers, Wright and Decker found that the vast majority of the robbers that they interviewed noted a need for cash as a primary motivation. Consider the following responses noted by the interviewees (Wright & Decker, 1997:33):

> Being broke [gets me to thinking about doing an armed robber]... cause being broke, man, you don't feel good. You ain't got nothing in your pocket, so you want to take something out of someone else's pocket. (Bill Williams—No. 78)

> [The idea of committing an armed robbery] comes into your mind when your pockets are low; it speaks very loudly when you need things and you are not able to get what you need. It's not a want, it's things that you need, basic things that if you don't have the money, you have the artillery to go and get it. That's the first thing on my mind; concentrate on how I can get some more money. (Black—No. 79)

[Armed robbery] was a big joke more or less when I was younger. It ain't no joke now. It's survival. That's how I look at it now. (James Minor—No. 14)

So, viewed objectively, robbery is a crime committed by less powerful individuals in society. Robbers want money. However, given their occupational and social status, they have a rather limited range of opportunities from which to choose just how they will get the money. Compare the situation of a robber from that of a physician, an accountant, a stock broker, a banker, or the Chief Executive Officer of a large corporation. Greed, need and want are not confined to lower socioeconomic classes. If a physician feels that she wants money, then the opportunities available to act on this want are very different. A physician may turn to other means to acquire money through illegal means, such as defrauding Medicaid, engaging in tax evasion, or possibly embezzlement

Death by Pintos or Pizzas: Is There Really a Difference?

As opposed to street crimes, white-collar crimes and other transgressions of the affluent are defined as much less serious. Nobody gets hurt by these crimes, right? Wrong! Consider the Ford Pinto, a case study of corporate greed that has become a bit of a classic illustration of the harm that can result from white collar crime. During the 1970s, there was a big of an international car war being waged. The American economy was threatened by the growing popularity of foreign car imports like Toyotas, Datsuns, and Volkswagens. In order to compete, executives at Ford Motor Company rushed the Pinto, a small, inexpensive subcompact, into production. The Pinto became very popular and by the late 1970s was the number one selling car in its class.

Unfortunately, in their haste to begin production, engineers at Ford Motor Company ignored one important problem with the Pinto: The rear-mounted gas tank of the Pinto had a tendency to explode in rear end collisions. The engineers knew about the problem prior to the mass production of these dangerous vehicles. Since the assembly line had already been configured to install the gas tanks according to the original unsafe design, any changes would have delayed production, added costs, and impacted profits. It was estimated that it would have cost less than six dollars per car to line the gas tank with a rubber bladder, making the Pinto safer. Apparently this cost was too great. For eight years after the problem was discovered, the Pinto continued to be sold and used with the originally design flaw. Nearly 30 burn deaths were "officially" attributed to the exploding gas tank, while some estimates put the number in the hundreds. Finally, after the federal government intervened and ordered new safety standards, Ford recalled 1.5 million Pintos to implement the new improvements to the gas tanks (Dowie, 1982; Feagin & Feagin, 1990).

I did not grow up in a wealthy family, so my parents could easily have fit the demographic of a "typical" Pinto customer: less affluent, working class people bought Pintos (gee, I wonder what would have happened if a car marketed to the wealthy, like the Lincoln Town Car, had been found to have a similar problem). Let's say I'm driving to high school one day and bam...I get rear-ended. The car bursts into flames and I become another statistic in the Ford Pinto scandal. A crime of greed has resulted in the death of an innocent victim. Now, let's say I'm closing down the old pizza shop and an armed robber walks in, shoots me dead, and runs off with the day's receipts. Once again, a crime of greed has resulted in the death of an innocent victim. In the case of the Pinto, no one was convicted of homicide, and no prison sentences were served (for a fascinating discussion of the Pinto case, please see Cullen, Maakestad & Cavender, 1987). While Ford Motor Company paid for its crimes in civil lawsuits, no criminal penalties were levied. However, in the case of the pizza shop robbery, one could be certain that the perpetrator would be hunted down by police officers and the full force of the criminal justice system, possibly including the death penalty, would be brought to bear—especially since the perpetrator would, in all likelihood, be a poor person with only a public defender to look out for his rights. To me, as the innocent victim in all of this, it really doesn't matter. Either at the hands of the Ford executives or the robber, I'm just as dead.

Thinking Outside of the Box: The Radical Perspective

Some time has been spent discussing two specific types of radical criminological theories: conflict theory and Marxist theory. To help keep them separate, conflict theory tends to be used to help us better understand cases of culture conflict while Marxist theory is usually employed when analyzing rich-versus-the-poor type issues. Sometimes the distinction can get a bit blurred. However, the important thing to remember is that this family of theories forces us to think about "crime," "criminals," and crime reduction strategies in a much different way. The rest of this chapter will be devoted to a critical evaluation of the various intervention strategies that were previously presented in this text. As this discussion will suggest, there is often more to consider than what immediately meets the eye.

Radical Critiques

First and foremost, radical criminologists would charge that too much emphasis is focused on crimes committed by individuals from lower socioeconomic classes. Indeed, the focal point of our entire criminal justice system places far too much weight on "street crimes" and not enough importance on crimes of the powerful. Crime analysis, crime mapping, and other high tech enforcement tools of law enforcement are used to better control the "dangerous classes" of society. Consider the cases of corporate greed exhibited by the companies Enron and Worldcom. Thousands of employees and investors lost everything due to the deceptive accounting practices used by these corporate giants. The individuals responsible for these crimes will never show up on any crime analysis bulletin, nor will their homes be identified on a crime map. Local police agencies do not monitor the criminal actions of the wealthy or privileged. This is in spite of the fact that one is at least as likely to be injured or killed due to an occupation injury or disease, unnecessary medical procedures, or poor emergency medical services as being the victim of aggravated assault or a homicide. Further, society has lost more money from embezzlement, price fixing, and consumer deception than the combined losses of all of the property crimes included in the all-important list of FBI Part I Index crimes (Reiman, 1998). A number of crime reduction policies have been discussed in this text. Regardless of the specifics of the policy, all target the everyday behaviors and criminal actions of the less powerful.

What Could Be Wrong with Rebuilding Communities?

In the previous discussions of criminological theory, two other schools of thought were presented: Positivism and Classical criminology. Just as a point of review, a Positivist assumes that human behavior is not a matter of free choice. One's actions are, at least to some extent, determined by factors beyond one's immediate control. These factors may include both internal and external influences, such as psychological or biological defects, poor socialization within the family, or growing up in a low income, high crime neighborhood. Positivists believe that differences between criminals and non-criminals can be clearly identified.

The quality of the environment in which people live is an important difference between criminals and non-criminals. Certain communities have higher levels of crime than others. Poverty, social disorganization, higher levels of residential turnover, greater racial and ethnic diversity, higher number of single parent households, and lower levels of informal social control are oftentimes associated with high crime spaces. To reduce crime in these areas, the sense of community must be strengthened, educational and job opportunities improved, and the level of both formal and informal social control increased.

How would a radical criminologist view such community-building initiatives? Recall the discussion of the Chicago Area Project. The CAP, which is still in operation today, is based upon the work of Shaw and McKay. Designed to improve conditions in troubled neighborhoods and reduce social disorganization, the CAP advocated after school and weekend recreational, educational, and vocational programs. Local youths were provided with opportunities to engage in positive activities, such as sports programs and other structured events. Local business owners joined the executive boards of the CAP, providing financial support, volunteer hours, and other forms of philanthropy. What could possibly be bad about that?

A radical criminologist would attack such measures, arguing that these sorts of "feel good" programs are nothing more than a band-aid designed to make the rich feel better about themselves with little or no real concern given to the plight of poorer people in society. By focusing attention on social disorganization as a cause of delinquency, the real causes of crime and other social problems—the inequality and exploitation that are part and parcel of our capitalist system—were completely ignored. Of course the wealthy would support CAP programs that were designed to improve the living conditions of the poor—they would be crazy not to. These programs did alleviate some of the problems of the less fortunate. However, most importantly, these programs deflected attention away from the real problems and allowed the unequal distribution of wealth and resources to continue (Krisberg & Austin, 1978; Sheldon, 2001; Snodgrass, 1976).

Bear in mind that when thinking like a Marxist, violent revolution is always a possibility. Even though they may not have any real power, when one considers the sheer number of warm bodies, the proletariat is a much larger class than the ruling elite. The threat of an uprising in which the proletariat seizes power and redistributes wealth and resources is very real. Therefore, the proletariat must be pacified in some manner. It is not in the best interests of the bourgeoisie elite to have the proletariat dwell on their poor lot in life and blame the elite for their impoverished situation. By donating some money here and there, holding a charity banquet, or volunteering a few hours a month to some sort of cause, the bourgeoisie give the illusion that they are the "good guys." Anger, blame, and outrage are diverted away from the powerful elite even though it is their everyday business practices that have caused the neighborhoods to deteriorate and ensure that the impoverished conditions will continue.

The Dark Side of Community Policing: A Wolf in Sheep's Clothing?

What about community policing initiatives? Isn't community policing a better way for police officers to conduct themselves in lower income neighborhoods than say, zero tolerance policing? Well, yes and no. Zero tolerance policing (ZTP) is an aggressive, pro-active policing strategy that encourages police officers to target relatively trivial criminal offenses. In the City of New York, Rudolph Guiliani abandoned community policing, which he viewed was too soft on crime, in favor of ZTP. Hispanics, African Americans, and members of various immigrant groups have borne the brunt of these new aggressive tactics (Bass, 2001; Chambliss, 1994). The number of minorities stopped and frisked by the police has increased sharply, especially in neighborhoods where they constitute a clear minority. For example, in communities where African Americans and Hispanics comprise less than 10 per cent of the population, blacks comprised 30 per cent of those stopped by the police and Hispanics accounted for another 23.4 per cent (Bass, 2001). It should come as no surprise that complaints filed against the NYPD have risen 41 per cent since ZTP became the norm. Most of these complaints have been filed by racial and ethnic minorities (Bass, 2001; Greene, 1999).

While not all of these encounters with police end with a formal arrest, many of the encounters do. Even in cases where no formal arrest is made, the stop provides a great opportunity for the police to embark on a fishing expedition to gain valuable intelligence concerning "dangerous" individuals. One of the goals of zero tolerance policing is to have a record of the formal contact with the individual who has been stopped. This information gathering exercise assists in crime analysis — data gathered during the encounter is passed along to the crime analysis unit. The location and time of the stop, name, address, and identifying characteristics (scars, tattoos) of the individual stopped, and any known acquaintances are entered into a searchable database. If the police ever need to find the individual in the future, they have a good place to start. While law enforcement personnel herald the field interview report as an essential tool in fighting crime, a radical criminologist would attack this practice, arguing that the government is monitoring the comings and goings of innocent people who have been defined as potential criminals. Since a disproportionate number of minorities and lower income residents find themselves stopped and interviewed by the police, this practice is viewed as just another tool of exploitation designed to keep less powerful groups in check.

If an arrest is made, then the individual is fingerprinted (more data for crime analysts) and gets a formal arrest record. Since it is much easier to plead guilty to a minor offense than to fight the charge in court, more than likely the individual will have a criminal conviction (Walker, 1998). Now, if this same individual is ever arrested and convicted on a more serious charge, it will not be their first encounter with the criminal justice system. This removes the possibility of the arrestee being offered the opportunity to participate in various diversion programs for first time offenders and increases the likelihood of more serious sanctions being handed down. Once again, the issue of power and who gets targeted for arrest enters into the picture. The data suggest that under ZTP, minorities have been disproportionately arrested for less serious misdemeanor offenses (Harcourt, 1998). Given the problems associated with ZTP, some have gone so far as to label the practice "harassment policing" (Panzarella, 1998; Walker & Katz, 2002).

Since zero tolerance policing has been criticized so heavily, is community policing better? Not exactly. Community policing has a bit of a dark side. In a documentary on the Arts and Entertainment channel (A&E) on the history and changing role of the police, community policing was compared to vigilante justice. Under a system of vigilante justice, local residents monitor the behavior of those defined as criminal and often take the law into their own hands. While this sort of policing system is usually associated with the historical era of the frontier and the "Wild West," the concern is that this sort of "justice" is being replicated in many contemporary neighborhoods. Under the warm and fuzzy guise of community policing, some questionable tactics may be utilized to monitor and control the behavior of those defined as dangerous, different, or undesirable (A & E, 1996).

For example, my father lives in a neighborhood that has a rather strong neighborhood watch and community policing organization. The group holds regular meetings, distributes a newsletter, organizes various dinners and other community events, and even developed a rather complex communication system to report criminal activities in the neighborhood. When I visit, sometimes there is a crime watch sign posted at the main entrance to the neighborhood with a ribbon attached. Sometimes the ribbon is green; other times it is blue. This is a message to members of the neighborhood watch. A green ribbon indicates that a burglary had taken place, and a blue ribbon means that there was some sort of problem with juveniles. There are other codes, but the newsletter is needed to figure out what sort of incident had occurred.

In one unfortunate incident, one of the community watch members discovered that a local resident had a *15-year-old* conviction for exposing himself in public. Now, this sort of conviction can result from a number of different scenarios other than the image of a child molester driving around a playground in a trench coat. Perhaps he had been skinny-dipping, or had been caught parking with his girlfriend—even public urination could fall under this sort of charge. Based on the age of the man, the incident probably occurred during his college-age years. The exact circumstances surrounding the incident did not matter to the community watch, who distributed "important alert" fliers to all of the people in the neighborhood informing them that a "sexual predator" lived in their midst. Not surprisingly, he did not live there much longer.

The strongest community organization efforts tend to arise in neighborhoods dominated by white, older, middle class homeowners who perceive some sort of threat to their way of life. Oftentimes, this threat is centered on changes in the racial composition of the neighborhood, as members of racial or ethnic minorities purchase or rent homes in the area (Skogan, 1986). Under these sorts of conditions, community policing efforts may be utilized to legitimize and support a system of racism. Neighbors are encouraged to monitor the actions of "criminals" in their community in order to help the police in their war on crime. Additionally, community efforts to reduce decline and maintain neighborhood racial stability have been most successful in areas where the residents' mission was supported by what Skogan described as "large but immobile corporate actors (e.g. hospitals, banks, and universities) with a sunk investment to protect (1986:222)." In the words of a radical Marxist, the capitalist elite had a stake in ensuring that the "dangerous classes" of individuals be driven out of "their" neighborhood; thereby making sure that their real estate investments and personal safety remained undisturbed.

Too Much Weeding and Not Enough Seeding?

As noted earlier, community policing programs are most successful in white, middle class neighborhoods. In areas with high number of working and lower class minority residents or areas where a sense of community does not exist, community policing efforts are not as successful. In keeping with our radical critique, given the emphasis that the police and the criminal justice system places on street crimes, it should come as no surprise that minority, lower income areas tend to have higher rates of crime. In higher crime neighborhoods, another more aggressive law enforcement tactic has been used that is packaged as an offshoot of community policing: Operation Weed and Seed.

Operation Weed and Seed (OWS) started in 1991 when the United States Department of Justice provided grant opportunities to law enforcement agencies to target high crime neighborhoods. The goal of OWS is based on its name: First, violent offenders and drug dealers are "weeded out" through aggressive, pro-active law enforcement and dogged prosecution. The weeding phase is a coordinated effort between federal, state, county, and local police departments along with their prosecutor's offices. The underlying philosophy is that the neighborhoods cannot be improved without removing the dangerous elements from circulation. Then, after the criminal offenders have been removed, the area is "seeded" with various programs designed to improve the quality of life for the local residents, including economic opportunities, drug and alcohol treatment programs, juvenile intervention and diversion programs, community enrichment, and crime prevention strategies (Roehl et al.1996; Simons, 2002).

While the National Institute of Justice has heralded Operation Weed and Seed as a success, not all community members share the same level of enthusiasm. And, once again, the disparate evaluations often fall along race and class lines. "Regular" community policing projects are used in white, middle class neighborhoods, while OWS projects are more likely to be used in poorer, minority communities. It is the weeding phase of the projects that has raised concerns among residents of the communities targeted for such efforts. Consider the following statements by Elijah Gosier, an African American columnist, as he voices his concerns about a Weed and Seed project:

> No one argues with the seed portion of the equation. Who could argue with the prospect of federal money supporting jobs and businesses and other community enhancements? The only argument with the *seeding* is that it can be viewed as a bribe to coerce a hurting community to submit to the *weeding*. [emphasis in original]

> The weeding is the sticking point. Some perceive it as granting the police permission to trample the provisions of the constitution that are intended to protect citizens from police and governmental excesses. They see it as something just short of martial law....

> There is a history of mistrust—even enmity—between police and communities like the one targeted for St. Petersburg's Weed and Seed program, communities that are poor and black. [Officers in charge of the project] said little to dispel those sentiments among those who have acquired them over years of experience....

> If police in a Weed and Seed do the same thing they do in the rest of the city, why bother calling it something other than policing, especially when that something is as *tactless and dehumanizing* as weeding? Why couple the weed with the seed? [emphasis added] If you're looking to arrest major drug figures, why waste time mining for them in the poorest part of town, where only their flunkies work? (Gosier, 1997:C1)

Unfortunately, the concerns voiced by Gosier have not been unfounded in many communities. While weeding efforts have been successful, the seeding efforts have proven to be much more of a challenge. Police agencies and their community partners either do not know exactly what to do to increase education, vocational, and other quality of life measures, or, in other areas there simply is not enough funds left to do any seeding in the newly-weeded areas (Kennedy, 1996; Tien &

Rich, 1994). In sum, police agencies are good at the weeding phase, but not so good at the seeding component.

The net effect is that poor and minority residents may experience a very different form of community policing than more affluent, white residents. While white residents interact with "Officer Friendly" at community meetings and neighborhood picnics, many minorities experience aggressive law enforcement tactics, including increased "stop and frisks," crackdowns, heightened surveillance, undercover stings, and other intensive operations. It should also be noted that if federal law enforcement agencies get involved, drug cases may then be moved to federal court. Federal drug convictions carry much harsher penalties than state convictions. No matter which jurisdiction eventually tries the case, arrest and prosecution are the keys to success in the OWS areas.

Conversely, success in community policing efforts in more affluent, white neighborhoods is measured by the *absence* of arrests. An arrest is viewed as the last resort, since an arrest does nothing to address the underlying problems in a community. So, in the eyes of a radical criminologist, community policing is nothing more than an excuse to unleash an army of occupation on minority communities, whose residents will once again experience the full weight of the criminal justice system. In practice, community policing becomes indistinguishable from zero tolerance policing—though it may *sound* better. Wealthy business owners can support OWS efforts and appear charitable and caring—all the while supporting a system that emphasizes greater social control over less powerful groups in society.

In closing, radical criminologists would argue that community building efforts have a much darker agenda than assisting the less fortunate. But what about policies based on choice theories? Would a radical criminologist view these programs as potential harmful to less fortunate groups in society?

Radical Critiques of Choice Based Policies

As a point of review, choice-based policies are based on the theoretical perspective of Classical Criminology. A Classical Criminologist assumes that human beings exercise free will in making rational decisions. After careful consideration of a number of factors, including perceived effort, reward, risk of apprehension, and alternative courses of action, a rational offender selects the "best" location and time to commit a crime as well as the best form of crime to commit (robbery versus burglary, for example). In this text we have discussed a number of policy recommendations based on this school of thought, including various target hardening strategies such as defensible space, crime prevention through environmental design, and situational crime prevention.

It is important to mention that a radical criminologist would attack one of the core, basic assumptions held by a Classical Criminologist: the issue of free choice. Radical criminologists focus on issues related to the unequal distribution of power in our society. An affluent white male has much different choices and opportunities than an African American female born in a family of poverty. In order to understand how choices are structured, it is absolutely essential to consider how differently people are treated based on social class, race, gender, and other social and demographic characteristics. A radical criminologist would argue that the assumption of free choice for all members in our society given the inequalities of our social structure is absurd.

Monopoly, Anyone?

If it helps to understand what a radical criminologist is talking about, consider the game of Monopoly. The object of the game is to become the richest player by buying, selling, or renting properties. A player travels around the game board, landing on various properties. If someone else has not already purchased the property, the player may buy the property. Then, when another player lands on the property, that player must pay the owner of the property rent. The owner can improve the property by building houses and hotels, which allow the owner to charge even more rent. When you are broke, you are out of the game.

Monopoly can be viewed as a miniature replication of our capitalist system. Of course, there is one important consideration: In monopoly, all players are essentially equal. Everyone starts out the game with the same amount of money. Then, based on the luck of the dice, draw of the card, and individual strategy, the winner is decided. Both luck and skills enter into the equation of who will ultimately be the most successful.

Now, let's make the game more accurately reflect the realities of American society. The person who draws the shoe game piece is given $500 to start the game. The person who is the thimble is given $1,500, and the person with the dog starts the game with $5,000. Now, the person with the hat begins the game with $50,000 and ownership of Park Place and Boardwalk (the two most valuable properties). On top of that, the "hat" person also controls the bank and is allowed to set interest rates for loans and dole out money as they see fit. Also, the hat person may send other, less powerful pieces to jail if they complain too much or otherwise disturb the game.

As the game begins, who really has "free" choice? Would you be shocked if the "shoe" person grabbed some cash when the banker got up to use the restroom? A radical criminologist would argue that this unequal situation more accurately reflects the class-based realities of our society. Also, bear in mind that in the Monopoly illustration, we have not considered issues of discrimination based on gender, race, or ethnicity. What if the thimble person were not allowed to collect $200 upon passing "Go" for no reason other than being a thimble?

Because of the unequal nature of our society, the assumption of free choice is not a given for radical criminologists. Instead of free choice, minority citizens and members of lower socioeconomic classes experience **structured choice**. Proponents of this perspective argue that an individual's circumstances may be best understood when one considers how often meaningful, positive life chances and opportunities are made available to that individual (Lynch & Patterson, 1996; Stretesky & Lynch, 1999a). In our current social structure, one's race and social class factor heavily into how often positive life chances are presented. Greater constraints are placed on the choices available to minorities and less affluent individuals. For example, if a neighborhood begins to deteriorate, a more affluent white family has more choices than a less affluent minority family. The minority family may not have the financial resources to leave. Furthermore, due to discrimination in housing and employment, the minority family may experience greater difficulty in finding a new home and a new job. These constraints further limit the choices that are available to the minority family. Radical criminologists would argue that structured choice more accurately describes our class and race-based social system. Therefore, any policies based on flawed theoretical assumptions are doomed to failure.

Beyond the debate surrounding free choice, radical criminologists would have other concerns regarding choice-based policies. One of the more serious critiques surrounds the issue of displacement, or simply moving crime from one target to another. To summarize, radical criminologists would argue that the location where the crime ultimately moves might be linked to social class. Individuals with more money will be able to utilize target hardening strategies, hire security consultants, or even have their own private police force, while the poor will not. Targets that are not well protected are viewed as easier to violate, so it would follow that poorer people and their homes, cars, and businesses will experience higher levels of victimization.

Crime Displacement: Is the Glass Half Empty?

As mentioned in chapter 5, displacement occurs when crime simply moves or changes its form as a result of a crime fighting strategy. The specifics of the crime fighting strategy can take on a variety of forms: enhanced efforts by law enforcement, situational crime prevention, or various target hardening techniques. In their evaluations of the effectiveness of these strategies, researchers have identified a number of different types of displacement. Criminals can move from one location to another (called **spatial** or **territorial displacement**); move from one time to another (**temporal displacement**); select a more vulnerable target (**target displacement**); change their methods to adapt to the new design modification (**tactical displacement**); or change to a completely new form of crime. Regardless of the type of displacement, the important point is that there is no net reduction in the level of crime—the criminals have simply adapted to the heightened level of risk, modifying their behavior to reduce the threat of apprehension.

Of the various forms of displacement, spatial displacement is the most prevalent (Lab, 2000). Interestingly enough, individual police agencies may not be very concerned with spatial displacement, as long as the crime moves out of their jurisdiction. Over the years of my research on various police issues, I have interacted with a number of officers from many different agencies. Occasionally, the issue of displacement has come up, especially if an agency's crime fighting efforts have been well publicized in the media. One municipal agency had received a great deal of positive publicity after their FBI UCR numbers experienced a dramatic drop. I asked an agency representative about his perception of the drop, and he began to laugh quite heartily. Apparently a large lower income housing project had been deemed uninhabitable and was demolished. The former residents—predominately poor and minority—had a great deal of difficulty finding landlords who would accept their housing vouchers within the city limits. The displaced residents ultimately found new housing—in the county, outside of the city limits. While the official crime statistics for the city experienced a sharp decline, the numbers from the county sheriff's department reported a similar increase. The displacement of the local residents—and the crime problems that followed them—was quite a source of amusement for the municipal police officers.

Illustrations of calculated displacement are not difficult to come by. In one-on-one conversations, I have been told that it is relatively common for police personnel to pick up vagrants in their jurisdiction, only to drop them off in a nearby city. The neighboring city will then return the favor. The "sport" in this activity is not to get caught in the act. Prostitution stings chase women and their customers out of one area and into another agency's space. Of course, it is much easier to make an arrest than it is to try to address the underlying root cause of why the women have turned to prostitution in the first place. When planning various evaluation studies, I have been met with incredulous stares and told not to worry about measuring displacement. The police knew where the crime would move. In some cases, agency personnel provided me with the specific cross streets where the crime would be channeled. As long as the crime was out of their jurisdiction, the project was to be labeled a success.

Law enforcement agencies are not the only guilty parties with respect to a lack of concern over the issue of displacement. As noted by Lab (2000), there are not many studies of various crime fighting efforts that explicitly address the issue of displacement. One of the reasons for this omission is the fact that displacement is not a primary concern of the law enforcement agency, business, commercial development, or apartment complex that has initiated the crime prevention effort. As long as the crime problem was moved out of their realm of concern, the effort was a victory. Even now, as I reflect back on my previous life as a private business owner, I would share in this guilt. If I had spent several thousand dollars in surveillance cameras, locking devices, safes, increased lighting, and other target hardening measures, I would not be concerned with whether or not the robbers had decided to go down the street to victimize a less protected target. My only concern was whether or not my chances of becoming a victim had been reduced. So what if the robbers drove by my place of business to hit the more vulnerable local 7-11; as long as it was NIMBY—not in my back yard. This, of course, is a very selfish, shortsighted view, but most business owners are not interested in changing the world—only their little part of it.

In a review of the issue of displacement, Lab (2000:88) summarizes with the following:

> These studies find that displacement is a viable concern for discussions of crime prevention. Although the list of studies supporting each type of displacement is limited, this is probably due to the failure of most evaluations to consider displacement. In many other studies, displacement of one type or another is a realistic rival hypothesis to the claims of crime prevention. Interestingly, two reviews that claim to find little evidence of displacement argue that it should not be a major concern (Eck, 1993; Hesseling, 1994) actually uncover a significant level of various forms of displacement. Both Hesseling's (1994) and Eck's (1993) analyses show that roughly one-half of the studies show evidence of displacement, particularly territorial and target forms. The fact that the authors do not find 100 percent displacement, or displacement in all studies, leads them to conclude that it is not a major problem. This is an unrealistic criterion and any evidence of displacement is a concern that should be addressed.

A proponent of various crime prevention and target hardening strategies would probably argue that while half of the studies reviewed did show evidence of displacement, that would imply that half did not. The glass is half full, not half empty. Felson (1998:141, 142) goes so far as to describe displacement as an "illusion," stating that the displacement model is "extremely dubious." Felson further argues, "it is a disgrace to use 'displacement' as an excuse to hold back creativity in preventing crime" (1998:142).

The Ethics of Crime Prevention

Part and parcel of the displacement debate is where and against whom crimes are displaced. A radical criminologist would argue that wealthy people, who can afford protections, deflect crime and criminals into less powerful communities. Therefore, minorities and people from lower socioeconomic communities will experience heightened levels of crime. The wealthy will enjoy greater safety and protection at the expense of the poor.

Felson and Clarke (1997), both supporters of routine activities theory and situational crime prevention, recognize the issues surrounding the displacement of crime into less powerful communities. In order to ensure equal protection from crime to all members of society, Felson and Clarke (1997:200) provide the following principles that they feel should guide crime control policy:

1. Situational prevention should not serve as a means for one segment of the community to displace its crime risk onto another element.

2. Situational prevention should not serve just one social class, nor should its costs be borne by another social class or stratum of society.

3. Situational prevention should be attentive to the victimization risks of minorities and disempowered segments of society.

These are truly noble goals that radical criminologists would embrace wholeheartedly. However, it should also be noted that Felson and Clarke (1997) do not perceive that situational crime prevention disproportionately favors the wealthy. According to Felson and Clark, individuals who argue that the rich reap greater benefits than the poor do not fully understand the basic principles of situational crime prevention. The poor can benefit from crime prevention efforts just as the wealthy can—the positive successes of the various strategies are not confined solely to affluent residents. Less affluent communities can experience a **diffusion of benefits,** a sort of spillover of the positive effective of crime prevention strategies.

Furthermore, Felson and Clarke argue that policies that appear to disproportionately target individuals from lower socioeconomic classes are not really hurting the poor. For example, if the police stop and question teenagers in lower income areas when they are out late at night, enforce curfews, or otherwise restrict the teens' freedom, this official action by the police should not be viewed as a bad, discriminatory action. In fact, this form of social control is quite helpful in lower income communities. According to Felson and Clark (1997:204), "wealthier groups tend to restrict more closely the freedom of their children to wander, especially at night, thus containing the amount of trouble they get into. If we wish to treat equally those lower in income, especially those living in inner cities, *facilitating equality of supervision* is one method" [emphasis added]. So, it is really in the interests of equality that the police pick up, question, gather intelligence data, and monitor the actions of lower income kids.

By now, you should be able to recognize that a radical criminologist would take great issue with this assertion. A radical criminologist would argue that there really is no difference between wealthy teenagers and poor teenagers—except in how their very similar behaviors are defined. Poor kids hanging out on a street corner are viewed as dangerous potential criminals and are more likely to be picked up by the police (who are disproportionately assigned to poor and minority communities). Teens from wealthy families are more likely to have cars and hence be mobile and less obvious to the eyes of the public and the police. Further, fewer police patrols in wealthy neighborhoods leads to fewer official contacts. The assertion that more aggressive monitoring of teens in lower income neighborhoods enhances equality of supervision provides even greater justification for police to stop and question poorer youths.

A radical criminologist would argue that the answer to the crime problem is not to engage in various crime prevention strategies, but instead to provide a more level playing field for poor and minority youths. Improve educational, vocational, and occupational opportunities for residents of our inner cities. Change the existing social structure to ensure that all members of society, regardless of race, ethnicity, or socioeconomic class truly do have free choice, and not just structured choice. Inequality is the root cause of all crime. Without addressing this basic issue, any crime control effort will fail.

Felson and Clarke (1997) argue that pursuing these sorts of programs may very well be a waste of time and effort. In their words (1997:205), "However liberal and attractive [social improvement programs] might sound, it violates our basic notion that people are not very prone to long-term improvement. Social prevention implies improving people, which we regard as a goal almost sure to produce frustration." Social prevention programs designed to improve education, recreation, and employment opportunities must take a back seat to situational crime prevention in any serious discussion of crime prevention. In this view, programs advocated by radical criminologists will certainly fail. You cannot change people by increasing their education levels or improving their economic status. This charge goes back to the very basic principles of Classical Criminology: People are basically evil. Left to our own devices, we will return to our evil nature. If you want to control crime, you need to go back to certain, swift, and proportionate punishments. If people perceive that they will get caught and punished, they will not commit crimes. For a Classical Criminologist, the answer to the crime problem is quite simple. To a radical criminologist, the answer is also quite simple — it is just a very different answer.

And so the debate continues. Before the close of this chapter, it is important to recognize a new movement that is slowly picking up speed among more traditional criminologists: the study of environmental justice. Research in this area forces one to consider new issues in the study of crime and space.

Is There Something Truly Sinister Going on in Lower Income Communities? The Issue of Environmental Justice

Environmental justice puts a new spin on why crime and other social problems are concentrated in lower income and/or minority communities. Thus far, various policies designed to improve the quality of life in higher crime areas have been examined, such as community building efforts. Various crime prevention strategies that attempt to increase the perception of effort and risk of apprehension, thereby encouraging a rational potential criminal to rethink his or her actions have also been discussed. In this section, it is suggested that something much worse is happening in some communities that may lead the local residents to engage in impulsive, antisocial behavior. Without addressing these underlying conditions, even the best policy will be ineffective.

The study of environmental justice really began to take off in the late 1970s (Stretesky & Lynch, 1999a). Environmental justice is a rather broad area that includes study of the relationship between social demographic characteristics (such as race, ethnicity, income, and education levels) and exposure to various environmental hazards. These environmental hazards may include such things as the geographic locations of storage and dump sites for hazardous wastes, accidental chemical releases, lead poisoning, and various forms of pollution (air, water, soil). The principles of environmental justice argue that all things being equal, these environmental hazards should be distributed equally across society. One should be just as likely to find a hazardous waste dump site in an affluent white neighborhood as in a poorer community inhabited by racial and ethnic minorities (Bullard, 1994; Stretesky & Lynch, 1999a). No one group should be exposed to higher concentrations of air pollution than another.

As one might suspect, this is not the case. Exposure to various pollutants and environmental hazards has been linked to the demographic characteristics of a community. Higher levels of exposure to various environmental hazards and risks are much more likely to be found in less affluent African American and Hispanic neighborhoods than in more affluent white neighborhoods (Krieg, 1995; Reiman, 1998; Stretesky &

Lynch, 1999a, 1999b; United Church of Christ, 1987). The concentration of pollutants in these neighborhoods has a number of implications for the residents. Depending on the nature of the toxin, local residents may experience higher levels of various forms of cancer, respiratory diseases, cardiovascular disease, miscarriages, birth defects, and other health problems (Edelsein, 1988; Gould, 1986; Lave & Seskin, 1970; Morello-Frosch, Pastor & Sadd, 2001). It should also be noted that the quality of health care that one receives varies with race and social class. If a less affluent minority resident contracts a life threatening disease like cancer, then he or she is less likely to have health insurance and ready access to state of the art medical treatments. Not surprisingly, the mortality rate for African Americans diagnosed with cancer is higher than the mortality rate for whites (for a more detailed discussion, see Reiman, 1998).

Lead Exposure and Crime

Environmental pollutants have also been linked to various behavioral changes. In particular, exposure to lead has been studied by criminologists and other behavioral researchers. While lead exposure is detrimental at any age, it is particularly harmful to the developing brains of small children, especially children age five and under. Lead exposure may lead to irreversible brain injuries which impact social and behavioral development including language acquisition, attention, memory, sensory perception and fine motor processes (Lidsky & Schneider, 2000). In a review of the medical literature, Stretesky (in press) reports that lead exposure has been linked to lower IQ scores, lower educational success, higher levels of hyperactivity and impulsive behaviors, and delinquency (see, for example, Banks, Ferretti & Shucard, 1997; Bellinger, Stiles, & Needleman, 1992; Needleman et al., 1996; Needleman & Gatsonis, 1990).

The issue of lead poisoning becomes particular troubling when considering that exposure to lead is not distributed equally across all segments of society. According to the Centers for Disease Control (1997, cited in Stretesky, in press), minority children are much more likely to be exposed to lead than white children. African American children suffer from lead poisoning at a level that is over five times the rate for white children. Lead poisoning also appears to be concentrated among those living in our inner city, urban areas. Whereas 21 per cent of inner city youths had bloodlead levels above the CDC's maximum allowable level, only 5.8 per cent of youths residing in rural and suburban areas had high bloodlead levels (Lidsky & Schneider, 2000). Social class also appears to be related to lead exposure. While 16 per cent of children from low-income families were found to have high bloodlead levels, the percentage was lower in more affluent families: only 5.4 per cent of middle class children and 4 per cent of high income children were found to have bloodlead levels above the maximum recommended amounts (Lidsky & Schneider, 2000).

Furthermore, as argued by Stretesky (in press), the detrimental effects of lead poisoning are often wrongly attributed as characteristics of individuals. Consider for a moment the debate surrounding intelligence scores and race. It has been argued by some researchers that certain racial and ethnic groups are less intelligent than other groups based on their IQ scores. Since these same researchers also argue that IQ has a genetic component, it would follow that they would make the argument that certain groups are inherently intellectually inferior (Herrnstein, 1988; Herrnstein & Murray, 1994). However, because of social inequalities in our society, minority children are exposed to higher rates of lead. Lead exposure has been linked to lower intelligence scores. Therefore, it would follow that minority children would have lower IQ scores—not because of inherent racial differences, but because of their exposure to lead.

Lead and Space:
Hot Spots of Crime, or Hot Spots of Lead?

Just as crime is not equally distributed across all geographic areas, risk for lead exposure is concentrated in certain places. For most of us, the most commonly thought-of source of lead poisoning is lead-based paint. Before the harmful effects of lead exposure were known, it was common for homes to be decorated using lead-based paint. As the paint cracked and peeled the small pieces were often eaten by children, who then suffered lead poisoning. People living in newer homes do not have to concern themselves with exposure to lead-based paint. However, people who live in older housing units are more likely to be exposed to lead, especially in inner city areas. Since many minorities and/or less affluent individuals tend to be concentrated in communities with older rental units, it would follow that children growing up in these areas are exposed to higher levels of lead.

Furthermore, exposure to lead and other toxins can also occur through the air. Stretsky (in press) reported that black youths were much more likely than white youths to live in counties that have higher concentrations of lead in the air. In effect, there are identifiable lead "hot spots" that are often found in lower socioeconomic areas with higher number of minority residents. The higher concentration of lead in these communities causes irreversible biochemical changes in the residents. These changes may lead to concentrated geographic patterns of crime, delinquency, and other social problems. Since lead exposure has been linked to higher levels of aggression, violence, and delinquency, it would follow that geographic areas with high levels of lead would have high levels of crime (Klug, 2000; Lidsky & Schneider, 2000). For example, Stretesky and Lynch (2001) found a positive relationship between air lead concentrations and the occurrence of homicides: Geographic areas with higher levels of lead in the air also reported more homicides. Assuming that there is a relationship between lead exposure and crime, individuals who are exposed to lead suffer irreversible brain damage that leads to various behavioral problems including impulsive behaviors, poor school performance, memory problems, violence, and aggression. Certain neighborhoods experience higher levels of exposure than others, which would imply that certain areas have higher numbers of exposed individuals than others. If a community with high levels of lead exposure is targeted with a few of the policies explored in this text, will even the best community building efforts have any impact in areas in which the very air that the residents breathe is poison? Can a policy based on the assumption of a rational offender have any effect if many of the residents suffer from a condition that causes impulsive, aggressive behavior? Probably not.

Unfortunately, while interest in the area of environmental justice is growing, there are very few criminologists who study the link between exposure to environmental contaminants and crime. Clearly, this is an area of great importance with implications for any crime control policies that our society chooses to enact. A crime hot spot may actually be deflecting our attention away from something much worse. While people can certainly be arrested, addressing the underlying cause of the problem is a much more difficult process.

Summary

I do hope that this closing chapter has encouraged you to take a closer look at some of the various theories and policies that have been discussed in this text. Nothing is ever simple. Even the most carefully considered policy driven by the best of intentions might backfire, causing even more problems for residents living in high crime areas. You, the reader, may very well be the next police chief, city council representative, mayor, or governor. You may hold an influential office where your opinions and actions truly have an impact on the lives of other people. I hope that in some small way, this text has helped to sharpen your critical thinking skills regarding crime, criminals, and public policy.

Bibliography

A&E Home Video (1996). *Police* [Film]. (Available from New Video Group, 126 Fifth Avenue, New York, NY 10011).

Akers, R. (1992). *Drugs, alcohol, and society.* Belmont: Wadsworth.

Akers, R. (1994). *Criminological theories: Introduction and evaluation.* Los Angeles: Roxbury Publishing Company.

Banks, E., Ferretti, L., & Shucard, D. (1997). Effects of low-level lead exposure on cognitive function in children: A review of behavioral, neuropsychological and biological evidence. *Neurotoxicology, 18,* 237–282.

Barnes, G. (1995). Defining and optimizing displacement. In J. Eck & D. Weisburd (Eds.) *Crime and place* (pp. 95–114). Monsey: Willow Tree Press.

Barnes, H. & Teeters, N. (1959). *New horizons in criminology* (3rd ed.) Englewood Cliffs: Prentice Hall.

Bartollas, C. & Hahn, L. (1999). *Policing in America.* Boston: Allyn and Bacon.

Bass, S. (2001). Out of place: Petit apartheid and the police. In D. Milovanovic and K. Russel (Eds.) *Petit apartheid in the U.S. criminal justice system: The dark figure of racism* (pp. 43–55). Durham: Carolina Academic Press.

Beccaria, C. (1963). *On crimes and punishments.* (H. Paolucci, Trans.). Indianapolis: Bobbs-Merrill. (Original work published 1764).

Becker, H. (1973). *Outsiders.* New York: Free Press.

Bellinger, D., Stiles, K., & Needleman, H. (1992). Low-level lead exposure, intelligence and academic achievement: A long-term follow-up study. *Pediatrics, 90,* 855–861.

Bennett, J. (1981). *Oral history and delinquency: The rhetoric of criminology.* Chicago: University of Chicago Press.

Blau, J., & Blau, P. (1982). The cost of inequality: Metropolitan structure and violent crime. *American Sociological Review, 47,* 114–129.

Block, C. (1998). The geoarchive: an information foundation for community policing. In D. Weisburd & T. McEwen (Eds.). *Crime mapping and crime prevention* (pp. 27–82). Monsey: Willow Tree Press.

Block, R. & Block, C. (1995). Space, place and crime: Hot spot areas the hot places of liquor-related crime. In J. Eck and D. Weisburd (Eds.) *Crime and place* (pp. 145–184). Monsey: Willow Tree Press.

Boarnet, M. and Bogart, W. (1996). Enterprise zones and employment: Evidence from New Jersey. *Journal of Urban Economics, 40,* 198–215.

Boba, R. (2001). *Introductory guide to crime analysis and mapping*. Washington, D.C.: U.S. Department of Justice Office of Community Oriented Policing Services.

Bohm, R. (1997). *A primer on crime and delinquency*. Belmont: Wadsworth Publishing Company.

Bracey, D. (1992). Police corruption and community relations: Community policing. *Police Studies, 15*, 179–183.

Brantingham, P.J. & Brantingham, P.L. (1981). *Environmental criminology*. Prospect Heights: Waveland Press.

Brantingham, P.J. & Brantingham, P.L. (1991). *Environmental criminology* (2nd ed.). Prospect Heights: Waveland Press.

Brantingham, P.L. & Brantingham, P.J. (1998). Planning against crime. In M. Felson (Ed.) *Reducing crime through real estate development and management* (pp. 23–28). Washington DC: Urban Land Institute.

Brantingham, P.L. & Brantingham, P.J. (1999). A theoretical model of crime hot spot generation. *Studies on Crime and Crime Prevention 8*, 7–26.

Bruce, C. (2000, Spring). Mapping in action. Tactical crime analysis: Musings from the Cambridge, Massachusetts Police Department. *Crime mapping news, 2*, 10–12.

Bullard, R. (1994). *Dumping in Dixie: Race, class and environmental quality*. Boulder: Westview.

Bureau of Justice Assistance (1997). *Crime prevention and community policing: A vital partnership*. Washington, D.C.: United States Department of Justice.

Bureau of Justice Statistics (1999a). *Sourcebook of criminal justice statistics — 1998*. Washington, DC: National Institute of Justice.

Bureau of Justice Statistics (1999b). *Substance abuse and treatment in state and federal prisoners, 1997*. Washington, DC: National Institute of Justice.

Burgess, E. (1925). The growth of the city. In R.Park, E.Burgess, & R. McKenzie (Eds.) *The city* (pp. 47–62). Chicago: University of Chicago Press.

Bursik, R. Jr., & Grasmick, H. (1993). *Neighborhoods and crime: The dimensions of effective community control*. New York: Lexington Books.

Bursik, R., Jr. (1986). Delinquency rates as sources of ecological change. In J.M. Byrne & R.J. Sampson (Eds.) *The social ecology of crime* (pp. 63–76). New York: Springer-Verlag.

Bynum, T. (2001). *Using analysis for problem-solving: A guidebook for law enforcement*. Washington, D.C.: U.S. Department of Justice Office of Community Oriented Policing Services.

Byrne, J. & Sampson, R. (1986). Key issues in the social ecology of crime. In J. Byrne & R. Sampson (Eds.), *The social ecology of crime* (pp. 1–22). New York: Springer-Verlag.

Canter, P. (1990). *Baltimore County Police Department spousal abuse study*. Towson: Baltimore County Police Department.

Canter, P. (1995). State of the statistical art: Point pattern analysis. In C. Block, M. Dabdoub & S. Fregley (Eds.) *Crime analysis through computer mapping* (pp. 151–160). Washington, D.C.: Police Executive Research Forum.

Canter, P. (1998). Geographic information systems and crime analysis in Baltimore County, Maryland. In D. Weisburd & T. McEwen (Eds.) *Crime mapping and crime prevention* (pp. 157–192). Monsey: Willow Tree Press.

Canter, P. (2000). Using a geographic information system for tactical crime analysis. In V. Goldsmith, P. McGuire, J. Mollenkopf, & T. Ross (Eds.) *Analyzing crime patterns: Frontiers of practice* (pp. 3–10). Thousand Oaks: Sage Publications.

Centers for Disease Control and Prevention (1997). *Screening young children for lead poisoning: Guidance for state and local public health officials.* Atlanta: CDC.

Chambliss, W. (1996). The Saints and the Roughnecks. In R. Berger (Ed.), *The sociology of juvenile delinquency* (pp. 43–54). Chicago, IL: Nelson-Hall.

Clarke, R. (1983). Situational crime prevention: Its theoretical basis and practical scope. In M. Tonry & N. Morris (Eds.), *Crime and justice: A review of research* (pp. 225–256). Chicago: University of Chicago Press.

Clarke, R. (1992). *Situational crime prevention: Successful case studies.* New York: Harrow and Heston.

Clarke, R. (1995). Situational crime prevention. In M. Tonry & D. Farrington (Eds.) *Building a safer society: Strategic approaches to crime prevention.* (pp. 91–150). Chicago: University of Chicago Press.

Clarke, R. (1997). *Situational crime prevention: Successful case studies Volume 2.* New York: Harrow and Heston.

Clarke, R. & Cornish, D. (1985). Modeling offenders' decisions: A framework for research and policy. In M. Tonry & N. Morris (Eds.), *Crime and justice: An annual review of research, volume 6* (pp. 147–185). Chicago: University of Chicago Press.

Clarke, R. & Felson, M. (1993). *Routine activity and rational choice: Advances in criminological theory volume 5.* New Brunswick: Transaction Publishers.

Clarke, R. & Harris, P. (1992). A rational choice perspective on the targets of automobile theft. *Criminal Behavior and Mental Health, 2,* 25–42.

Clarke, R. & Homel, R. (1997). A revised classification of situational crime prevention techniques. In S. Lab (Ed.) *Crime prevention at a crossroads.* Cincinnati: Anderson Publishing.

Clarke, R. & Mayhew, P. (1980). *Designing out crime.* London, UK: HMSO.

Clarke, R. & Mayhew, P. (1988). The British gas suicide story and its implication for prevention. In M Tonry and N. Morris (Eds.), *Crime and justice: A review of research.* Chicago: University of Chicago Press.

Cohen, L. & Felson, M. (1979). Social change and crime rate trends; A routine activity approach. *American Sociological Review, 44,* 588–608.

Cook, P. (1980). Research in criminal deterrence: Laying the groundwork for the second decade. In N. Morris & M. Tonry (Eds.) *Crime and justice: An annual review of research volume 2,* (pp. 211–268). Chicago: University of Chicago Press.

Coordinating Council and Juvenile Justice and Delinquency Prevention, (1996). *Federal efforts to prevent and reduce juvenile delinquency: FY 1995.* Washington, D. C.: U.S. Government Printing Office

Cornish, D. & Clarke, R. (1986). *The reasoning criminal*. New York: Springer-Verlag.

Cox, S. (1996). *Police: Practices, perspectives, problems*. Boston: Allyn and Bacon.

Crawford, A. (1998). *Crime prevention and community safety: Politics, policies and practices*. London, UK: Longman.

Crime Mapping Research Center (1998). *Hotspots: An exploration of methods*. Available online at www.usdoj.gov/cmrc.

Cromwell, P., L. Parker, & Mobley, S. (1999). The five-finger discount: An analysis of motivations for shoplifting. In P. Cromwell (Ed.) *In their own words: Criminals on crime* (pp. 57–70). Los Angeles: Roxbury Publishing.

Cromwell, P., Olson, J. & Avery, D. (1991). *Breaking and entering: An ethnographic analysis of burglary*. Newbury Park: Sage.

Crowe, T. & Zahm, D. (1994, Fall). Crime prevention through environmental design. *Land Development*, 22–27.

Crowe, T. (2000). *Crime prevention through environmental design: Applications of architectural design and space management concepts* (2nd ed.). Boston: Butterworth-Heinemann.

Cullen, F., Maakestad, W., & Cavender, G. (1987). *Corporate crime under attack: The Ford Pinto case and beyond*. Cincinnati: Anderson.

Curran, D., & Renzetti, C. (1994). *Theories of Crime*. Boston: Allyn and Bacon.

Curran, D., & Renzetti, C. (2001). *Theories of Crime* (2nd ed.). Boston: Allyn and Bacon.

Davis, P. (1998, September 18). Altering the landscape for criminals. *The Washington Post*, pp. B1, B5.

DeLeon-Granados, W. (1999). *Travels through crime and place*. Boston: Northeastern University Press.

Department of Justice (1978). *Response time analysis*. Washington, D.C.: Government Printing Office.

Durkheim, E. (1965). *The division of labor in society* (G. Simpson, Trans.). New York, Free Press. (Original work published 1893).

Eck, J. & Spellman, W. (1987). *Problem solving: Problem oriented policy in Newport News*. Washington, D.C.: Police Executive Research Forum.

Eck, J. & Weisburd, D. (1995). Crime places in crime theory. In J. Eck & D. Weisburd (Eds.) *Crime and place* (pp. 1–34). Monsey: Willow Tree Press.

Eck, J. (1993). The threat of crime displacement. *Criminal Justice Abstracts*, 25, 527–546.

Eck, J. (2001). Problem-oriented policing and crime event concentration. In R.Meier, L. Kennedy, & V. Sacco (Eds.), *The process and structure of crime*. Piscataway: Transaction Press.

Eck, J., Gersh, J. & Taylor, C. (2000). Finding crime hot spots through repeat address mapping. In V. Goldsmith, P. McGuire, J. Mollenkopf, & T. Ross (Eds.) *Analyzing crime patterns: Frontiers of practice* (pp. 49–64). Thousand Oaks: Sage.

Edelstein, M. (1988). Contaminated communities: The social and psychological impacts of residential toxic exposure. Boulder: Westview.

Einstadter, W., & Henry, S. (1995). *Criminological theory: An analysis of its underlying assumptions*. Fort Worth: Harcourt Brace College Publishers.

Elliott, D., & Huizinga, D. (1983). Social class and delinquent behavior in a national youth panel. *Criminology, 21*, 149–177.

Environmental Systems Research Institute (1999). *Getting to know ArcView GIS: The geographic information system (GIS) for everyone*. Redlands: Environmental Systems Research Institute Inc.

Farrel, G. & Sousa, W. (2001). Repeat victimization and hot spots: The overlap and its implications for crime control and problem oriented policing. In G. Farrel and K. Pease (Eds.). *Repeat Victimization* (pp. 221–240). Monsey: Willow Tree Press.

Feagin, J. & Feagin, C. (1990). *Social problems: A critical power-conflict perspective* (3rd ed.). Englewood Cliffs: Prentice Hall.

Feagin, J., & Feagin, C. (1993). *Racial and ethnic relations* (4th ed.). Englewood Cliffs: Prentice Hall.

Federal Bureau of Investigation, (1975). *Crime in the U.S.: Uniform crime report*. Washington, DC: U.S. Government Printing Office.

Federal Bureau of Investigation (2001). *Crime in the United States*. Washington D.C.: U.S. Department of Justice.

Feins, J.D., Epstein, J.C., & Widom, R. (1997). *Solving crime problems in residential neighborhoods: Comprehensive changes in design, management, and use*. U.S. Department of Justice: National Institute of Justice.

Felson, M. (1986). Linking criminal choices, routine activities, informal control, and criminal outcomes. In D. Cornish & R. Clarke (Eds.) *The reasoning criminal* (pp. 119–128). New York: Springer-Verlag.

Felson, M. (1998a). *Crime and everyday life*. (2nd ed.). Thousand Oaks: Pine Forge Press.

Felson, M. (Ed.). (1998b). *Reducing crime through real estate development and management*. Washington D.C.: Urban Land Institute.

Felson, M. & Clarke, R. (1995). Routine precautions, criminology, and crime prevention. In H. Barlow (Ed.) *Crime and public policy: Putting theory to work* (pp. 179–190). Boulder: Westview Press.

Felson, M. & Clarke, R. (1997). The ethics of situational crime prevention. In G. Newman & R. Clarke (Eds.), *Rational choice and situational crime prevention: Theoretical foundations* (pp. 197–218). Brookfield: Ashgate Publishing.

Felson, M. & Clarke, R. (1998). *Opportunity makes the thief: Practical theory for crime prevention*. London: Home Office.

Ferrell, J. (2001). Trying to make us a parking lot: Petit apartheid, cultural space, and the public negotiation of ethnicity. In D. Milovanovic & K. Russell (Eds.) *Petit apartheid in the U.S. criminal justice system: The dark figure of racism* (pp. 55–68). Durham: Carolina Academic Press.

Fleming, Z. (1999). The thrill of it all: Youthful offenders and auto theft. In P. Cromwell (Ed.) *In their own words: Criminals on crime* (pp. 71–79). Los Angeles: Roxbury Publishing.

Foucault, M. (1977). *Discipline and punish*. Harmondsworth: Allen Lane.

Fowler, F., Jr. & Mangione, T. (1982). *Neighborhood crime, fear, and social control: A second look at the Hartford program. Washington, D.C.: Department of Justice.*

Gibson, C., & Lennon, E. (1999). *Population Division Working Paper No. 29.* Washington, DC: United States Bureau of the Census.

Goddard, H. (1914). *Feeblemindedness: Its causes and consequences.* New York: Macmillan.

Gold, M. (1987). Social ecology. In H. Quay (Ed.) *Handbook of Juvenile Delinquency* (pp. 62–105). New York: John Wiley & Sons.

Goldstein, H. (1979). Improving policing: A problem-oriented approach. *Crime and Delinquency, 25,* 236–258.

Goldstein, H. (1987). Toward community-oriented policing: Potential, basic requirements, and threshold questions. *Crime and Delinquency, 33,* 6–30.

Goldstein, H. (1993). *The new policing: Confronting complexity.* National Institute of Justice, Research in Brief, Washington, D.C.: U.S. Department of Justice.

Gosier, E. (1997, August 20). 'Weeding' might sow more seeds of distrust. *St. Petersburg Times,* 1C.

Gordon, M. (1964). *Assimilation in American life.* New York: Oxford University Press.

Gottlieb, S., Arenberg, S., & Singh, R. (1998). *Crime analysis: From first report to final arrest* (2nd ed.). Montclair: Alpha Publishing.

Gould, J. (1986). *Quality of life in American neighborhoods: Levels of affluence, toxic waste, and cancer morality in residential zip code areas.* Boulder: Westview.

Gould, S. (1981). *The mismeasure of man.* New York: W.W. Norton.

Greek, C. (1992). *Religious roots of American sociology.* New York: Garland.

Green, J. (1999). Zero tolerance: A case study of police policies and practices in New York City. *Crime and Delinquency, 45,* 171–187.

Greenwood, P. (1975). *The criminal investigation process.* Santa Monica: RAND Corporation.

Haley, K. Todd, J. & Stallo, M. (1998). Crime analysis and the struggle for legitimacy. Presented at the annual meeting of the Academy of Criminal Justice Sciences in Albuquerque, New Mexico, March 10–14, 1998.

Harcourt, B. (1998). Reflecting on the subject: A critique of the social influence conception of deterrence, the broken windows theory, and order maintenance policing New York style. *Michigan Law Review, 97,* 291–389.

Harries, K. (1999). *Mapping crime: Principles and practice.* Washington, D.C.: U.S. Department of Justice.

Herrnstein, R. (1988). Crime and human nature revisited: A response to Bonn and Smith. *Criminal Justice Ethics, 7,* 10–15.

Herrnstein, R. & Murray, C. (1994). *The bell curve: Intelligence and class structure in American life.* New York: The Free Press.

Hesseling, R. (1994). Displacement: A review of the empirical literature. In R. Clarke (Ed.), *Crime prevention studies, volume 3.* Monsey: Criminal Justice Press.

Hibbert, C. (1966). *The roots of evil: A social history of crime and punishment.* London: Weidenfeld and Nicolson.

Hirschi, T. (1969). *Causes of delinquency.* Berkeley: University of California Press.

Hirschi, T. (1986). On the compatibility of rational choice and social control theories of crime. In D. Cornish & R. Clarke (Eds.) *The reasoning criminal* (pp. 105–118). New York: Springer-Verlag.

Hope, T. (1995). Community crime prevention. In M. Tonry & D. Farrington (Eds.), *Building a safer society: Strategic approaches to crime prevention* (pp. 21–90). Chicago: University of Chicago Press.

Howell, J. & Hawkins, J. (1998). Prevention of youth violence. In M. Tonry & M. Moore (Eds.), *Youth violence*, (pp. 263–316). Chicago: University of Chicago Press.

Jacobs, J. (1961). *Death and life of great American cities.* New York: Vintage Books.

Jeffery, C. (1971). *Crime prevention through environmental design.* Beverly Hills: Sage Publications.

Kappeler, V. Sluder, R., & Alpert, G. (1994). *Forces of deviance: Understanding the dark side of policing.* Prospect Heights: Waveland Press.

Karp, D. (2001, May 18). Strawberry is spared jail term. *St. Petersburg Times,* p. 1A.

Katz, J. (1988). *Seductions of crime.* New York: Basic Books.

Kelling, G., Pate, T., Dieckman, D., & Brown, C. (1974). *The Kansas City preventive patrol experiment: A summary report.* Washington, DC: Police Foundation.

Kennedy, D. (1996). Neighborhood revitalization: Lessons from Savannah and Baltimore. *National Institute of Justice Journal, 231,* 13–17.

Klug, E. (2000). Lead poisoning may be linked to delinquency. *Corrections Today, 62,* 14.

Kobrin, S. (1959). The Chicago Area Project—A 25 year assessment. *Annals of the American Academy of Political and Social Science, 322,* 20–29.

Kornhauser, R. (1978). *Social sources of delinquency.* Chicago: University of Chicago Press.

Krieg, E. (1995). A socio-historical interpretation of toxic waste sites. *The American Journal of Economics and Sociology, 54,* 1–14.

Lab, S. (2000). *Crime prevention: Approaches, practices and evaluations* (4th ed.). Cincinnati: Anderson Publishing Co.

Langworthy, R. & Jefferis, E. (2000). The utility of standard deviation ellipses for evaluating hot spots. In V. Goldsmith, P. McGuire, J. Mollenkopf, & T. Ross (Eds.) *Analyzing crime patterns: Frontiers of practice* (pp. 87–104). Thousand Oaks: Sage.

Lave, L. & Seskin (1970). Air pollution and human health. *Science, 169,* 723–733.

Laverty, I. & MacLaren, P. (2002, Summer). Geographic profiling: A new tool for crime analysts. *Crime Mapping News, 4,* 5–8.

LaVigne, N. & Groff, E. (2001). The evolution of crime mapping in the United States: From the descriptive to the analytic. In A. Hirschfield and K. Bowers (Eds.) *Mapping and analyzing crime data: Lessons from research and practice* (pp. 203–222). New York: Taylor & Francis Inc.

LeBeau, J. (1992). Four case studies illustrating the spatial-temporal analysis of serial rapists. *Police Studies, 15*, 124–145.

Lidsky, T. & Schneider, J. (2000). Evaluating the poisoned mind. *Trial, 36*, 32–40.

Lynch, M. & Patterson, E. (1996). *Justice with prejudice*. Boston: Harrow and Heston.

Lundman, R. (1993). *Prevention and control of juvenile delinquency* (2nd ed.). New York: Oxford University Press.

Mamalian, C. & LaVigne, N. (1999). *The use of computerized crime mapping by law enforcement: Survey results*. Washington, D.C.: National Institute of Justice.

Martin, D., Barnes, E., & Britt, D. (1998). The multiple impacts of mapping it out: Police, geographic information systems (GIS) and community mobilization during Devil's Night in Detroit, Michigan. In N. Lavigne & J. Wartell (Eds.) *Crime mapping case studies: Successes in the field* (pp. 3–14). Washington, D.C.: Police Executive Research Forum.

Martin, R., Mutchnick, R., & Austin, W. (1990). *Criminological thought: Pioneers past and present*. New York: Macmillan Publishing Company.

Martinson, R. (1974). What works? Questions and answers about prison reform. *The Public Interest* (Spring), 25.

Maxfield, M. (2001). *Guide to frugal evaluation for criminal justice: Final report*. Washington, D.C. National Institute of Justice.

Maxfield, M., & Babbie, E. (1995). *Research methods for criminal justice and criminology*. Belmont: Wadsworth Publishing Company.

Mayhew, P., Clarke, R., & Elliot, D. (1989). Motorcycle theft, helmet legislation and displacement. *Howard Journal, 28*, 1–8.

McDonald, P. (2002). *Managing police operations: Implementing the New York Crime Control Model-CompStat*. Belmont: Wadsworth.

McEwen, T. & Taxman, F. (1995). Applications of computerized mapping to police operations. In J. Eck & D. Weisburd (Eds.) *Crime and Place* (pp. 259–284) Monsey: Criminal Justice Press.

McGahey, R. (1986). Economic conditions, neighborhood organization, and urban crime. In A. Reiss, Jr. & M. Tonry (Eds.) *Communities and crime* (pp. 231–270). Chicago: University of Chicago Press.

McLafferty, S., Williamson, D., & McGuire, P. (2000). Identifying crime hop spots using kernel smoothing. In V. Goldsmith, P. McGuire, J. Mollenkopf, & T. Ross (Eds.) *Analyzing crime patterns: Frontiers of practice* (pp. 77–86). Thousand Oaks: Sage.

Merry, S. (1981). Defensible space undefended: Social factors in crime control through environmental design. *Urban Affairs Quarterly, 16*, 397–422.

Michalowski, R. (1985). *Order, law and crime: An introduction to criminology*. New York: Random House.

Miethe, T. & McCorkle, R. (2001). *Crime profiles: The anatomy of dangerous persons, places, and situations* (2nd ed.). Los Angeles: Roxbury.

Miller, W. (1962). The impact of a "total community" delinquency control project. *Social Problems, 10*, 168–191.

Morello-Frosch, R., Pastor, M., & Sadd, J. (2001). Environmental justice and Southern California's riskscape: The distribution of air toxics exposures and health risks among diverse communities. *Urban Affairs Review, 36,* 551–578.

Morgan, P. (2002, December 3). Fighting urban scrawl. *The Tampa Tribune,* Baylife 1,5.

Monachesi, E. (1955). Pioneers in criminology IX: Cesare Beccaria (1738–1794). *Journal of Criminal Law, Criminology and Police Science, 46,* 439–449.

Moore, M., & Tonry, M. (1998). Youth violence in America. In M. Tonry & M. Moore (Eds.) *Youth violence* (pp. 1–26). Chicago: University of Chicago Press.

Murray, C. (1995). The physical environment. In J. Wilson & J. Petersilia (Eds.), *Crime* (pp. 349–362). San Francisco: Institute for Contemporary Studies.

National Advisory Commission on Civil Disorders (1968). *Report.* New York: Bantam Books.

National Advisory Commission on Criminal Justice Standards and Goals (1973). *Report on police.* Washington, D.C.: U.S. Government Printing Office.

National Institute of Justice, (2000). *Excellence in Problem-Oriented Policing: The 1999 Herman Goldstein Award Winners.* Washington, D.C. National Institute of Justice.

Needleman, H. & Gatsonis, C. (1990). Low-level lead exposure and the IQ of children: A meta-analysis of modern studies. *Journal of the American Medical Association, 263,* 673–678.

Needleman, H., Riess, J., Tobin, M., Biesecker, G., & Greenhouse, J. (1996). Bone lead levels and delinquent behavior. *Journal of the American Medical Association, 275,* 363–369.

Newman, G., Clarke, R., & Shohan, S. (1997). *Rational choice and situational crime prevention: Theoretical foundations.* Brookfield: Ashgate Publishing Company.

Newman, O. & Franck, K. (1980). *Factors influencing crime and instability in urban housing developments.* Washington, D.C.: United States Government Printing Office.

Newman, O. (1972). *Defensible space.* New York: Macmillan.

Office of Juvenile Justice and Delinquency Prevention, 1995. *Matrix of Community-Based Initiatives.* Washington, D.C.: U.S. Department of Justice, Office of Juvenile Justice and Delinquency Prevention.

Panzarella, R. (1998). Bratton reinvest 'harassment model' of policing. *Law Enforcement News,* June 15/30, 13–15.

Papke, L.(1994). Tax policy and urban development: Evidence from the Indiana Enterprise Zone Program. *Journal of Public Economics.* 54:37–49.

Paternoster, R. (1987). The deterrent effect of perceived certainty and severity of punishment: A review of the evidence and issues. *Justice Quarterly, 42,* 173–217.

Peak, K., & Glensor, R. (2002). *Community policing and problem solving: Strategies and practices* (3rd ed.). Upper Saddle River: Prentice Hall.

Peterson, M. (1998). *Applications in criminal analysis: A sourcebook* (2nd ed.). Westport: Praeger.

Phillips, P. (1980). Characteristics and typology of the journey to crime. In D.E. Georges-Abeyie & K.D. Harries (Eds.), *Crime: A spatial perspective* (pp. 167–180). New York: Columbia University Press.

Pilant, L. (1999, January). Going mobile in law enforcement technology. *National Institute of Justice Journal, 238*, 11–17.

Plaster, S. & Carter, S. (1993). *Planning for prevention: Sarasota, Florida's approach to crime prevention through environmental design*. Tallahassee: Florida Criminal Justice Executive Institute.

Poyner, B. (1983). *Design against crime: Beyond defensible space*. London: Butterworths.

President's Commission on Law Enforcement and Administration of Justice (1967). *The challenge of crime in a free society*. Washington, D.C.: U.S. Government Printing Office.

Rand, M. & Rennison, C. (2002). True crime stories? Accounting for differences in our national crime indicators. *Chance, 15*, 47–51.

Reiman, J. (1998). *The rich get richer and the poor get prison: Ideology, class, and criminal justice* (5th ed.). Boston: Allyn and Bacon.

Reno, S. (1998). Using crime mapping to address residential burglary. In N. Lavigne & J. Wartell (Eds.) *Crime mapping case studies: Successes in the field* (pp. 15–22). Washington, D.C.: Police Executive Research Forum.

Rich, T. (1999). *Mapping the path to problem solving*. Washington, D.C.: National Institute of Justice.

Roehl, J., Huitt, R., Wycoff, M., Pate, A., Rebovich, D., & Coyle, K. (1996, October). National process evaluation of Operation Weed and Seed. *National Institute of Justice Research in Brief*. Washington, D.C.: U.S. Department of Justice.

Roncek, D. (1981). Dangerous places: Crime and residential environment. *Social Forces, 60*: 74–96.

Rosenfeld, R. (1986). Urban crime rates: Effects of inequality, welfare dependency, region, and race. In J. Byrne & R. Sampson (Eds.) *The social ecology of crime* (pp. 116–132). New York: Springer-Verlag.

Rossmo, D. (2000). *Geographic profiling*. Boca Raton: CRC Press.

Rossmo, D. (1995). Place, space, and police investigations: Hunting serial violent criminals. In J. Eck & D. Weisburd (Eds.) *Crime and Place* (pp. 217–236). Monsey: Criminal Justice Press.

Sacco, V. & Kennedy, L. (2002). *The criminal event: Perspectives in space and time* (2nd ed.). Belmont: Wadsworth.

Sampson, R. (1985). Neighborhood and crime: The structural determinants of personal victimization. *Journal of Research in Crime and Delinquency 22*: 7–40.

Sampson, R. (1986). Neighborhood family structure and the risk of personal victimization. In J. Byrne & R. Sampson (Eds.) *The social ecology of crime* (pp. 25–46). New York: Springer-Verlag.

Sampson, R. (1995). The community. In J. Wilson & J. Petersilia (Eds.) *Crime* (pp. 193–216). San Francisco: Institute for Contemporary Studies Press.

Sampson, R., & Groves, W. (1989). Community structure and crime: Testing social-disorganization theory. *American Journal of Sociology, 94,* 774–802.

Sampson, R., & Raudenbush, S. (1999). Systematic social observation of public spaces. *American Journal of Sociology, 105,* 603–651.

Sampson, R., & Raudenbush, S. (2001). Disorder in urban neighborhoods — Does it lead to crime? *National Institute of Justice Research in Brief.* Washington D.C.: U.S. Department of Justice.

Sampson, R., Raudenbush, S., & Earls, F. (1997). Neighborhoods and violent crime: A multilevel study of collective efficacy. *Science, 277,* 918–924.

Schafer, J. (2002). Community policing and police corruption. In K. Lersch (Ed.), *Policing and misconduct,* (pp. 193–218). Upper Saddle River: Prentice Hall.

Schlossman, S., & Sedlak, M. (1983). The Chicago Area Project revisited. *Crime and Delinquency, 29,* 298–462.

Schlossman, S., Zellman, G.,and Shavelson, R. (1984). *Delinquency prevention in South Chicago: A fifty-year assessment of the Chicago Area Project.* Santa Monica: RAND.

Shaw, C., & McKay, H. (1969). *Juvenile delinquency and urban areas* (Rev. ed.). Chicago: The University of Chicago Press.

Shearing, C.D. & Stenning, P.C. (1992). From the panopticon to Disney World: The development of discipline. In R. Clarke (Ed.) *Situational crime prevention: Successful case studies* (pp. 249–255). New York: Harrow and Heston.

Sheldon, R. (2001). *Controlling the dangerous classes: A critical introduction to the history of criminal justice.* Boston: Allyn and Bacon.

Sherman, L. (1995). Hot spots of crime and criminal careers of places. In J. Eck & D. Weisburd (Eds.) *Crime and place* (pp. 35–52). Monsey: Willow Tree Press.

Sherman, L. Gartin, P. & Buerger, M. (1989). Routine activities and the criminology of place. *Criminology, 27,* 27–55.

Sherman, L. Gottfredson, D. MacKenzie, D., Eck, J. Reuter, P. & Bushway, S. (1997). *Preventing crime: What works, what doesn't, what's promising.* Washington D.C.: U.S. Office of Justice Programs.

Sherman, L., & Weisburd, D. (1995). General deterrent effects of police patrol in crime 'hot spots': A randomized, controlled trial. *Justice Quarterly, 2,* 625–648.

Sherman, L., Schmidt, J., & R. Velke (1992). *High crime taverns: A RECAP project in problem-oriented policing.* Washington, D.C.: Crime Control Institute.

Sherman, L., Shaw, J. & Rogan, D. (1995, January). The Kansas City gun experiment. *National Institute of Justice: Research in Brief.*

Silverman, E. (1999). *NYPD battles crime: Innovative strategies in policing.* Boston: Northeastern University Press.

Simons, C. (2002). The evolution of crime prevention. In D. Robinson (Ed.) *Policing and crime prevention* (pp. 1–18). Upper Saddle River: Prentice Hall.

Skogan, W. (1986). Fear of crime and neighborhood change. In A. Reiss, Jr. & M. Tonry (Eds.) *Communities and Crime*, (pp. 203–229). Chicago: University of Chicago Press.

Skogan, W. (1988). Community organizations and crime. In M. Tonry & N. Morris (Eds.), *Crime and justice: A review of research*, (pp. 39–78). Chicago: University of Chicago Press.

Skogan, W. (1990). *Disorder and decline: Crime and the spiral of decay in American neighborhoods*. New York: Free Press.

Smith, D., & Jarjoura, G. (1988). Social structure and criminal victimization. *Journal of Research in Crime and Delinquency 25*, 27–52.

Snodgrass, J. (1976). Clifford R. Shaw and Henry D. McKay: Chicago criminologists. *British Journal of Criminology, 16*, 1–19.

Sorrentino, A., & Whittaker, D. (1994). Chicago Area Project: Addressing the gang problem. *FBI Law Enforcement Bulletin, 63*, 8–12.

Stretesky, P. & Lynch, M. (1999a). Corporate environmental violence and racism. *Crime, Law & Social Change, 30*, 163–184.

Stretesky, P. & Lynch, M (1999b). Environmental justice and the predictions of distance to accidental chemical releases in Hillsborough County, Florida. *Social Science Quarterly, 4*, 830–846.

Stretesky, P. & Lynch, M. (2001). The relationship between lead exposure and homicide. *Archives of Pediatrics and Adolescent Medicine, 155*, 579–582.

Stretesky, P. (in press). The distribution of air lead levels across U.S. counties: Implications for the production of racial inequality. *Sociological Spectrum*.

Swanson, C., Territo, L., & Taylor, R. (1998). *Police administration: Structures, processes, and behavior* (4th ed.). Upper Saddle River: Prentice-Hall.

Swartz, C. (2000). The spatial analysis of crime: What social scientists have learned. In V. Goldsmith, P. McGuire, J. Mollenkopf, & T. Ross (Eds.) *Analyzing crime patterns: Frontiers of practice* (pp. 33–46). Thousand Oaks: Sage Publications.

Tafoya, W. (1998). Foreward. In S. Gottlieb, S. Arenberg, & R. Singh *Crime analysis: From first report to final arrest* (2nd ed.). Montclair: Alpha Publishing.

Taylor, I., Walton, P., & Young, J. (1973). *The new criminology: For a social theory of deviance*. New York: Harper Torchbooks.

Taylor, R. & Gottfredson, S. (1986). Environmental design, crime and prevention: An examination of community dynamics. In A. Reiss, Jr., & M. Tonry (Eds.) *Communities and crime* (pp. 387–416). Chicago: University of Chicago Press.

Taylor, R. & Harrell, A. (1996). *Physical environment and crime*. Washington, D.C.: National Institute of Justice.

Taylor, R., Gottfredson, S. & Brower, S. (1980). The defensibility of defensible space: A critical review and a synthetic framework for future research. In T. Hirschi & M. Gottfredson (Eds.) *Understanding crime* (pp. 64–75). Beverly Hills: Sage.

Tien, J. & Rich, T. (1994). The Hartford COMPASS program: Experiences with a weed and seed-related program. In D. Rosenbaum (Ed.) *The challenge of community policing: Testing the promises*. Beverly Hills: Sage.

Tittle, C., Villemez, W., & Smith, D. (1978). The myth of social class and criminality: An empirical assessment of the empirical evidence. *American Sociological Review, 43*, 643–656.

Trojanowicz, R., & Bucqueroux, B. (1990). *Community policing: A contemporary perspective.* Cincinnati: Anderson Publishing Co.

Tunnell, K. (1992). *Choosing crime.* Chicago: Nelson-Hall Publishers.

United Church of Christ Commission for Racial Justice (1987). *Toxic wastes and race in the United States: A national report on the racial and socioeconomic characteristics of communities with hazardous waste sites.* New York: United Church of Christ.

Velasco, M. & Boba, R. (2000, Spring). Tactical crime analysis and geographic information systems: Concepts and examples. *Crime mapping news, 2,* 1–4.

Vellani, K. & Nahoun, J. (2001). *Applied crime analysis.* Boston: Butterworth-Heinemann.

Vold, G., Bernard, T., & Snipes, J. (2002). *Theoretical criminology* (5th ed). New York: Oxford University Press.

Walker, S. & Katz, C. (2002). *The police in America.* Boston: McGraw-Hill.

Walker, S. (1998). *Sense and non-sense about crime*, (4th ed.). Belmont: Wadsworth.

Walker, S. (1999). *The police in America* (3rd ed.). Boston: McGraw Hill.

Weisburd, D. & Mazerolle, L. (2000). Crime and disorder in drug hot spots: Implications for theory and practice in policing. *Police Quarterly, 3,* 331–349.

Weisburd, D. & McEwen, T. (1998). Crime mapping and crime prevention. In D. Weisburd & T. McEwen (Eds.) *Crime mapping and crime prevention* (pp. 1–26). Monsey: Willow Tree Press.

Weisburd, D. (1997). *Reorienting crime prevention research and policy: From the causes of criminality to the context of crime.* Washington, D.C.: National Institute of Justice.

Weisel, D. & Eck, J. (1994). Toward a practical approach to organizational change: Community policing initiatives in six cities. In Rosenbaum, D.P. (Ed.), *The challenge of community policing: Testing the promises,* (pp. 110–126). Thousand Oaks: Sage Publishing.

Wekerle, G. & Whitzman, C. (1995). *Safe cities: Guidelines for planning, design, and management.* New York: Van Nostrand Reinhold.

Wilder, M. and Rubin, B. 1996. Rhetoric vs. reality: A review of studies on state enterprise zone programs. *Journal of the American Planning Association, 62,* 473–491.

Williams, J., & Gold, M. (1972). From delinquent behavior to official delinquency. *Social Problems, 20,* 209–222.

Wilson, J., & Kelling, G. (1982). Broken windows: Police and Neighborhood Safety. *The Atlantic Monthly, 249,* 29–38.

Wilson, W. (1980). *The declining significance of race.* Chicago: University of Chicago Press.

Wilson, W. (1987). *The truly disadvantaged* (2nd ed). Chicago: University of Chicago Press.

Index